Creative Business Education

Philip Powell • Bhabani Shankar Nayak
Editors

Creative Business Education

Exploring the Contours
of Pedagogical Praxis

Editors
Philip Powell
Business School - Creative Industries
University for the Creative Arts
Epsom, UK

Bhabani Shankar Nayak
Business School - Creative Industries
University for the Creative Arts
Epsom, UK

ISBN 978-3-031-10927-0   ISBN 978-3-031-10928-7   (eBook)
https://doi.org/10.1007/978-3-031-10928-7

This Palgrave Macmillan imprint is published by the registered company Springer Nature Switzerland AG.
The registered company address is: Gewerbestrasse 11, 6330 Cham, Switzerland

Acknowledgements

We acknowledge the research funding from University for the Creative Arts that enabled to us to organise the conference from which this text emerged. We are thankful to all colleagues in the Business School for the Creative Industries for their participations and contributions in the making of this volume. We particularly thank Victoria Kelley, Charlotte Rutter, Mark O'Connor, Janja Song, Hannah Mason, Bruce McGowen, Martin Charter, Claire Joyce, Katie Griffiths, Julian Sims, Jennifer Perumal, and Elizabeth Baxter for all their support as well as the Vice-Chancellor of the University for the Creative Arts who was instrumental in the founding of the Business School for the Creative Industries. Thanks to Barlow and Paul Smith Jesudas for all editorial support.

University for the Creative Arts, UK   Philip Powell
London   Bhabani Shankar Nayak
20th of May 2022

Contents

Notes on Contributors

Julie Blanchard has taught at UCA in its various guises for twenty-two years, as well as at Goldsmiths College, London and Southampton Solent University, teaching at undergraduate, postgraduate and, more recently, at doctorate level. Her specialisms are fashion history and theory, cultural and gender studies, and media and communications. Julie's own educational background involved master's degrees in History of Dress and Textiles at Winchester School of Art and in Media and Communications at Goldsmiths. Her PhD thesis '*Feeling your age: Pre-teen Fashionable Femininity*' was a sociological study carried out whilst at the University of Southampton.

Simon Das is a Senior Lecturer, BSCI, UCA Epsom. Dr. Das is a media management scholar, with a particular interest in magazine publishing, Simon is the lead editor of a new Routledge book *Innovations in Magazine Publishing*, having taught on journalism and publishing courses in the UK and in Europe for the last 14 years. Before becoming an academic, he was the managing editor of UK black music monthly *Touch* magazine (the magazine arm of Kiss FM), a supplement editor for *TimeOut* and a freelance journalist for a number of magazines including *Arena* and *i-D* in London, *el* Pais newspaper in Madrid and *The Fader* in New York. Simon holds a first degree in Business Studies, a Master's (with Distinction) in Higher and Professional Education and a PhD in media management and cultural theory from the University of Westminster, where he researched managing creativity. Simon is a member of the Chartered Institute of Marketing and was the co-founder of the Creative Industries Management Research Hub (CIMRH) at the University of the Arts London (UAL).

David Faulkner works as Professor of Doctoral Studies and Corporate Strategy in the Business School for the Creative Industries, University for the Creative Arts. He is also Dean of Magna Carta College, Oxford and Emeritus Professor in the University of London, UK.

Frank Fitzpatrick has extensive experience of working in leadership and academic roles in international business and education across several continents and diverse cultural contexts. He has a PhD in Cross-Cultural Business Communication and a Master's degree in Business Administration (MBA) and has published internationally on intercultural issues in the globalised workplace.

Lynda Fitzwater is Senior Lecturer in Critical Theory in the Business School for the Creative Industries at the University for the Creative Arts. She has published on critical pedagogy; neurodiversities; institutional support for student mental health; materiality of memory. Their current work considers support structures for LGBTQIA+ students and affective spaces of collectivity in the university as well as emerging discourses of the Global Citizen in the context of neo-imperialism.

Kathleen Hinwood has been a Lecturer at the University for the Creative Arts, Business School for the Creative Industries for the past 3 years. Currently, she is working across a number of different courses, primarily Marketing and Advertising, as well as Critical and Theoretical Studies for both UG and PG courses. Kathleen is also the Course Lead for Level 4 & 5 Advertising. Previously, Kathleen worked in both creative advertising and strategic marketing roles in both corporate and agency environments for over 20 years. She is able to share her expertise and unique experiences with the students, enabling them to keep up to date with contemporary marketing and advertising practices.

Abdul Jabbar is an Associate professor in Strategy and data analytics at Leicester Business School. He has professional experience in a software development environment and has expertise in developing web-based content management systems. His areas of expertise encompass big data, business analytics, information systems, software development, blockchain and programmatic marketing. His current research to data has a focus on Blockchain, Smart Contracts, Sentiment analysis and IoT data sources. Abdul has published in numerous academic and press publications including the International Journal of Production Research, Computers and Human Behaviour, Technology and Social Forecasting and Industrial Marketing Management to name a few.

Charles Lambert worked as a broadcast journalist for 20 years, as reporter, presenter and producer for the BBC and ITV. He became a full-time academic in 2013 as course leader for BA Sports Journalism at the University of East London and moved to the University for the Creative Arts the following year. His first book *Digital Sports Journalism* (Routledge, 2019) looks at the changes that journalism has undergone since the inventions of the world wide web and smartphones and is on the reading lists at many British universities.

Elisabetta Lazzaro is Professor of Creative and Cultural Industries Management at UCA Business School for the Creative Industries. She holds a PhD in Economics jointly from Paris 1-Panthéon-Sorbonne University and Université Libre de Bruxelles (Fellow), a Master in Economics & Culture from Paris 1-Panthéon-Sorbonne University (Fellow), and a Master in Business Economics from Ca' Foscari Venice University (Fellow), in addition to other degrees and fellow studies in economics, music, fashion, art history and applied technologies in Europe, the USA and Australia. She has formerly been professor of business, economics and entrepreneurship of the arts, culture and creative industries at the HKU University of the Arts Utrecht, the ULB in Brussels and Southern Methodist University in Dallas Elisabetta is Executive Board Member of the Association for Cultural Economics International (ACEI), and has served in several scientific and steering committees of major international, European and national cultural organisations and institutions, and governments. Her research interests and professional experience deal with current academic and industry needs and trends.

Shawn Li is a Lecturer at the University for the Creative Arts. Before joining academia, he has over ten years of experience in data-driven marketing across many sectors. As an early practitioner in digital marketing in the UK, Dr Li focuses on marketing strategies led by customer behaviour, analytics, and insight. He is specialised in data and evidence-based marketing planning, implementation, and evaluation. DrLi received his PhD from the University of Exeter; he has a particular interest in social media text mining, customer segmentation, behavioural prediction, CHAID and regression modelling for marketing. He has worked on many transformation projects to deliver an enhanced digital experience for customers and optimise the marketing channel performance.

Bhabani Shankar Nayak is a political economist working as Professor of Business Management, University for the Creative Arts, UK. He worked in the universities in Sussex, Glasgow, Manchester, York and Coventry for last eighteen years. His research interests consist of four closely interrelated and mutually guiding programmes i.e. (1) political economy of sustainable development, gender and environment in South Asia, (2) market, microfinance, religion and social business, (3) faith, freedom, globalisation and governance and (4) Hindu religion and capitalism. The regional focus of his research is on the impacts of neoliberalism on social, cultural and economic transition of indigenous and rural communities in South Asia. He is the author books like; '*Nationalising Crisis: The Political Economy of Public Policy in India*', '*Hindu Fundamentalism and Spirit of Capitalism in India*' and '*Disenchanted India and Beyond: Musings on the Lockdown Alternatives*', *China: The Bankable State (2021)*.

Terry Newman worked in the fashion industry for more than twenty years, both as an editor at *i-D, Attitude*, and *Self Service* and as a contributing writer for newspapers including the *Guardian*, the *Independent*, the *Times*, and the *Sunday Times*. She has also written and presented fashion programs in the United Kingdom for Channel 4 (*She's Gotta Have It* and *Slave*). The author of *Legendary Authors and the Clothes They Wore* and *Legendary Artists and the Clothes they Wore* (Harper Design), she has contributed to books including *i-D's Fashion Now, Fashion Now 2,* and *Soul i-D.* She currently lectures at the University for the Creative Arts in Epsom and lives in Paddington with her husband and two children.

Philip Powell is Professor of Creative Business and Director of the Business School for the Creative Industries, University for the Creative Arts, UK. Philip is a socio-technical researcher concerned with surfacing and explaining difference. Much of this work has been undertaking in the information systems/information management domains and explores the differing outcomes in organisations employing new technologies. He has focused a lot of work on small and medium-sized businesses. He has also researched many aspects of 'e-', including e-enabled supply chains, e-auctions, hubs and infrastructure. He researches knowledge management, strategy and planning. More recently, he has focussed my work on the management of higher education at sector and institutional level, and on developing enterprise and entrepreneurial support. He has published more than 355 articles, authored five books, two edited books, 50 book chapters and 110 conference proceedings. Philip was previously Executive Dean, Pro Vice-Chancellor (Enterprise and Innovation), and Professor of Management at Birkbeck, University of London and Dean of the Faculty of Business, Law and Politics at the University of Hull. He was Editor-in-Chief of the Information Systems Journal. He has held an honorary chair in the University of Groningen, Netherlands since 2006 and has an honorary chair at the University of Stirling and he holds an emeritus chair at Birkbeck, University of London. Before becoming Dean at Birkbeck in 2009, Philip was deputy dean of the School of Management at the University of Bath having worked at Hull, Warwick, Adelaide, Southampton and Nova de Lisboa. He is a Fellow of Birkbeck, of the British Computer Society, of the Academy of Social Sciences, of the Centre for Distance Education, of the HEA and is a Senior Scholar of the Association of Information Systems. He was president of the UK Academy for Information Systems. Prior to becoming an academic, Philip worked in insurance, accounting and systems analysis. He has served on a variety of public bodies concerned with skills development, enterprise and entrepreneurship and currently sits on the Institute for Apprenticeships Business and Management Route Panel.

Sarah Scarsbrook is an artist, researcher, and Lecturer in Management for the Creative Industries, in the Business School for the Creative Industries, University for the Creative Arts, Epsom, UK. Her artistic, research, and teaching interests include; artists' identities, myths, professional development, and careers; pathways into the creative industries; museums and galleries management; understanding arts marketing and audiences; cultural policy, policymaking, and its relationship to arts management; and qualitative research methods and methodologies. Sarah holds a BA in Fine Art from Kingston University (2004), and an MA in Arts Policy and Management from Birkbeck College, University of London (2011). In 2021, she completed her PhD at Birkbeck, with the thesis, Artists and The Art School: Experiences and Perspectives of Fine Art Education and Professional Pedagogies in London Art Schools, 1986–2016. Sarah's professional experience spans over fifteen years working as an arts manager across London's arts and cultural sector, including at the Saatchi Gallery, ICA, and Barbican Arts Centre. For eight years she worked as a freelance arts marketing manager, building bespoke campaigns for a wide range of arts and cultural organisations and individual artists, spanning all art forms from theatre and classical music to visual arts and spoken word. She has extensive industry knowledge of audience engagement and arts marketing practices.

Gareth Shaw is Professor of Retail and Tourism Management at the University of Exeter Business School. In the past 10 years has completed an ESRC project on innovation in the hotel industry and an ESRC follow-on project on Sustainable Travel and Social Marketing. Professor Shaw has worked on numerous research projects related to retail and tourism development all of which have been funded by major grant awarding bodies. In addition, he has written widely within tourism and produced key texts on tourism studies. Professor Shaw has acted as a consultant for many local, national and international organisations; these include UNESCO, American Express, Coca Cola and Amoco Oil, Visit England and South West Tourism. He is an elected member of the Tourism Research Centre at Modul University, Vienna and the International Academy of Tourism. In addition, he was also an Innovation Fellow at the Advanced Institute of Management and a currently a member of the Innovation Caucus which is an initiative funded jointly by Innovate UK and the ESRC. He was the Chair of the EU COST Action on Tourism, Wellbeing and Ecosystem services (2012–2017) and also Leader of Theme 5 on the EU Smartline project which involves the development of SMEs and e-Health in the Cornish economy (2017–2020).

Gareth Thomas began his career in journalism as a news reporter in France, working for a year as a reporter and producer at the 24-hour channel Euronews. He then worked as a news journalist for the BBC and ITV in Norwich before being appointed news editor at KLFM Radio in King's Lynn. Moving to London in 2000, Gareth took up the position of music editor at Billboard magazine, Music & Media. Following the folding of the title, Gareth went freelance, for publication and websites including Q, What's On In London, The Daily Mirror, The Sun and The Londoner. Gareth began teaching music journalism at the University for the Creative Arts in Surrey in 2010. In 2014 he presented a paper on '*The New Journalism*' at the ICCMS XII International Conference on Communication and Media Studies in Venice. The paper was subsequently published in the Volume 8, Number 11 of the International Science Index Journal. In 2016 he was commissioned by Penguin/Puffin to write a children's book on the 1960s to coincide with the V&A exhibition '*You Say You Want A Revolution? Records and Rebels 1966–1970*'. He is currently Senior Lecturer in Music & Communications where he specialises in the live music industry, music media, audio-visual production and public relations, as well as cultural theory as applied to music. He is a Senior Fellow of the Higher Education Academy and External Examiner for the Media & Communications course at the University of West London. Gareth is a member of the International Association for the Study of Popular Music (IASPM).

Shajara Ul-Durar is a Senior Lecturer in Management and Organisational Behaviour at University for the Creative Arts, UK. She has expertise in organisational behaviour, business ethics and environmental management. She is the projects' lead of the Association of Physicians and Surgeons of the UK. She holds memberships of Higher Education Academy as a Fellow, Chartered Management Institute as CMgr MCMI, Chartered Association of Business Schools as Certified Management and Business Educator,

Academic Associated CIPD, Professional Member Young Professionals' Society and a member of The British Academy of Management. She is an enthusiastic interdisciplinary researcher who wants to create an impact through research. She is experienced in cross-cultural researches. She has won several research grants/projects and has published in high profile international academic journals.

Anita Walsh is a Professor of Work Based Learning at Birkbeck, University of London, and a UK National Teaching Fellow. She sees herself as a practitioner researcher, in that her research interests focus on epistemologies of practice and the pedagogies required to support the recognition of the full range of knowledges, both conceptual and applied, in the academic curriculum. Anita is an internationally recognised expert on pedagogies associated with the academic recognition of experiential learning, and has national recognition for her expertise in innovative curriculum design.

Yue Wang gained her Ph.D. degree in Arts Management and Cultural Industry at Peking University, master's degree in Design Management for the Fashion Industry at UAL and bachelor's degree in Graphic Design in CAFA (Central Academic of Fine Arts). Before returning to academia, she worked for almost ten years in the fashion industry, as a jewellery and product designer for brands including Swarovski.

List of Figures

List of Tables

1

Future of Creative Business Education

Bhabani Shankar Nayak and Philip Powell

Abstract This introductory chapter argues that creative business education curriculum needs to break away from the narrow silo of disciplinary boundaries to outline the pedagogical praxis of creative and critical business education that challenges existing knowledge traditions, power relations, dominant narratives and institutions while offering alternative pedagogic approaches to learning, teaching and research. The future of creative business education depends on its abilities to engage with pluriversal knowledge traditions.

Introduction

The need for creative business education is obvious. The mainstream knowledge traditions, and their positivist approaches within business and management curriculums, are somewhat discredited.

B. Shankar Nayak • P. Powell (✉)
Business School for the Creative Industries, University for the Creative Arts, Farnham, UK
e-mail: Philip.Powell@uca.ac.uk; bhabani.nayak@uca.ac.uk

© The Author(s), under exclusive license to Springer Nature Switzerland AG 2022   **1**
P. Powell, B. Shankar Nayak (eds.), *Creative Business Education*,
https://doi.org/10.1007/978-3-031-10928-7_1

There are four main reasons for the demise of mainstream business education. First, it represents narrow market-determined skill-based essentialism. Second, it has failed to understand and explain the crisis and uncertainties of our times. Third, mainstream business education curricula have failed to offer any viable alternatives. Last, it has failed to develop its own methods and languages concomitant with disciplinary requirements. Business management continues to develop its interdisciplinarity by borrowing methods and languages of its research, study, learning and teaching from other disciplines. Such a crisis within business and management education has led to the return of critical social constructivist ideas based on the principles and values of participation, democratic representation and empowerment to expand the creative potentials of people and their planet.

The pedagogy of creative business education is under conceptualised, both in theoretical and practical terms. Its empirical significance is outsourced to the 'corporates', 'service sectors' and 'third sectors' as if it has little to do with the materiality of everyday lives of people and our planet. The cost benefit analysis has reduced human experience to numbers in spreadsheets. Such reductionist, essentialist, and functionalist approaches ignore the historical and philosophical perspectives within creative business education. This is the context within which this volume attempts to address the philosophical gaps of creative business education. It is important to articulate and outline the critical lineages of creative business education and its potentials.

This volume on the 'Contours of Creative Business Education' is rooted in the praxis of three paradigms i.e., (1) creativity and business education, (2) creativity of business education and (3) creativity in business education. The volume aims to explore six fundamental questions. What constitutes 'creative business education'? How to define 'creative business'? What is the nature and scope of creative business education? What are the theories, methods and approaches to study 'creative business education'? What are the values and ethics of creative business education? What are the challenges and barriers to creative business education? These research questions run through the volume to identify, understand, analyse and advance the essence and emancipatory potentials of a creative business education curriculum. The essence of creative business education curriculum can address the skills gaps within the market whereas the emancipatory logic can look at issues and crisis of our time by focusing on people and on our planet.

The underlying focus of the volume is to expand eclectic knowledge traditions combined with creative business education practices. The volume aims to move away from narrow silo of positivist disciplinary perspectives, and their ontological and epistemological foundations that are largely devoid of the social, cultural, religious, political, regional and economic conditions that determine the business and management education. Fitzpatrick's chapter questions the dominant paradigm in Cross-Cultural Management (CCM) and outlines the significance of interculturality in higher education (HE) and in the development of a creative business management curriculum. The chapter argues that interculturality as an approach is central to higher education. Das' chapter argues that complexities in conceptualising *creative* through the cultural and historical narratives that have influenced, and been influenced by, the modern study of creativity—and more recently computational creativity and artificial intelligence (AI).

Fitzwater, in her chapter, argues to reclaim global citizenship within the context of transnational education. Hinwood focuses on the ubiquity of storytelling in recent years and its implications for business education. Her chapter argues that the use of storytelling in different contexts help in greater understanding of developing an ethical framework for business education. Blanchard's chapter outlines the processes of commercialisation of childhood and socialisation of pre-teen femininity with the help of fashion industry. The chapter is a critique of fashion industry that seeks to expand the commodification and sexualisation of childhood.

Wang's chapter argues for an inclusive teaching strategy while framing the curriculum for the growth of creative industry. Jabbar and UL-Durar's paper explores the pedagogical approaches for business school academics who teach ethnically diverse international students in northern English universities. The paper argues for cultural consciousness to avoid cultural stereotypes by highlighting the problematic nature of pedagogical disassociation in higher education in UK universities. Newman's chapter helps to understand and explain the importance of collaboration for growth of creative practice within fashion industry. The curriculum needs to incorporate the ideals of collaboration for collective working environment. Lambert locates students voices within the field of journalism and creative education. It argues that students in journalism have engaged with contentious political issues. Faulkner argues that hyperreality is a dangerous modern phenomenon which affect all sections of society including education sector. Li and Shaw's chapter conceptualises new types of creative and sustainable tourism by moving away from tangible destinations to the intangible heritage sites. Thomas makes a critique of capitalism and outlines self-ethnography of an educator of music industry pedagogy.

Walsh and Powell argued that higher education research neglects local research, which supports both pedagogical engagement and practice based research which would be valued by communities. The pedagogical innovation and engaged learning is central to mode 2 knowledge and intrareneurship. In her chapter, Sarah frames the relationship between UK Higher Arts Education (HAE), government policy, and the emergence and maintenance of professional pedagogies in creative education. She outlines the socio-political history of UK art schools, focussing on significant cultural and higher educational policy that shaped the adoption of professionalisation in creative pedagogical activity alongside the institutionalisation of art schooling. Lazzaro provides an overview of different types and features of cultural and creative districts and their theoretical backgrounds. Her chapter investigates different types of governance and models of administration models, elements of monitoring and indicators that are usually used for the measurement of performance of cultural districts. It finally offers a taxonomy based oncase studies of successful districts, where they are located, and their characteristics at start, growth and maturity phases of their life.

The final chapter by Nayak investigates the disciplinary denials of subjectivities and pluriversal nature of creative business education, examining the interdisciplinary limits of its curriculum produced in response to neoliberal crisis in business education. While creative business education is depicted as an alternative way out to regain the legitimacy of mainstream business school education and its dynamism, the programmes often recycled that upholds market values of compliant culture that destroys creativity of labour and the criticality of educational process. It highlights the continuity and growth of alienation within the interdisciplinary praxis of creative business education. It argues against the use of language, methods and conceptual narratives of traditional business education within creative business education for a radical transformation of business praxis that values people, planet and society.

This volume critically analyses the conceptual contours of pedagogical transformations in the field of creative business education. It calls for an integrated and ethnographic approach to understand, to analyse and to innovate creative curricula that is different from traditional business and management educations and its compliant culture. The book argues for a pluriversal vision based on social intelligence, critical thinking, inclusivity and creativity resulting in a holistic pedagogy that understands the social needs of people and of the planet. The critical reflections on everyday realities of life is central to this intercultural pedagogic approach to understanding and explaining different forms of contemporary crisis. The book brings together interdisciplinary academic practitioners and their praxis with different philosophical orientations within a single ethnographic and theoretical narrative to reclaim global citizenship rights in the age of artificial intelligence, democratic deficit, hyperreality and alienation.

In this way, the volume breaks away from the narrow silo of disciplinary boundaries to outline the pedagogical praxis of creative and critical business education that challenges existing knowledge, power and institutions while offering alternative pedagogic approaches to learning, teaching and research.

2

Towards Interculturality in International Creative Business and Management in Higher Education

Frank Fitzpatrick

Abstract Increasing diversity in global business has had an impact on the nature and structure of international business education. The provision of international education courses for students studying business has continued to grow, while universities have quite deliberately targeted enhanced internationalisation strategies as a business model worldwide. Such trends have compelled higher education institutions, in general, and business schools, in particular, to reflect upon how to engage with students from diverse cultural backgrounds and how to respond to their potentially different prior educational experiences. The response of higher education institutions to cultural diversity, however, is considered by many as broadly inadequate and heavily reliant on a largely discredited essentialist and deterministic view of culture. This manifests itself in two ways. First, the content of business management courses in higher education tends to draw upon the dominant paradigm in Cross-Cultural Management, which is

F. Fitzpatrick (✉)
Business School for the Creative Industries, University for the Creative Arts, Farnham, UK
e-mail: Philip.Powell@uca.ac.uk

© The Author(s), under exclusive license to Springer Nature Switzerland AG 2022
P. Powell, B. Shankar Nayak (eds.), *Creative Business Education*,
https://doi.org/10.1007/978-3-031-10928-7_2

7

increasingly considered to lag behind current thinking in conceptual trends in social science. This has consequences for the treatment of culture and diversity when analysing and explaining behaviours and issues in the globalised workplace. Second, a poor understanding of the concept of cultural diversity has an impact on how administration and academic systems and structures in universities actually engage with international students to overcome what are perceived as problems or difficulties in adjustment to university life in an unfamiliar context. Addressing these two issues requires, on the one hand, a better understanding of the concepts of culture and cultural diversity in the teaching of international business, drawing on contemporary research and approaches within the broader social sciences, and, on the other, a sense of how cross-cultural and intercultural processes work to develop a true sense of '*interculturality*' both in the experience of internationalised business education and in what students will eventually take into the global workplace. This chapter explores these concepts and issues and proposes that an understanding of interculturality should be at the heart of a global approach to higher education.

Introduction

The nature and focus of international business is changing fast with the rate of economic growth in the emerging economies of the global East and South having doubled in the last decade to now equal the value of trade in developed countries, as they look to expand their share of global business (UNCTAD 2016). This has led to an increase in international mobility and diversity in the global workforce (OECD 2009) and the need to adapt to alternative perspectives and definitions (Fitzpatrick 2019).

Increasing diversity in global business has had an impact on the nature and structure of international business education (AACSB International 2011; Calderon 2018). The provision of international education courses for students has continued to grow, while HEIs have adopted enhanced internationalisation strategies as a business model worldwide (British Council 2016; Zhu Hua et al. 2016).

Such trends have compelled higher education institutions, in general, and business schools, in particular, to reflect upon how to engage with students from diverse cultural backgrounds and how to respond to their potentially different prior educational experiences. The response of higher education institutions to cultural diversity is, however, considered by many as broadly inadequate and heavily reliant on a largely discredited essentialist and deterministic view of culture (Dervin and Layne 2013). This manifests itself in two ways. First, the content of business management courses in higher education tends to draw upon the dominant paradigm in *Cross-Cultural Management* (*CCM*), which is increasingly considered to lag behind current thinking in conceptual trends in social science (Bjerregaard et al. 2009). This has the consequences for the treatment of culture and diversity when analysing and explaining behaviour and issues in the globalised workplace. Second, a poor understanding of the concept of cultural diversity has an impact on how administration and academic systems and structures in universities actually engage with international students to overcome what are perceived as problems or difficulties in adjustment to university life in an unfamiliar context (Crawford and Bethell 2012). Addressing these two issues requires, on the one hand, a better understanding of the concepts of culture and cultural diversity in the teaching of international business, drawing on contemporary research and approaches within the broader social sciences, and, on the other, a sense of how cross-cultural and intercultural processes work to develop a true sense of '*interculturality*' in the experience of internationalised business education and what students will eventually take into the global workplace. This article explores these concepts and issues and proposes that an understanding of interculturality should be at the heart of a global approach to higher education.

Culture as Product: The Dominant Paradigm in International Business Education

In some respects, the origins of CCM can be traced back to Hall's work in developing the field of Intercultural Communication (ICC) at the Foreign Service Institute (FSI) of the U.S. Department of State, as described by Leeds-Hurwitz (1990). From Hall's perspective, culture and communication are seen as somewhat mysterious and sinister, a '*silent language* (Hall 1959) a *'hidden dimension'* (Hall 1966), unconsciously moulding our interactions with strange and exotic others in distant locations. Alternatively, culture is often described anthropologically, as a way of life (Williams 1981), observable within a particular, bounded location, relating to shared traditions and customs, embodied in dress, cuisine, rituals, celebrations and so on. In this sense, culture is seen to provide continuity across generations and influences how individuals interpret their world, how they behave and the choices that they make.

Such approaches have led CCM theorists to focus on *national cultures* defined by *dimensions* (Hofstede 1991; Trompenaars and Hampden-Turner 1997). In such models, culture is characterised as external to individuals, with values and behaviours passed down the generations through socialisation. National cultures are categorised and explained in *essentialist* terms, defined by national characteristics and behaviours deemed to be typical and immutable of a national population. Such categorisation creates the idea of homogeneity across entire populations, including large countries or geographical regions (e.g. *'Arab'*, *'Asian'*, *'European'*, *'Latin'*), where individuals can be expected to respond and behave in a predictable way as a result of their cultural programming or *'software of the mind'* instilled in them through their upbringing (Hofstede 1991). This has engendered lists and league tables of cultural typologies that dominate managerial and leadership approaches in particular and typical environments (House et al. 2004; Lewis 1996), designed to provide guidance for managers on how to overcome seemingly irreconcilable cultural differences in the workplace and succeed in international markets.

While CCM theorists claim that their work is empirically sound and widely researched, this has been deeply contested (McSweeney 2002; Søderberg 1999) based on the notion that culture and cultural identity are socially constructed, dynamic and open to interpretation. Further, such an approach to culture tends to rest on intuitive perceptions, appealing to acquired stereotypes or commonly held, imagined views drawn from prejudice or anecdotal accounts of supposedly typical behaviour (Anderson 1991). In this sense, moving away from a *'billiard board'* model of culture (Wolf 1982), which inspires the view of essentialist incompatibility of different cultural perspectives knocking against each other, towards a more pluralist and constructionist approach is critical to ensuring inclusivity and diversity.

The idea of creating describable categories and typologies of culture or through comparative dimensions is an approach that is heavily influenced by a positivist perspective, which seeks to understand behaviour on the basis of identifiable '*types of people*' (Moghaddam 2012) with set characteristics, not dissimilar to approaches to social categories and roles, such as race or gender, in which individuals from a certain category or background are assumed to be alike or determined by their fixed and immutable essential nature. Likewise, persisting with the idea that culture can stretch across a whole national population as a '*national culture*' belies the growing diversity of many national populations as a bricolage of diaspora, hybridity and fusion. Such a vision of cultural homogeneity perceived in large communities can be said to be largely conceptualised, or imagined (Anderson 1991), depicted through symbolic representation. It is often the case that individuals and groups identify with such conceptualisations and associated cultural categorisations, believing them to represent a presumed inherent cultural heritage. However, culture, viewed as a product of nationhood or a similarly large construct, such as ethnicity or religion, can also encourage the discourse of ethnocentric cultural superiority over others and potential intolerance of other ways of life that could lead to intercultural conflict.

Culture as Process: Culture Large and Culture Small

In contrast, an interpretive perspective sees culture and identity in a *non-essentialist* way, as socially constructed, created and negotiated by individuals in a social context across multiple sites and locations through interaction. This is to see culture more as a *process*, one of dynamic social construction (Berger and Luckman 1967), rather than a static *product* or imagined construct that individuals continually relate back to as a notional or imagined concept. In contrast, treating culture as a process, driven by interaction, allows us to entertain the idea that culture and cultural identity can evolve as a result of negotiation and experience.

Building on this, Holliday (1999) introduces the notion of '*two paradigms*' of culture, described as '*large cultures*' and '*small cultures*' The notion of *large culture* relates to a reified concept of culture focusing on notions and descriptions of cultural influences such as nationhood, community, background, upbringing and so on, which we often use to describe where we are from and are open to interpretation. On the other hand, the idea of *small cultures* refers to how we construct and negotiate shared understanding and cultural meaning at a group level through everyday interaction and language and is more concerned with social processes (Holliday 1999). For Holliday, the paradigm of large cultures can tend towards cultural reductionism or *culturalism*, in which the notion culture has become stabilised and reified by particular parties with particular interests and which can lead to a process of *otherisation*, '*whereby the "foreign" is reduced to a simplistic, easily digestible, exotic or degraded stereotype*' (ibid., p. 245). A *small culture* approach, on the other hand, can liberate definitions of culture from the *large*, imagined notions of ethnicity or nationhood as determining influences and thereby explore the full complexity of culture and identity. In this sense, culture is seen as a complex and dynamic *process* as individuals interact with each other at small group level to create shared cultural understanding at all levels of social existence through *universal cultural processes* (Holliday 2011).

This does not exclude external influences on individuals, which may be identified as tradition, national symbols and values, popular media or cultural artefacts, symbols, resources and narratives, which people may choose to identify with, but it does not accept socialisation as a *determining* factor. The increasing diversity of spaces and sites of intercultural interaction, and the increasing assortment of resources and media for international connectivity and mobility militates against a simplistic identification of individuals with stable and static identities based on a fixed location or social role.

Culture as Context: A Dialectical Approach

Critical in all of this is the existence of free will and choice as our identity evolves. However, culture is constructed and sustained through structures set within a framework of authority and power relations that govern and regulate a particular social and economic order, both from the wider institutional organisation of society to the concertive informal way that individuals and groups negotiate everyday issues through universal inter-cultural processes at the discourse level (Holliday 2011). Thus, the social construction of culture takes place within particular *contexts* influenced by wider economic, socio-political and ideological influences. This is not a static environment, however, and the concept of context goes further than simply location. While context suggests a physical location, relating to a local infrastructure and conditions of life, it also entails a social or behavioural environment, formed through sociocultural practices and processes, regulated by socially constructed conventions and created and sustained through a discursive and historical dialectical process, embracing also broader extra-situational forces that impinge upon the location from broader socio-economic and geo-political frameworks (Duranti and Goodwin 1992).

This adds a further dimension to the social constructionist approach, bringing into view the dynamics of power and conflicting agendas of the context that frames the purely constructive process and negotiation of meaning. In this sense, a *dialectical* approach becomes apposite, one of opposing and contradictory forces and interests pitched against each other, which acknowledges the relational tensions that larger sociocul-tural constructs can generate (Martin and Nakayama 2009). Context, then, should be viewed more as a dynamic process, rather than a static environment in which implicit norms and conventions and inherent power relations, inequities and ideologies pervade the social construction of shared meaning and understanding in all facets of sociocultural behav-iour. In this sense, it is the context of cultural behaviour and the loca-tional, behavioural and extra-situational dynamics that create and sustain cultural interaction, rather than innate and immutable cultural charac-teristics, locationally determined.

Culture as Universal: The Omni-Cultural Imperative

Culture can also be seen as a universal phenomenon in that all biological and cognitive and interactive processes can be considered common to all human groups as members of the same species. Through language and instinct, we have a natural predisposition to be able to interpret the behaviour of other humans regardless of cultural variance and negotiate shared understanding of what is considered acceptable group (cultural) behaviour (Berger and Luckman 1967). This approach has been supported by a long tradition of anthropological research and identifies the commonalities in the way humans live together in groups and societies, referring to such areas as, for example, social organisation and governance, the structure of belief and value systems and social living and behaviour relating to such things as rituals, rites, feasts, greetings, gift-giving, games, body adornment, dancing, gestures, language and so on (Antweiler 2016; Brown 1991; Fitzpatrick 2020).

The existence of universals could indicate that behaviour, which might be identified as culturally distinct across different societies, is actually the result of differences in contextual or dialectical dynamics created and sustained through the application of distinct systems of power and control, driven by self or by group interest, rather than being essentially distinguishable.

This has resulted in a more dispassionate approach to culture and diversity in multicultural education, with a focus on *omniculturism* (Moghaddam 2012), as an imperative to avoiding the potential pitfalls of diversity policies and practices, such as exoticisation, tokenism or otherisation, in which those from alternative cultural backgrounds can be persistently labelled or defined by their difference from the mainstream within society and denied opportunities to integrate more widely (Fitzpatrick 2020). Thus, in this it is the shared human commonalities and cultural universals that are sought and emphasised, removing focus from essential cultural differences. The benefit of such an approach is to defuse the narrative of cultural discourse as a potentially divisive exercise and replace it with the exploration reflection of what is fundamentally human in social interaction and organisation.

Culture as Identity: Personal Cultural Narrative

Primary socialisation, or, principally, *enculturation*, is the process by which an individual learns and internalises the accepted norms and values of their cultural group or society in early life (Kottak 2013). However, as pointed out above, while we are born into a social order and way of life which existed before us and we learn to interact within a social and institutional framework of relationships that ascribe identity and roles to us through cultural categories and representations, we are not determined or constrained by this (Berger and Luckman 1967).

In this sense, culture can be defined as membership of 'a discourse community that shares a common social space and history, and common imaginings' in which individuals share '*a common system of standards for perceiving believing, evaluating and acting*' (Kramsch 1998: 10). Such standards have also been described as '*regularities*' (Spencer-Oatey and Zegarac 2018), or consistencies, in how people behave and articulate their understanding of their world, the legitimacy of which is shared and adhered to by individuals within a given group and which, consequently, govern the group's behaviour. The assumption here is that, even when individuals move away from their community of origin, such standards and regularities will continue to influence them to some extent and are often identified as their *culture*. With this definition, however, while it is understood that there is a process based in heritage, socialisation and the early stages of learning to live in communities (enculturation), all of which influences individuals in their cognitive, emotional and sociocultural development and sense of identity, if we accept that individuals are able to make choices as free agents, their sense of identity is likely to evolve over the course of their lifetime as a result of their experiences.

Thus, individuals will continue to construct and forge their cultural identity through what can be described as a *personal cultural trajectory* (Holliday 2011) across multiple discursive sites of interaction, influenced by the sociocultural groups that they belong to, the spaces and institutions that they frequent and the narratives that they draw upon and identify

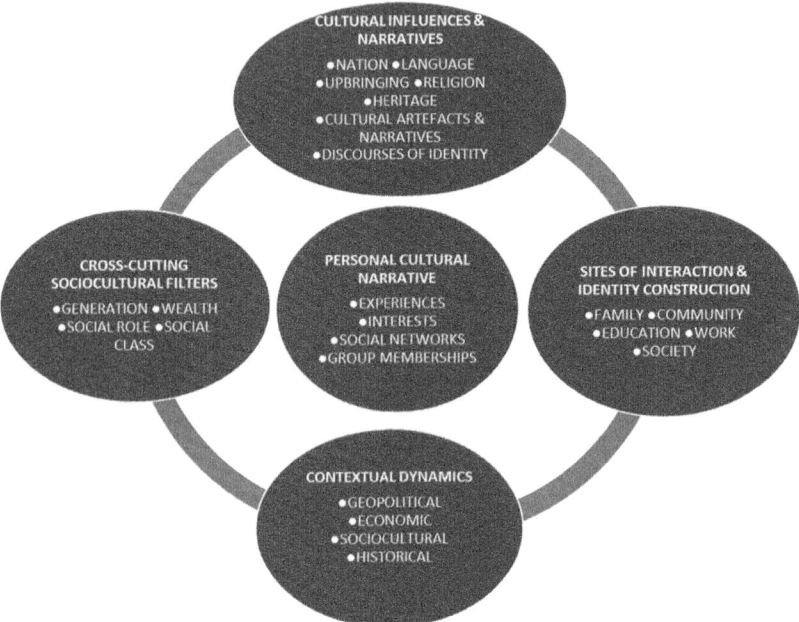

Fig. 2.1 The construction of personal cultural narrative (cultural identity)

with over time (Benwell and Stokoe 2006). As depicted in Fig. 2.1, then, cultural identity, then, can be seen as a personal cultural narrative or auto-biography that we construct over time about who we are culturally, although this is a static representation of the processes involved and is merely a heuristic device to help us explore such complexity. By drawing on the particular cultural narratives that have influenced us in our sociali-sation and through engagement with particular sites of interaction, social networks and discourse communities, we shape our own personal cultural narrative and identity as we navigate the ongoing opportunities, relation-ships and experiences that we encounter, albeit subject to contextual dia-lectical constraints and the sociocultural contextualities and filters that frame our interactions.

Approaching Culture in International Creative Business Education: Cross-Cultural or Intercultural?

Given this overview, how then should we approach culture and cultural identity in international business education in order to nurture interculturality? The approach taken in international business and business education has tended to favour a *cross-cultural* analysis, with an *intercultural* focus being used when focusing specifically on communication issues and, in this sense, the cross-cultural approach tends to dominate the paradigm, as indicated by the predominant use of the name *Cross-Cultural Management* (*CCM*) (French 2015). Breaking this down, CCM studies tend to take a *cross-cultural* comparative approach to how people behave across different cultural settings, while an *intercultural* focus analyses interaction amongst individuals from different cultural backgrounds within a particular cultural context (Gudykunst 2003; Fitzpatrick 2020). An example of a cross-cultural analysis might be to compare how meetings are conducted in different cultural contexts by looking at, for example, how individuals from the same cultural context address each other, how formal they are, what sort of dress code exists or what types of gestures, non-verbal cues, body language and communicative scripts or discourse features dominate and compare and contrast these features with other cultural contexts. In research terms, this approach takes an *etic* focus in that it is an external analysis of cultural behaviour. On the other hand, an intercultural analysis would focus more on the nature and outcomes of intercultural contact amongst individuals from different backgrounds when they meet together or interact with each other in a particular cultural context. This is more of an *emic* focus in research terms in that the motive of the analysis becomes the intercultural processes within group encounters. While both levels of analysis have value, there is a tendency to favour a cross-cultural focus both in dealing with internationalisation and through the use of essentialist dimensional models of culture in Cross-Cultural Management content, such as those mentioned above. The danger with a cross-cultural comparative approach, however, is that it tends to extrapolate observations of behaviour, or accounts of what is perceived as typical behaviour, and reify these as part of a set of immutable cultural dimensions to be associated with set contexts or territories embodied in *national cultures* (as in Hofstede 1991).

Cross-cultural analysis does not need to be like this, but to avoid the pitfalls of essentialism and reification, it would need to concentrate on particular cultural settings and take into account the contextual elements that frame intercultural behaviour at the time of observation, rather than *a priori* and immutable notions of assumed or imagined stereotyped national characteristics. On the other hand, an intercultural approach is more favourable for exploring the notion of identity and personal cultural narrative as individuals reflect upon and develop their cultural perspective as a consequence of their international experience. Through this, an awareness of interculturality amongst students of varying cultural backgrounds can be encouraged.

The Intercultural Process: Interstitial Culture and Third Space

By taking an intercultural approach, then, it is possible to focus on the processes of change and growth that international students and workers experience in their time in a new environment. This can help create a more fruitful understanding amongst those that administer international programmes of study of the nature of cultural diversity and how intercultural engagement can evolve amongst individuals from varied backgrounds.

The approach here, then, is to explore what is known as the *Third Space* or *interstitial* space (Bhabha 1994) in which, in this case, students from different cultural backgrounds have the opportunity to interact with each other to form relationships and friendship and collegiate groups without the baggage of cultural labelling. This can be considered a neutral domain in which individuals come together as themselves, rather than members of a distinctive cultural or national grouping (Holliday 2013: 110). Through their interactions in their everyday course work, group work, extra-curricular activities and participation on campus in social and academic spaces they can form new relationships and forge new memberships to enhance their own identity beyond their cultural origins. In other words, students from all backgrounds use this interstitial space to develop their own intercultural reference points and *interculturality*, together, as a unique group in a unique context, drawing on, but distancing themselves from, the polarising perception of their own cultural background and influences, as they experience identity convergence through growing *symbolic interdependence* (Imahori and Cupach 2005) and mutually shared commonalities in their perspectives as a common group.

This can be demonstrated in the model in Fig. 2.2. As a group comes together with a sense of belonging and common purpose, individuals from different cultural backgrounds and perspectives can build interculturality through their shared experience in the third space amongst them, which in turn may influence their own sense of cultural identity and personal cultural trajectory as they adapt to and integrate other cultural perspectives associated with a more ethno-relative outlook (Bennett and Bennett 2004). In effect, their experience in an international setting results in an evolving personal perspective on the world, which may

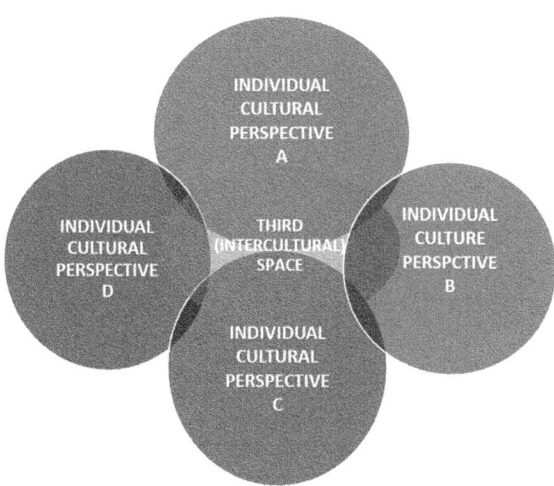

Fig. 2.2   Developing interculturality

incorporate views, values, tastes, choices, reflections and such, which may have been previously unfamiliar to them, or may have begun to influence them to alter their view of the world, their own cultural origins and their evolving personal cultural narrative.

With this approach, the role of the educator is to promote and provide the opportunities for intercultural understanding, focusing on team and group dynamics, ensuring tolerance and inclusion and avoiding cultural stereotyping.

Understanding and Overcoming Obstacles to Building Interculturality

While this may seem straightforward, it is important to understand the challenges of adjustment to unfamiliar cultural contexts and the processes and resources that are in play within the third or intercultural space, as the obstacles to building interculturality can be considerable. First, it is questionable as to whether interaction takes place amongst students on equal terms. International students, for example, may come from very different educational contexts in which their experience of learning and teaching might not prepare them for approaches and methods in an alternative context without being given specific support or without scaffolded intervention (Peacock and Harrison 2008). Likewise, diversity in communications styles or aspects of observable cultural differences may lead to cultural or behavioural labelling, setting them apart from home students. Consequently, the question arises as to how to create equity of treatment within the formation of relationships amongst students, who may struggle to engage or integrate with local networks and groups and who may prefer the psychological comfort of their own national and cultural groupings.

Likewise, it is also important to be aware of the challenges of cross-cultural adjustment, commonly known as '*culture shock*', in which students are faced with affective, behavioural and cognitive challenges in navigating an unfamiliar cultural context, where they will need to make both sociocultural and psychological adjustments in their daily lives

(Ward et al. 2001). While international students have increasingly established *personal resources* to deal with adjustment, in terms of linguistic and intercultural skills, experience and means to access support, educators and, in particular, university support staff should ensure that they provide adequate *institutional resources* to ensure that students are supported in their new environment and able to build new *social networks* to facilitate their cross-cultural integration (Fitzpatrick 2016, 2017).

Towards Interculturality in Creative Business Management Education

Overall, then, the benefits of building a genuine understanding, space and opportunities for intercultural growth in international higher education programmes are considerable. As we have seen, global workforce mobility and diversity are on the increase and becoming progressively wide-ranging. Workforce diversity has long been considered a strength for organisational effectiveness for a number of assumed reasons, including wider market knowledge and insight, access to local networks and connections across international markets, greater diversity of skills and an increasing sense of ease and ethnorelative perspective in the face of cultural difference (Brett et al. 2006). Diverse workforces are likely to be less ethnocentric and more comfortable with culturally novel situations and intercultural interaction, reducing the likelihood of misunderstanding and conflict at work (Fitzpatrick 2020).

Further, some research suggests that taking an intercultural perspective can enhance the performance and creativity of teams (Fontaine 2017). Focusing on interculturality, then, can bring a number of advantages to creative business management education in the way that teams and group-level processes construct and stabilise culture and how diverse individuals can work together to build an evolving and dynamic interactive experience and shared understanding within an interstitial or third and unique space.

Much work has to be done, however, to engage academic and support staff in understanding the challenges of international students and to provide institutional resources and conditions in the form of support systems that will facilitate inclusive engagement for all students regardless of background and experience and ensure their full integration into university life. By understanding the educational and personal challenges of international students and by building intercultural sensitivity within the host university community and amongst individuals, interculturality can bring benefits to both the creative international educational experience and help build critical intercultural skills and perspectives for future global working.

References

AACSB International (2011) *Globalization of Management Education: Changing International Structures, Adaptive Strategies, and the Impact on Institutions.* Emerald Publishing: Bingley, available at https://www.aacsb.edu/-/media/aacsb/publications/research-reports/aacsb-globalization-of-management-education-task-force-report-2011.ashx?la=en&hash=46B805416C12C419DCFEE8FC4C36DBCB3AE2519A

Anderson, B. (1991) *Imagined communities: Reflections on the origins and spread of nationalism.* London: Verso.

Antweiler, C. (2016) *Our Common Denominator: Human Universals Revisited.* Berghahn Books: Oxford.

Bennett, J.M. and Bennett, M.J. (2004) 'Developing Intercultural Sensitivity: An Integrative Approach to Global and Domestic Diversity' in: Landis, D., Bennett, J.M., and Bennett, M.J. (Eds.) *Handbook of Intercultural Training.* Thousand Oaks: Sage Publications pp. 147–165.

Benwell, B. and Stokoe, E. (2006) *Discourse and Identity.* Edinburgh: Edinburgh University Press.

Berger, P. and Luckman T. (1967) *The Social Construction of Reality.* London: The Penguin Press.

Bhabha, H.K. (1994) *The Location of Culture.* London: Routledge.

Bjerregaard, T., Lauring, J. and Klitmøller A. (2009) 'A critical analysis of intercultural communication research in cross-cultural management' *Critical Perspectives on International Business*, 5 (30) pp. 207–228

British Council (2016) The shape of Global Higher Education: national Policies Framework for International Engagement. At: https://www.britishcouncil.org/

sites/default/files/f310_tne_international_higher_education_report_final_ v2_web.pdf

Brown, D. E. (1991) *Human Universals*. New York: McGraw-Hill.

Calderon (2018) 'Massification of Higher Education Revisited'. RMIT University. At: http://cdn02.pucp.education/academico/2018/08/23165810/ na_mass_revis_230818.pdf

Crawford, B., & Bethell, L. (2012) Internationalized Campuses Just Don't Happen: Intercultural Learning Requires Facilitation and Institutional Support. In: S. Ahola & D. M. Hoffman (Eds.) *Higher Education Research In Finland: Emerging Structures and Contemporary Issues* (pp. 189–213). University of Jyväskylä. At: https://www.oamk.fi/files/8115/5429/1432/978-951-39-5189-4.pdf

Dervin, F. and Layne, H. (2013) 'A guide to interculturality for international and exchange students: an example of Hospitality?' *Journal of Multicultural Discourses* 8 (1) pp. 1–19.

Duranti, A. and Goodwin, C. (1992) *Rethinking Context*. Cambridge: CUP.

Fitzpatrick, F. (2016) *Voices from Cuba: Redefining culture shock*, Saarbrucken: Lambert Academic Publishing.

Fitzpatrick, F. (2017) 'Taking the 'culture' out of 'culture shock': A critical review of literature on cross-cultural adjustment in international relocation' *Critical Perspectives on International Business* 13 (4) pp. 278–296.

Fitzpatrick, F. (2019) 'Coping with authoritarianism in international relocation' *Critical Perspectives on International Business* 15 (1) pp. 2–19.

Fitzpatrick, F. (2020) *Understanding Intercultural Interaction: An Analysis of Key Concepts*. Bingley: Emerald Publishing.

Fontaine, G. (2017), 'Intercultural Teams' in: Y. Y. Kim (Ed.) *The International Encyclopaedia of Intercultural Communication*. London: Wiley.

Gudykunst, W.B. (Ed.) (2003) *Cross Cultural and Intercultural Communication*. London: Sage.

French, R. (2015) *Cross-Cultural Management in Work Organisations*. London: CIPD.

Hall, E.T. (1959) *The Silent Language*. New York: Anchor Books.

Hall, E.T. (1966) *The Hidden Dimension*. New York: Anchor Books.

Brett, J., Behfar, K. and Kern, M.C. (2006) 'Managing Multicultural Teams' *Harvard Business Review* November pp. 84–91.

Hofstede, G. (1991) *Cultures and Organisations: Software of the mind*. New York: McGraw-Hill.

Holliday, A. (1999) 'Small cultures' *Applied Linguistics* 20 (2) pp. 237–64.

Holliday, A. (2011) *Intercultural Communication and Ideology*. London: Sage.

Holliday, A. (2013) *Understanding Intercultural Communication: Negotiating a Grammar of Culture* London: Routledge.

House, R.J., Hanges, P.J., Javidan, M., Dorfman, P.W., & Gupta, V. (Eds.) (2004) *Culture, Leadership, and Organizations: The GLOBE Study of 62 Societies*. Thousand Oaks: Sage Publications.

Imahori, T. and Cupach, W. R. (2005) 'Identity Management Theory: Facework in Intercultural Relationships' in: Gudykunst, W.B. (Ed.), *Theorizing About Intercultural Communication*. London: Sage pp. 195–210.

Kottak, C. (2013) *Window on Humanity: A Concise Introduction to General Anthropology*. New York: McGraw-Hill Education.

Kramsch, C. (1998) *Language and Culture*. Oxford: Oxford University Press.

Martin, J. & Nakayama, T. (2009) *Intercultural Communication in Contexts*. New York: McGraw-Hill Education.

Leeds-Hurwitz, W. (1990) 'Notes in the history of intercultural communication: The Foreign Service institute and the mandate for intercultural training' *Quarterly Journal of Speech* 76 (3) pp. 262–281

Lewis, R. D. (1996) *When Cultures Collide* Boston: Nicholas Brealey Publishing.

McSweeney, B. (2002) 'Hofstede's model of national cultural differences and their consequences: A triumph of faith—a failure of analysis' Human Relations, 55 (1) pp. 89–118.

Moghaddam, F. M. (2012) 'The omnicultural imperative' in: *Culture and Psychology* 18 (3) pp. 304–330.

OECD (2009) *Globalisation and Emerging Economies*. At: http://www.oecd.org/ tad/globalisation-and-emerging-economies-9789264044814-en.htm

Peacock, N., & Harrison, N. (2008) 'It's so much easier to go with what's easy: "Mindfulness" and the discourse between home and international students in the United Kingdom' *Journal of Studies in International Education* 13 pp. 487–508.

Søderberg, A-M. (1999) 'Do National Cultures Always Make a Difference?' in T. Vestergaard (Ed.), *Language, Culture and identity*. Aarhus, Denmark: Aarhus University Press.

Spencer-Oatey, H. & Zegarac , V. (2018) 'Conceptualising culture and its impact on behavior' in: C. Frisby & W. O'Donohue (Eds.) *Cultural Competence in Applied Psychology: An Evaluation of Current Status and Future Directions*. New York: Springer pp. 211–242.

Trompenaars, F. and Hampden-Turner, C. (1997) *Riding the Waves of Culture: Understanding Diversity in Global Business*. New York: Mc-Graw-Hill.

UNCTAD (2016) *Key Statistics and Trends in International Trade 2016, United Nations Conference on Trade and Development.* At: http://unctad.org/en/PublicationsLibrary/ditctab2016d3_en.pdf

Ward, C. Bochner, S. and Furnham, A. (2001) *The Psychology of Culture Shock.* London: Routledge.

Williams, R. (1981) *Culture.* London: Fontana.

Wolf, E.R. (1982) *Europe and the People Without History.* Berkley: University of California Press.

Zhu Hua, Handford, M. & Young, T.J. (2016) 'Framing interculturality: a corpus-based analysis of online promotional discourse of higher education intercultural communication courses' *Journal of Multilingual and Multicultural Development* 38 (3) pp. 283–300.

.

3

The Meaning of Creativity Through the Ages: From Inspiration to Artificial Intelligence

Simon Das

Abstract Given the relatively new pedagogic contexts of creative business education and creative industry business schools, this chapter aims to examine the complexity tied-up in the word '*creativity*' through the cultural and historical narratives that have both influenced, and been influenced by, the modern study of creativity—and more recently computational creativity and artificial intelligence (AI). The chapter illustrates that despite creativity appearing in modern dictionaries only after Guilford's inaugural speech as chair of the APA in 1950, its modern origins belie Western historic myths and cultural assumptions such as genius, intelligence and imagination that have endured into present day '*confluence theories*' of creativity by social psychologists such as Amabile—models largely about creativity as intrinsic psychology and cognitive abilities. It is argued that along this historical journey towards an ontology of creativity '*in the mind*', the creativity of the person in social systems (first

S. Das (✉)
Business School for the Creative Industries, University for the Creative Arts, Farnham, UK
e-mail: Philip.Powell@uca.ac.uk

© The Author(s), under exclusive license to Springer Nature Switzerland AG 2022
P. Powell, B. Shankar Nayak (eds.), *Creative Business Education*,
https://doi.org/10.1007/978-3-031-10928-7_3

outlined by Whitehead in the 1920s) has been overlooked, especially in the new field of AI. Rising to a call from Still and D'Inverno's paper at an *International Conference of Computational Creativity* (2016), the chapter reviews the facets and features of what they term '*G creative*' (perhaps God like) and '*N creative*' (perhaps nature like)—and point to the problem of psychology's hijacking of the subject of creativity from 1950s onwards with its adopted closed system intelligence in the development of AI programs and '*thinking*' machines. The case is made for a place in the creative academy, therefore, to help the field of AI move beyond '*closed system*' creativity AI by pointing to more '*open system*' approaches, including a recent AI artwork algorithm employing Csikszentmihalyi's sociocultural creativity model of external '*rating*'.

Introduction

The responsibility of the creative academy is to aid the field of AI and machine learning, helping it move beyond '*closed system*' creativity algorithms inspired by individualistic '*thinking power*' theories. Though much AI in everyday modern technology remains akin to Boden's closed-system '*combinational*' computational creativity of the 1990s, a recent example in the chapter will examine the AI artwork algorithm by the Obvious Collective in 2018, against Csikszentmihalyi's sociocultural creativity model, highlighting its value in human-and-machine creative futures beyond complex problem solving and '*in-the-mind alone*' analogous creativity.

Creativity a Modern Concept?

A rich history of concepts and ideas related to the act of creativity has brought many ideas—some more rational than others—to the table of contemporary creativity research, despite no formal definition or even entry into modern dictionaries existed until after World War II.

In a contemporary industrial context, the world of creative industries, creative labour and creative work examined by scholars such as labour economists Hesmondhalgh and Baker point out the nebulous '*catch all*' term, saying '*the terms "creativity" and "creative" have been abused and over-use*' (2011, p. 2) in recent years. This is largely because, although there is some agreed definition of what creativity is in terms of the generation of '*novel and appropriate*' ideas / products / concepts, academic literature on creativity lacks unified theory or explanations of its causes. Creativity, as a result, can be at best, according to Runco, a 'syndrome or complex, *labels that capture the idea that creativity can be expressed in diverse ways (e.g. art vs. science), and sometimes involves different processes (e.g. cognitive or social)*' (2007, xi) or a worse something so subjective, it is like defining humour.

Philosophising that creativity is '*not like height or acidity, but more like, say, humor or beauty, a quality that people—although they may concur in many of their actual judgments—are prone to disagree about*' (Klausen 2010, p. 348), Klausen, and others, see creativity as consensual, real, measurable but at the same time *subjective*, and therefore best grouped in three directions (Klausen 2010, p. 350)—as '*people*', '*products*' and '*processes*'. Each 'P', according to Klausen, places emphasis on a different location, depending on context. However, regardless of scientific approach or '*direction*' and its philosophical approach, any modern creativity theory has to be judged against the weight of cultural history and engrained ideas about how creativity works and where creativity functions. Holland and Quinn (1987) define an anthropological system of cultural assumptions as a '*cultural model*', one that Sawyer explains in his preface to his book on *Explaining Creativity* (2012) exists and influences the various beliefs and assumptions underpinning the experts' research in the field of creativity.

Although Sawyer (2012) cites as many as ten separate assumptions or beliefs, some of them not entirely supported by scientific evidence—though many '*partially true*' (Sawyer 2012, pp. 12–14), most creativity authors acknowledge a number of these. What could be called a series of discourses on the subject, representing different beliefs and power relations (Foucault 1972), or what has been termed the '*rhetorics of creativity*' by sociologists of creativity (Banaji et al. 2006), can be summarised as involving a number beliefs in differing '*locations*', by different theorists and schools of thought, for example: Weisberg on '*eminent*' creativity located in talent (1993); Sawyer on creativity as an emergent property via collaboration 1999); Amabile on creativity as a form of intrinsic motivational psychology 1983), Csikszentmihalyi on creativity located in affective '*flow*' states of mind (1996), Simonton on creativity as a form of '*intelligence*' (2009) and perhaps at the fringes of this chapter, the cognitive research of creativity in neurological locations in the brain (Sawyer 2011).

These theories and theorists '*locate*' creativity in different ways and places, and their explanations of creativity have emerged via a long history of interest in the term, the phenomena and what it can add to various fields, for example the psychologists' search for problem-solving talent Post-War (Torrance 1959), the educational and sociological proponents of creativity (Banaji et al. 2006; Gauntlett 2011) and those with a post Schumpeterian political economy of a new '*creative class*' of workers (Florida 2004). This varied and interdisciplinary field has created varying assumptions; and it has led to businesses reinforcing long-established '*tools*' of creativity (such as brain storming and Google's 'skunk works') and the creative industries (a sector defined by DCMS 2001, to include advertising, publishing, design, film, music and the arts) failing to debunk '*myths*' around creativity. In the twenty-first century, creativity is still seen through a number of historically-derived ways, such as the work of '*genius*', creativity as the '*art*' of inspired individuals, creativity as the outcome of '*play*' and collaboration or even creativity as form of mental illness (Freud 1924)—talent being a '*silver lining*' to madness in the creativity '*beliefs list*' by Sawyer (2012, p. 13).

A History of Creativity Theory

Throughout various historical discussions on creativity, the concept, the values attributed to it and the various usages we give to the term, are widely said to be relatively modern (Weiner 2000; Sawyer 2012; Kaufman and Glaveneau 2019). According to Sawyer (2012), no historical period would understand today's concept of creativity. It is a term that has evolved over a short period of time, and to put some context to this, he provides there is no reference to the word '*creativity*' in the English language before the nineteenth Century (Sawyer 2012, p. 19). The first modern usage of '*creativity*' emerges as late as 1875, well into the Victorian Age. Cited by Kaufman and Glaveneau (2019) as appearing in the text of *A History of Dramatic English Literature* by Adolfus William Ward, this was said to be first used in language to define some talent or force across all disciplines—although Sawyer points out (2012, p. 20) that in the French and Italian speaking world, no reference to the word in this sense would emerge until some 50 years hence. Even a formal usage entry into English dictionaries did not happen until after World War II.

This modernity, however, is not meant to mean that '*creativity*' has no ancient origins and history. Indeed, the study of its origins, according to Kaufman and Glaveneau (2019), is recommended to help shed light on, not just '*our species' past*' but '*its present and beyond*' (Kaufman and Glaveneau 2019, p. 9)—especially considering the contemporary definitional debate about what creativity means today and the cultural value placed upon it in the fields of the arts, humanities, science and technology (Batey 2012). Scholars interest in the phenomenon, emphasises the need for socio-political, technological and economic context—and that is a historical one. In the preface to Weisberg's eponymous volume on the subject (2006), he gives over the entire purpose of the book to '*demonstrate how something as seemingly difficult to pin down as creativity can be **defined** and brought under scientific study*' [emphasis added] (Weisberg 2006, p. 4).

Over the last six decades, a wide body of knowledge on the subject has emerged in wide variety of fields of research—fields such as: human psychology (Torrance 1959; Gruber 1981; Simonton 1976, 1989; Sternberg and Lubart 1991), social psychology (Amabile 1983, 1996; Csikszentmihalyi 1988), the study of genius (Weisberg 1993), digital sociology (Gauntlett 2011), pedagogy and education and cultural anthropology (Niu and Sternberg 2002). According to a review by Sternberg and Lubart (1999), over the decades these many approaches, however, lack a '*theory of creativity*', being merely practical approaches to enhance creativity of the mind, perhaps led in this direction by its mythical origins in Western thought.

Researchers are said to have not provided a clear idea of what the characteristics of creativity exactly are. Given this lack of clear definition, the '*confluence*' theories or explanations of creativity (ones that mix creativity of the mind, talent and motivation) are recommended for research by Sternberg and Lubart (1999) and Runco (2007), who cite contributions by Amabile (1983, 1998, 1996; Amabile and Pratt 2016); Gruber and Davies (1988) and Csikszentmihalyi (1996) as well as their own '*investment theory*' of creativity where creativity is explained in metaphorical market-like context, where creatives '*buy low and sell high*' in the world of ideas (Sternberg and Lubart 1991, p. 30).

In the Beginning … Creativity and Inspiration

The word 'creativity' itself has deeply historic roots. Its etymology from the Indo-European root word *ker* or *kere*, meaning '*to grow*', and arrives into the Latin *creatio* or *creatus* meaning the same. In classical usage, linguists point out that in spoken Latin, create would have implied to biologically grow, as opposed to the Latin *artis* to '*make*' (Kaufman and Glaveneau 2019, p. 10). God created; people just made—a distinction that in the West endured for centuries, reinforced by the impact on thinking of the Old Testament and the Abrahamic story of God as creator and '*his Creation*' which brought with it the idea that man was made in the image of God. The message was that man could be fruitful and multiply, but man's participation in creativity, in every sense, was therefore limited, according to Weiner (2000, p. 25), who cites 13th Christian theologian Saint Anselm (then Archbishop of Canterbury) as making analogy between the craftsman who first conceives a project in his mind and God's pre-existing idea of Creation, before emphasising the analogy as '*very incomplete*' as the artisan follows existing models and '*God who is the first and sole cause and creates through himself alone*' (Weiner 2000, p. 44).

Over the centuries, in an enduring world where only God created, the nearest thing to a usage of the modern term '*creative*' was, according to Sawyer (2011, 2012), the idea of *inspiration*—to draw on its Latin meaning, to breath into, akin the Creator breathing life into the world. Man is not superhuman, but sometimes he can be inspired, a belief that stayed within Western culture well into the Middle Ages, is said by Weiner (2000, p. 76) to have arrived from the classical Platonic Greek myths of the inspiration by muses or deities. In Shrine of Wisdom on Plato and the Four Inspirations, Greece, musical and poetic inspiration came from the muses (and water nymphs), whereas prophetic inspiration came from Apollo: different deities gave different creativity. This tradition is something that is consistent within a number of religions of the world—for example in Hinduism, the Goddess Saraswati has been invoked to inspire music for thousands of years (Kinsley 1988). In Hackforth's translation of Plato's Phaedrus (1972), a dialogue between his protagonist Socrates and Phaedrus, he explains that madness and Devine inspiration were described as going hand in hand, contrary to the understanding of Plato as a rationalist. According to Sawyer (2012, p. 20), this form of creative *'insight'* about nature, problem solving and the world itself through inspiration was a superhuman force, as only the work of the God could be truly novel: the gods took away thinking and reason before bestowing the gift of inspiration. As given by art historians Honour and Flemming (1999), art and not poetry, however, was only ever a poor imitation of the perfection of the world of ideas, explaining why ancient Greek artists did not try to imitate what they saw in reality, but always sought to depict the pure forms of underlying identity.

The Origins of Creative Genius

This history of genius, reflected linguistically, over centuries also provides evidence of the ancient, the something special about someone being *their* 'genius'. Although not popular in modern idiomatic English, the phrasing of someone *'having a genius for cookery'*, or maths or anything else, relates better to other European languages, where the *'genius'* is more clearly *separate* to the person, and therefore closer to its historical root as a spirit. One linguistic example in a modern European language, using the exact Latin word for genius, *genio*, exists in Spanish, where a bad temper might be referred to having *'un mal genio'*, literally, having *'a bad genius'*. Simonton explaining in Spanish, one is not saying the person is an 'evil genius' but has a *'disagreeable disposition'* (Simonton 1994, p. 13). *Geniality* existing in someone today, illustrates the genius spirit in them derived from an ancient cultural meaning in the term.

In the classical world, if being inspired was therefore the explanation of the act of human creativity, then the force behind someone who achieved extraordinary feats of creativity over time was his '*genius*'. Another superhuman historical factor in the history of creativity, no modern researcher of creativity entirely avoids raising of examples about '*extraordinary people doing extraordinary things*' (Simonton 1976; Sternberg 2000; Csikszentmihalyi 1988); and of the genius over the recent centuries, people who in their place and context so influential, Simonton asks us: imagine Spain without Cervantes, France without Napoleon, England without Shakespeare and America without Jefferson? (Simonton 2009, p. 2). A creativity scholar with an interest in genius (his 1976 study sample size of eminent creators reached into the thousands), he divides the study and meaning of genius into two parts: one contemporary, scientific and measured by psychometric methods, and a second, '*humanistic*'—and one measured by '*a long history*' (2009, p. 13), explaining roots of the humanistic definition of genius as therefore '*story-based*'. In the Roman period, genius is an idea of a personal deity, a '*guardian angel*', according to Simonton (2009) very similar ancient Greek tradition of *daemon*, described as good and bad tutelary spirits in Liddell and Scott (1925). In Roman times people had deities; personal ones and ones that resided in locations (Struck 2019). The belief in this type of guiding genius carried over into Christianity (where it still exists today in Catholic school pedagogy), and endures thousands of years after the Roman idea of a spirit belonging to each person, Simonton (2009, p. 13) provides a vestige residing in contemporary art and culture via the 1946 film *It's a Wonderful Life* where an angel '*Clarence*' intervenes to show '*George Bailey*' that life is worth living (portrayed by actor James Stewart).

Creative Imagination

It is only in the last century that the more individualistic notion of a person not *having* a genius but *being* one comes to the fore (Murray 1989), one that has a more Western interpretation and one that forms part of a cultural model. What elevates the idea of creativity as art, artistry and the modern concept of the creative, is in particular, the portrayal of a solitary individual. This specific belief, according to Keith Sawyer is one that is barely 200 years old, along with the concept of the artist having high social status. Explaining that, 'before the Renaissance creativity was associated with the need to imitate established masters' (Sawyer 2012, p. 20), history, artists in the Middle Ages needed to survive on patronage by nobility. The role of the artist being exclusively commissioned by royalty, the church or rich merchant (Clark 1997, p. 11).

Long before the establishment of capitalism in Europe (widely recounted in Marxist analysis as developing in the seventeenth century by Braudel (1981–1984 and Holton 1978), Weiner's (2000) examination of the history of creative works in an earlier thirteenth Century world, outlines one of technological developments and the growing individual value of art and artefacts were already becoming less craft and craftsmen based. Drawing on various technological and sociocultural changes Weiner (2000, p. 47) describes a changing cultural meaning of creativity, between the thirteenth and fifteenth century, a period when Thomas Aquinas established a natural law theory against unjust rule, the Magna Carta sets out basic rights and freedoms of the individual and St Francis of Assisi inspired a new movement to elevate the individual as a '*dignified creature of God*' (Weiner 2000, p. 47). Surely the genesis of what, centuries later would become the Human Rights movement world, people are becoming liberated, and with that, the *creators* of their own destiny.

In the last two centuries, this more individualistic idea of creativity developed into what De Fillippi et al. (2007) calls creativity of the '*Western Tradition*'. A cannon of philosophy that starts with Plato, the development of the individual in the thirteenth Century, before the influence of modern psychology through Sigmund Freud and the philosophy through Karl Popper. However, within this tradition, the elevation of the fine arts to become synonymous with creativity is often attributed to the eighteenth century writing of Immanuel Kant (Simonton 2009; Banaji et al. 2006). In his *Critique of Judgement*, creativity is described as the making of the '*sublime*', of genius that can be revered and understood as set apart from the everyday—raising what in modern creativity research is frequently described as the divide between 'Big C' and 'Small C' creativity—the everyday from the extraordinary. This distinction, in Simonton's view (2009), shows us, from a Western cultural perspective, creativity discourses are dominated by the extraordinary things made by extraordinary people. Creativity therefore '*embodied in a particular kind of personality*' (De Fillippi et al. 2007, p. 511)—is a genius of things by genius people, and historically gave rise to the close association with domains of the fine arts, theatre, music, literature and architecture, during a period when the art world becomes less reliant on aristocratic patronage, emphasising the rise of the individual talent.

Science, however, had not yet become part of creativity in Kant's Age of Enlightenment. Thought as a function of methodology, of replicable process, Simonton cites Kant himself as saying Newton's *Principa Mathematica* was an '*immortal work*' but could have been produced by anyone with sufficient learning, 'whereas only a **genius** like Homer could have written the Illiad and the Odyssey' [emphasis added] (Simonton 2009, p. 25). Although the mysterious ancient world of the inspired and the genius seem present in the Kantian view of creativity, in the Classical era painting and art was imitation, and only poetry could be *inspired* (Weisberg 1993), reminding us of Polycleitos and his prescribed proportions for drawing the human form, called *canon* or '*measure*' (Pollit 1995). In the Classical worldview, creativity in art was perceived in a way more akin to the eighteenth Century Kantian views on science, something than can be quantified, is rule-based and recreated only by method—not by the inspiration of genius.

In the late Enlightenment period, the idea of Kant's sublime inspiration can be seen evolving towards providing a clear cultural notion of artists being special. Artists were seen to have an ability to create works without a specific ultimate consumer—worthy of creativity in its own right. By the time of the British Industrial Revolution, a new concept and belief about creativity was cystalising and evolving from the old—especially the idea individual talent as '*imagination*' (Sawyer 2012, p. 21). Into the eighteenth Century the establishment of art institutions, galleries and a marketplace for artefacts nourished by the development of art history, art schools and apprenticeships formed the modern conception of an artist as a person set-apart from the rest, isolated, talented and inspired.

By the dawn of the twentieth Century, these unchanged ideas about innate imagination and being set-apart, formed part of the new Freudian science of psychoanalysis. Creativity in this new field of examining the human mind was theorised, like many other facets of human character, as an *'unconscious'* act by Freud. Driven by the forces now often used as cliché of his ideas, the *ego* and *libido*, were theorized as an artist's form of defence mechanism against neurosis. Playing out his fantasies in a socially acceptable way (in a similar way that play for children provides a form of meaning and control), the artist in Freud's psychoanalysis makes unconscious daydreams a controllable reality. On his essay *Creative Writers and Daydreaming* (1908), Drobot (2018) provides that although the much quoted Freudian illness of *'suppression'* was not theorised as being at work in artistry (but a more healthy form of *'sublimation'*), Freudian psychology is nevertheless said to have fuelled controversial ideas that endured into the twenty-first Century: ideas that artists (and by association all creative people) were *'disturbed—similar to the mentally ill'* (Sawyer 2012, p. 22), by being sexually driven and even criminally minded. Psychoanalysis, is in Sawyer's opinion, a factor aiding the enduring myth that a creative person is a tortured *'lone genius'*.

Creativity as Potential: The Birth of a Sociological View

Alongside these new theories of the mind (some have called pseudoscience) about the *'hidden'* workings of creative sublimation, the beginnings of a more scientific and philosophical modernity applied to creativity were emerging about a universal phenomenon—or even non phenomenon—not something subconscious, inspired or the property of the genius. One of Britain's leading nineteenth Century's philosophers, Whitehead, who while professor of philosophy at Harvard, made a bold intervention at separating out some of the inspiration myths of creativity in his philosophical and cosmological opus magnum *Process and Reality* (1978/1929). In this tome, he raises an almost pre-psychology and pre-sociological view on creativity. Coming from his complex philosophical discourse on the meaning of *'potentiality'* in humankind being both a *'general bundle of possibilities'* but also *'real'*, being conditioned by the actual world (1978/1929), hint at what later influences more sociocultural views of creativity (Csikszentmihalyi 1988) and the confluence models of creativity (Amabile 1996) that would later appear in mid-century.

To quote the words of one scholar on Whitehead: '*[he] insists that creativity is in no way to be limited to human activity or consciousness and that a wider understanding of creativity, based on the relativity of the potential and the actual, must be recognized*' (Halewood 2013, p. 76). Creativity, was by the 1930s, philosophised as being a universal and cosmological truth, a systemic potentiality process, and as Whitehead's magnificently named '*Category of the Ultimate*' stated: '*Creativity is without a character of its own ... It is that ultimate notion of the highest generality at the base of actuality. It cannot be characterized, because all characters are more special than itself*' (1978/1929, p. 31). By invoking the idea of the potential and actual, Whitehead's lectures at Harvard disseminated the first modern usage of the term '*creativity*' as more aligned to a natural process—the *creare* of bringing about in nature, rather than through a '*gift*' of inspiration of something in the mind alone. Creativity through this philosophical lens can therefore be associated with '*normal*' everyday processes—the sort of creativity far removed from the '*subliminal*' endeavours of fine art. In the words of those that saw creativity in this way, such as art historian John Dewey by the mid nineteenth century, creativity is about breaking convention, '*in re-creating them ... it brings refreshment, growth and satisfying joy to one who participates*' (1948)—definition adopted in twenty-first Century by neo-craft media philosophers such as Gauntlett (2011) who theorised the importance of social connections and role of improving social capital that a creative 'making' culture might have.

Despite this progressive and emerging view from philosophy on the campuses of American and British universities in the 1930s and 1940s, mainstream culture took much longer to change what Sawyer (2012) points out as an already established story. Summarising this view of creativity at the time, it was one of '*people with a unique vision*', being solitary with imagination expressed through their genius in art—and art alone. As a 'story of creativity' it was, in his words, '*fully formed*' by then (Sawyer 2012, p. 23). The myth busting challenges from Whitehead provided many unsolved questions about creatives and creativity. By Freud's own admission, as far as creativity went, he did not have all the answers in the mind—specifically not being able to explain the '*effect of joy and pleasure [as it was the artist's]… innermost secret*' or what he called '*talent*'—something that required Whitehead's '*potentiality*' of the '*real*' external world and not psychodynamic cognitive analysis in the way he applied it (Drobot 2018).

Creativity of the Mind: Intelligence, Divergent Thinking and Psychology

The quest for providing more science to the potentiality of the mind, became the domain of the emerging Post World War II field of cognitive psychology. Led by the quest by Skinner, its approach was to provide reason through observable data in psychology and not through a philosophical or conceptual neural process theorised by Freudian psychology. Although creativity was seen by '*behaviourists*' as a function of intelligence, some scholars in the area were not satisfied that it remained untestable and hidden. The loudest complainant of them all was US military psychologist Guilford. Numerous authors and texts cite Guilford's 1950 address to the American Psychological Association (upon his inauguration as president), one where he called for more study in the area, as the birth of modern research in creativity (Sternberg and Lubart 1991, p. 3).

It is said, historically, the motive for this type of research was the unreliability of IQ based studies, which assumed creativity was part of general intelligence. According to Runco and Albert (2010) as early as the 1920s, Cox a PhD student under Terman (the author of the IQ test itself), is said to have exposed that trait theories, confidence and persistence were not subconscious acts for creativity and therefore cautioned the overemphasis of the influence of IQ on determining creativity (Runco and Albert 2010, p. 15). According to Sawyer (2012), these early insights into personality and genius provided the basis for the interest in creativity theory in the US during World War II, where testing for individual cognitive skills gave early (but limited) insight into its usefulness (p. 16). Guilford himself worked in the US Air Force, developing tests for intellectual abilities for flying aircraft before developing his research at the

Institute of Personality Assessment at University of Southern California (Sawyer 2012, p. 17).

According to Kurtzberg and Amabile (2001), Guilford's first address as the president of the APA came as a great surprise, given the context of the field of psychology at the time: '*Suddenly, the appealing but nebulous concept of creativity had scope, depth, and breadth that could be measured and explored*' (p. 285). In the 1950s creativity was seen as something that could not be scientifically examined and the entrenched views, although challenged by Treman, Cox and even Galton in the 1920s (Sawyer 2012, p. 19), was that creativity was an obscure phenomenon, one theorised mainly through Freudian analysis as a subliminal drive (discussed above). It could not really be encouraged through the predominant behaviourist methods of reinforcement either, Sawyer pointing out that arch behaviourist Skinner did try to respond to this criticism in a paper on technology and pedagogy (1968) but failed (Sawyer 2012, p. 17). At the time of common usage of the IQ intelligence tests (such as the Standford-Binet test by Terman in 1916), one of the leading 1950s behaviourist psychologists Torrance, outlines creativity at the time as simply a problem-solving faculty: '*Whenever one is faced with a problem for which he has no practiced or learned solution, some degree of creativity is required*' (Herbert et al. 2002, p. 39). High IQ and problem solving to the world of psychology, was a relationship set in empirical stone.

Guildford's call for creativity research, however challenging, did not fall on deaf ears, and eventually led the field of psychology over the next two decades toward development of theory and measurement tools compatible with the measurement of IQ—creativity as an observable '*production*' using thinking skills, 'divergent thinking', given as *fluency of thought, flexibility, originality and elaboration* (Sawyer 2012, p. 47). Developed as a DT test (the most common of which being the TTCT the Torrence Test of Creative Thinking: Torrence, 1974), these thinking skills tests became a hugely popular psychometric tool, working hand in hand with IQ testing. Getzels and Jackson (1962) showed, through data, how these two parameters (IQ and DT) co-varied and were related to one another—proving a strong relationship. Getzels and Jackson's threshold theory showed that the two go hand in hand, but only up to the point of an IQ of around 120—after this, it's theorised that too much intelligence can hamper creativity. Today, although this idea of creativity belonging (mainly) to the outstandingly intelligent, is contentious. Sawyer states clearly that '*many decades of research show that creativity and intelligence are related*' (Sawyer 2012, p. 57). Proponents of this type of psychology, such as Dean Simonton, provide an example of a domain where this might be evidenced: '*intelligence level impacts everyday creativity, such as that involved in problem-solving … You need an IQ of around 140 to learn enough physics to be truly creative in it*' [emphasis added] (Simonton 1989, p. 40).

Simonton's mention of the potential to *learn* is seen as significant in this quote, as when testing for talent. As Sawyer points out, '*intelligence predicts less than half the variance in creativity measures, [while still] providing evidence for the discriminant validity of creativity tests*' (2012, p. 57). A history of Terman himself, shows he proved the point. Having had a number of high IQ participants in his experimental work on people's life outcomes based on intelligence (the so called 'Terman Termites' experiment), Shockley, a boy who failed the requisite criteria of IQ for his pool, showed more creativity in his life's work than anyone else in the group as a Nobel Prize winner for the invention of the transistor (Kaufman 2009). Given these limitations, historiometric researcher, Weisberg (1993, p. 97), explains how the psychometric approach of intelligence and divergent thinking skills '*led to the development of confluence models of creativity*'—one that recognises other less predictable or testable factors in determining creativity. By the end of World War II, according to Runco and Albert (2010), creativity was being increasingly explained by psychologists through '*the personalities, the values, the talents **and the IQs** of exceptionally creative men and women*' [emphasis added] (p. 15).

Today: A Legacy of Two Narratives G-Creative and N-Creative

Given this history of specialness, creativity in the mind and the alternative creativity through learning, and social even pleasurable process, two clear strands exist in present day research around creativity—and they are yet to be unified, say Still and D'Inverno (2016). '*N-creative*' (perhaps nature creative) or creativity defined by people '*living and acting in the*

world [that is] inherent in all activity,' (2016, p. 7) based on actions, attentive enquiry and the impact it makes and the dominant *'G-creative'* (perhaps God creative) or the *'creativity in the mind'* narrative, which lives in
the contemporary creativity in psychology and the cultural legacy of
genius. In Weisberg's review (2006), a confluence theory acknowledges a
number of factors coming together: *'Creativity requires a person with a
particular thinking style, knowledge base, and personality, who is in a particular environment'* (p. 97). Although a number of personal and extra-
personal factors were considered for some time in the mid twentieth
Century as causes of creativity, the two most cited contemporary confluence models of are undoubtedly from the late twentieth Century:
Amabile's Componential Model of Creativity (1983, 1996) where creativity is *judged* as being something novel and appropriate and explained
as arising from a person's *domain-relevant skills*, his or her *creativity-
relevant skills* and finally their *task motivation*; and Sternberg and Lubart's
(1991) Investment Theory of Creativity, where creativity is like an economic metaphor of a marketplace, where creative thinkers *'buy low and
sell high'* (Weisberg 2006, p. 100).

Perhaps the most well known N-creative—or socially constructed creative model—in recent decades, invoking the earlier work of Whitehead
in the 1920s, comes through the social *'systems'* explanation of creativity
as emerging from both minds, people, gatekeepers and tastemakers.
Within this model the individual and his or her mind is only one part of
the more complex process that perhaps leads to creativity that is *'domain
changing'*. While the model deals with explanations of any type of creativity, it is seen to be particularly useful in explaining creativity that is sometimes referred to as *'Big C'* creativity or historically important creativity—as
opposed to short range or *'Small C'* creativity, which may be no more
than an idea for a new bus journey. Creativity in this model is *'rated'* in a
cultural system—something its author Mihaly Csikszentmihalyi used to
explain why creativity has 'clustered' throughout history in scenes, milieu,
geographic places and in industrial contexts, for example renaissance
Florence in art or Sixties London in pop music.

According to Csikszentmihalyi's tripartite model (1996) in Fig 3.1,
*'Creativity results from the interaction of a system composed of three elements:
a culture that contains symbolic rules, a person who brings novelty into the*

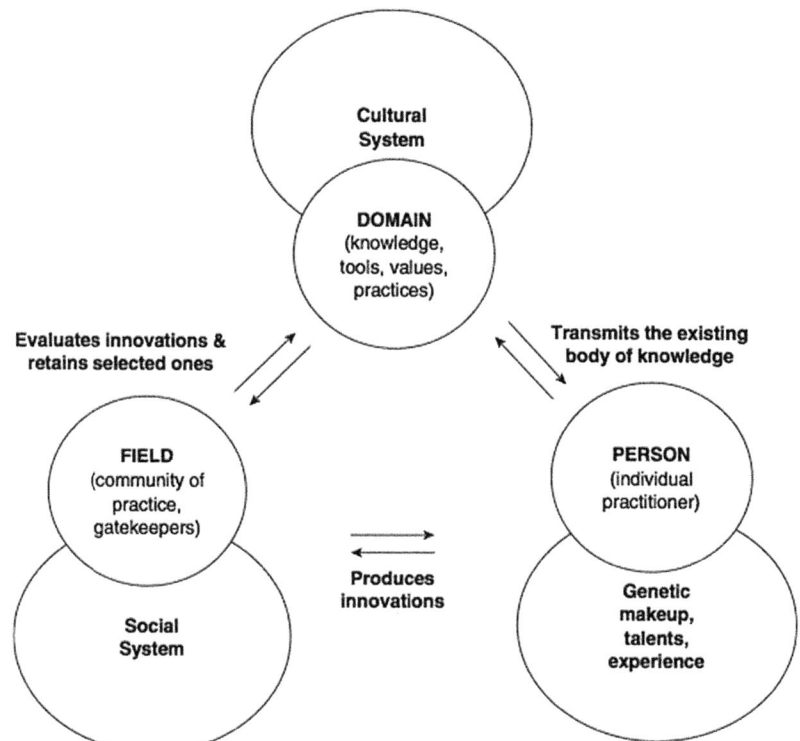

Fig. 3.1   An N Creative model of creativity. (Adapted from Csikszentmihalyi 2006)

symbolic domain, and a field of experts who recognise and validate innovation. All three are necessary for a creative idea, product or discovery to take place' (Csikszentmihalyi 1996, p. 6).

Csikszentmihalyi's model explains that real world creativity is only meaningful as a social process, after being an internal one. Figure 3.1 above conceptualises '*a process that can be observed only at the intersection where* **individuals, domains, and fields** *interact'* [emphasis added] (Csikszentmihalyi 2006, p. 3). Creativity seen this way is explained by a *person*, with a set of confluence and cultural factors making a change to a *domain*—a value and cultural system (a knowledge base, subject, or even an industry), which is rated (and selected therefore as creative) by its *field*—a community of gatekeepers, experts and tastemakers who form part of the social system for that domain. When it comes to the individual, alongside the various character, traits and abilities of the psychologists' confluence approaches, Csikszentmihalyi's provides a number of more culturally and historically formed ideas about *people*, such as a cultural capital, a person's ethnicity and cultural background and even marginality to a field (people from less conventional backgrounds), pointing to biographical accounts of some of the most eminent creative achievers in history, who often lived within uncomfortable unconventional contexts, such as India's Ghandi during his formative period under British rule in South Africa, the Catalan Picasso residing in the heart of the Parisian art scene at the turn of the twentieth century and Freud being a Jewish Catholic in Vienna (Csikszentmihalyi 2006, p. 13).

A Tale of Two Creatives: G-Creative and N Creative

We have seen that the historical narratives of where creativity comes from, how it is measured, considered a supernatural gift, a talent, a skill or many 'things' in the mind. These narratives, discourses or 'rhetorics' (Banaji et al. 2006) can be grouped loosely around two types of creativity: (1) creativity a closed '*in the mind*' cognitive process or (2) creativity as an open social process of a person in the '*real world*'. These two '*directions*' were termed by Still and D'Inverno (2016) as N-Creative (perhaps nature-like) and G-Creative (perhaps God like) in a paper made to the last International Conference of Computational Creativity, to aid the development of creative AI (artificial intelligence) systems, models and its development away from closed G-Creative '*in the mind*' analogous processes—a type of human-machine manifesto for AI development.

   The prising apart of these two differing narratives and theories: G-creative (largely psychological understanding of creativity) and N-Creative (largely socially constructed) is said by many to be important, and is summarised here in an analysis of creativity and AI in Table 3.1. A simplified ontology of creativity might suggest that, given the historical context we have seen, G-Creative aligns with a traditional idea of special people, who male special

Table 3.1   G Creative vs N creative narratives

Type of creativity	G creative (psychological creativity)	N creative (socially constructed creativity)
What is created?	Creation as separate from the creator	Creation as expressive part of the creative
What location or 'P of creativity' People, products, place	Focus on 'products' as novelty + appropriateness	Focus on 'people' and 'process'
How it happens (system)	A closed system inside the mind	An open system in a sociocultural context
Aiding, managing and developing it	Cognitive ability (IQ and DT) Brain storming Mind mapping Trial and error	Intrinsic motivation Confluence models: Knowledge + motivation + creativity skills) Play and pleasure
Theorists	Psychologists, computational creativity theorist, scientists, AI, business studies	Social psychologists, educationalists, historians, media and culture theorists
How is it assessed	Expert assessment (C.A.T. consensual assessment technique)	Field and wider cultural assessment
Creative industry relevance	New product ideas Invention Problem solving Ground-breaking	New product categories Innovation Problematising Taste-making
Cultural narratives	Individualistic Genius Inspiration Trial and error Specific rules and methods Brains	Collaborative Talent Effort Experimentation Interdisciplinary methods Skills
Development in artificial intelligence AI	Computational creativity (Turing tests)	Generative adversarial network Augmented technologies

things and are somehow gifted with unique and increasingly measurable and '*unlockable*' abilities (especially problem-solving ones) located in the mind. N-Creative, on the other hand, hails from the Latin meaning of *creare* (to bring forth) aligned to humanistic ideas of creativity through exploration, intrinsic motivation, joy and only meaningful in relation to a 'real world' setting.

AI and Computational Creativity

Boden's seminal work on artificial intelligence (AI) and computational computing (1998) outlined three types or categories of computer creativity, namely: *combinational, exploratory and transformative*. This hierarchy of computational creativity is akin to what creativity theorists have discussed as '*Big C*' and '*Small C*' creativity, the former being creativity of the type akin to combining two new ingredients in a food recipe (something we all do often), and latter being creativity that is historically important or to use the Csikszentmihalyi model (above), is domain changing, like the Bauhaus' break with decorative architecture or 1970s rap music's redefining of disco music.

Computational '*combinational*' creativity by machines has been a feature for at least last five decades. Boden explains that this might specifically mean the autonomous combining of two types of improbable yet familiar ideas / things. As far back as 1957 a computer algorithm was used to compose the Illiac Suite, a string quartet in the Classical style. When played by real musicians, it passed the '*Turing Test*' of it being indistinguishable from something that might have been written by a composer judged by a human bystander. In 1997 the JAPE (Joke Analysis and Production Engine) went a step further, and could create jokes and puns such as '*what do you call a Martian who drinks beer? An ale-ien!*', passing a type of Turing Test good enough, perhaps, as something drafted by a person for a Christmas cracker.

The problem, acknowledged by Boden herself, was that for machines to be transformative or Big C in their creativity, it '*depends largely on unarticulated values, including social considerations of various kinds. These social evaluations are often invisible to scientists*' (1998, p. 355). Describing a distant future where machines might be able to make these kind of evaluative and even persuasive processes (like those of Sternberg's, 1991, investment model of creativity where an idea is '*sold*'), a recent example in 2018 by a group of experimentalist coders in France called Obvious Collective points in this transformative direction.

On the portrait of Edmond Belamy, by the Obvious Collective, a blurry canvas of art reminiscent of an Old Master, a telling signature by its algorithm makers '*min G max D x[log(D(x))] + z[log(1−D(G(z)))]*' makes a point of a bold AI project that that might not only pass a Turing Test of *'realness'*, but be transformative in the way Boden describes AI futures. The *'painting'* sold for around £300,000 in 2019, and although that might not signify *'creative success'* in itself, it was made by a programme that did consider its social context. From a computational creativity point of view, this painting was different from many other AI creativity attempts in the past, in that its algorithmic basis programmatically modelled a form of human evaluative system called a *'Generative Adversarial Network'*. It could be argued, therefore, that the Portrait of Edmond Belamy is perhaps one of the first creative AI projects that has responded in part to Still and D'Inverno's call for N-Creative computer creativity—and an end to closed system G-Creative computational processes that ignore a socially constructed view of how man and machine might co-create.

In many ways, the Obvious Collective developed their algorithm according to Csikszentmihalyi's *'systems'* model of creativity (1988), one largely explained in this chapter as an N-Creative model. Using his model Fig. 3.1 we can analyse the Portrait of Edmond Belamy thus:

- *Domain*: the team behind it fed 15,000 artwork images spanning 600 years of portraiture.
- *Person*: the generative network selected candidate images to adopt, just as an artist might.
- *Field*: the *'Generative Adversarial Network'* did the important art criticism part, acting as a gatekeeper of what to keep and what to cut in a form of machine learning.

Although this cannot be considered a part of a real cultural system, and the algorithm needed the human programming team to persuade the artworld of its novelty (and appropriateness), it represents a step towards more N-Creative software development, and perhaps an end to the assumption of machines as creators with defined machine learning algorithms. Individualistic models of creativity ignore group, team and incremental process. Computational creativity of the combinative type ignores the co-creative way creative work is organised by a human and therefore replicates such G-Creative theories, ones Still and D'Inverno (2016) suggest as unhelpful for the field to develop AI creativity (Fig. 3.2).

Fig. 3.2   The portrait of Edmond Belamy. (Open sources)

In Conclusion: A Manifesto for (Wo)Man and Machine in the Creative Academy

This chapter has shown the complexity tied-up in the meaning of creativity, outlining its origins, cultural history and etymology adding to the complexity of theories and narratives around it. In reviewing some of these, we see that there exists today two related but separate theories, ones Stills and D'Inverno called G-creative (creativity in the mind) and N-Creative (creativity in a socially defined person). The ontological facets of these two theories provided in Table 3.1, shows a leaning towards G-Creative theories in the development of computational creativity, something hinted at over 22 years ago in Boden's paper on the subject in

1998. In this light, AI developers have much to gain from working with creative art schools, technologists and creative business students in the N-Creative areas listed in Table 3.1 with regards to experimentation, interdisciplinary methods, taste-making and domain skills.

With regards to AI, to echo Still and D'Inverno's call for less psychology-inspired AI computational creativity closed-systems and more human and sociocultural related ones, AI system designers should be grounded in the theory of sociocultural processes and less reliant on the post war '*Guilford School*' of intelligence and divergent thinking with its implied computational creativity. The portrait of Edward de Belamy is not only an example of an attempt at employing this, with its machine learning '*gatekeeper*' factoring of sociocultural of fields and domain knowledge, it also challenges the art world about its long cultural history discussed here around genius and the deification of fine artistry.

Knowing that N-creative human design and cultural context is realistically the only way machines can become part of a '*Big C*' or transformative creative process, can anyone really imagine a Blade Runner 'replicant' android in the next two decades, against present examples of anthropomorphic innovation of Amazon Alexa? As a journalist once joked, if a computer alone was creative enough to '*fool*' us (Turing Test) into being the next Banksy or Top Ten record producer, we would probably never know, as its first job would be to eliminate us! Creativity ultimately is a social process and one where researchers, students, experimentalists need to develop AI research (such as augmented technologies) in the way that creative people, teams and disciplines work and learn collaboratively when incredible things are achieved. The clear message here, is that when it comes to creativity, it is not *all* located in the gift of a '*mind*'—be that a person's or a one of a computer.

References

Amabile, T.M. (1983). 'The social psychology of creativity: A componential con-ceptualization', *Journal of Personality and Social Psychology*, 45, pp. 357–376.
Amabile, T. (1996). *Creativity in Context*. Boulder: Westview Press
Amabile, T. (1998). 'How to Kill Creativity', *Harvard Business Review*, 76, pp. 77–89

Amabile, T., & Pratt, M. (2016). 'The dynamic componential model of creativity and innovation in organizations: Making progress, making meaning', *Research in Organizational Behavior* 36, pp. 157–183

Banaji, S., Burn, A., & Buckingham, D. (2006). *The rhetorics of creativity: A review of the literature.* London: Arts Council.

Batey, M. (2012). 'The Measurement of Creativity: From Definitional Consensus to the Introduction of a New Heuristic Framework', *Creativity Research Journal,* 24(1), pp. 55–65.

Boden, M (1998). 'Creativity and Artificial Intelligence', *Artificial Intelligence,* 103(1) pp. 347–356

Braudel, F. (1981–1984). *Capitalism and Civilization, 15th to 18th Century,* 3 vols. New York: Harper & Row

Clark, T. (1997). *The Theory of Inspiration.* Manchester: University of Manchester Press.

Csikszentmihalyi, M. (1988). 'Society, culture, person: A systems view of creativity', in R.J. Sternberg (ed.) *The Nature of Creativity.* Cambridge: Cambridge University Press, pp. 325–339

Csikszentmihalyi, M. (1996). *Creativity Flow and the Psychology of Discovery and Invention.* New York: Harper Collins

Csikszentmihalyi, M. (2006). 'A Systems Perspective on Creativity'. In: Jane Henry (ed.) *Creative Management and Development,* The Open University Business School, 3rd edn, London: SAGE Publications. pp. 3–17

DCMS (2001). *Creative Industries Mapping Document 2001* (2nd ed.), London, UK: Department of Culture, Media and Sport

De Filippi, R, Grabher, G. and Jones, C. (2007). 'Introduction to paradoxes of creativity: manager and organizational challenges', *Journal of Organizational Behavior.* 28(5), pp. 511–521

Drobot, A. (2018). '*The Process of Creativity. Psychoanalysis and Creativity'.* Freudfile. Available at http://www.freudfile.org/psychoanalysis/papers_9. html (Accessed 10 December 2021).

Florida, R. (2004). *The rise of the creative class... And how it's transforming work, leisure, community and everyday life.* New York: Basic Books.

Foucault, M. (1972). *The Archaeology Of Knowledge.* (S. Smith, Trans.). London: Tavistock.

Freud, S. (1924). *A General Introduction to psychoanalysis.* (G.S. Hall Trans). New York: Boni & Liveright

Gauntlett, D. (2011). *Making Is Connecting: The Social Meaning of Creativity, from WDIY and knitting to YouTube and Web 2.0.* London: Polity Press

Getzels, J. W. & Jackson, P. W. (1962). *Creativity and intelligence: Explorations with gifted students.* New York: Wiley.

Gruber, H. (1981). *Darwin on Man: A psychological Study of Scientific Creativity.* (2nd ed) Chicago: University of Chicago Press.

Gruber, H.E. and Davies, S.N. (1988). 'Inching our way up Mount Olympus: the evolving system approach to creative thinking'. In R.J. Sternberg (ed.), *The Nature of Creativity: Contemporary and Psychological Perspectives,* pp. 243–70.

Halewood, M. (2013). *AN Whitehead and social theory: Tracing a culture of thought.* London: Anthem Press.

Herbert, T. P., Cramond, B., Neumeister, K. L. S., Millar, G., and Silvian, A. F. (2002). *E. Paul Torrance: His life, accomplishments, and legacy.* Storrs: University of Connecticut, The National Research Center on Gifted and Talented (NRC/GT).

Hesmondhalgh, D., & Baker, S. (2011). *Creative Labour: Media Work in Three Cultural Industries,* Oxford: Routledge

Holland & Quinn (1987). *Cultural Models in Language and Thought.* Cambridge: CUP

Holton (1978). *The Transition from Feudalism to Capitalism.* London: Palgrave

Honour & Flemming (1999). *World History of Art.* London: Lawrence King Publishing

Kaufman, J. (2009). 'The Truth about Terman's Termites', *Psychology Today.* Available at https://www.psychologytoday.com/gb/blog/beautiful-minds/200909/the-truth-about-the-termites (Accessed 15 November 2021)

Kaufman, J., & Glaveneau, V. (2019). 'A review of creativity theories: what questions are we trying to answer?' In J. Kaufman, & R. Sternberg (eds.), *The Cambridge Handbook of Creativity.* New York: Cambridge University Press.

Kurtzberg, T., and Amabile, T. (2001). 'From Guilford to Creative Synergy: Opening the Black Box of Team-Level Creativity', *Creativity Research Journal,* 13(4), pp. 285–294

Kinsley, D. (1988). *Hindu Goddesses: Visions of the Divine Feminine in the Hindu Religious Tradition.* Berkley: UCP

Klausen, S. (2010). 'The Notion of Creativity Revisited: A Philosophical Perspective on Creativity Research'. *Creativity Research Journal,* 22(4), pp. 347–360

Liddell, H. and Scott, R (1925). 'Greek-English Lexicon' *Perseus Digital Library.* Available at http://www.perseus.tufts.edu/hopper/text?doc=Perseus%3Atext%3A1999.04.0057%3Afrontmatter%3Dpref. (Accessed 3 December 2021)

Murray, P (1989). *Genius: the history of an idea.* Oxford: Basil Blackwell

Niu, W. & Sternberg, R. (2002). 'Contemporary Studies on the Concept of Creativity: The East and West'. *Journal of Creative Behaviour,* 36(4), pp. 269–288

Pollit, J (1995). 'The Canon of Polykleitus and Other Canons in Polykleitos, the Doryphoros and Tradition' In WG Moon (ed.) *Polykleitos, the Doryphoros, and tradition.* Wisconsin: UWP, pp. 19–24

Runco, M. (2007). *Creativity Research, Development and Practice.* London: Elsevier Academic Press

Runco, M. A. & Albert, R. S. (2010). 'Creativity research: A historical view'. In Kaufman, J. C. & Sternberg, R. J. (eds.), *The Cambridge Handbook of Creativity.* Cambridge: Cambridge University Press pp. 3–19

Sawyer, K (1999). 'The Emergence of Creativity'. *Philosophical Psychology,* 12(4), pp. 447–469

Sawyer, K. (2011). 'The Cognitive Neuroscience of Creativity: A Critical Review'. *Creativity Research Journal,* 23(2), pp. 137–154

Sawyer, K. (2012). *Explaining Creativity: the science of human innovation.* Oxford: Oxford University Press

Skinner, B (1968). *The Technology of Teaching.* New York: Appleton-Century-Crofts

Simonton, D. (1976). Biographical determinants of achieved eminence: A multivariate approach to the Cox data. *Journal of Personality and Social Psychology,* 33, pp. 218–226

Simonton, D. 1989 In Kersting, K (2003) *What Exactly Is Creativity,* Monitor Staff Vol 34, Accessed At http://Www.Apa.Org/Monitor/Nov03/Creativity.Aspx

Simonton, D. (1994) *Greatness: Who Makes History and Why.* New York: Guilford Press

Simonton, D. (2009) *Genius 101.* New York: Springer

Sternberg, R. J., & Lubart, T. I. (1991) An investment theory of creativity and its development. *Human Development,* 34(1), 1–31.

Sternberg, R. J. (2000) Identifying and developing creative giftedness. *Roeper Review,* 23, pp. 60–65.

Sternberg, R and Lubart T. (1999) The Concept of Creativity: Prospects and Paradigms. In R. Sternberg (Ed.) *The Handbook of Creativity.* Cambridge: CUP, pp. 3–15.

Still, A. and D'Inverno, M. (2016) 'A History of Creativity for Future AI Research', in Pachet, F. et al (eds.) *Proceedings of the 7th International Conference on Computational Creativity.* Paris: Sony CSL, pp. 147–156.

Struck, P. (2019). '*Greek and Roman Mythology Tools*'. University of Pennsylvania. Available at http://www.classics.upenn.edu/myth/php/tools/dictionary.php (Accessed 6 January 2022)

Torrance, E. P. (1959). *Explorations in Creative Thinking in the Early School Year: VI. Highly Intelligent and Highly Creative Children in a Laboratory School*. Minneapolis: University of Minnesota.

Weiner, R. (2000). *Creativity and Beyond: Cultures Values and Change*. New York: State University of New York Press

Weisberg, R. W. (1993). *Creativity: Beyond the Myth of Genius*. New York: W H Freeman

Weisberg, R. W. (2006). *Creativity: Understanding Innovation in Problem Solving, Science, Invention and the Arts*. New Jersey. NY. Wiley & Sons

Whitehead, A. N. (1978/1929) *Process and Reality: An Essay In Cosmology*. (Gifford Lectures of 1927–8). Corrected edition (eds. Griffin, D. and Sherburne, D.), New York: The Free Press

4

The Global Citizen, Globalized Lifestyles and Pedagogy

Lynda Fitzwater

Abstract Recent discussions around the digital nomad engendered by trends towards remote working in the post-covid expanded workplace border onto wider discourses of the Global Citizen. The longevity of the global citizen narrative can be explained through its adaptations to successive educational philosophies and frameworks. This highly contested and fractured subject position has been theorised through literatures of pedagogy, tourism, cosmopolitanism, consumerism, sustainability, Anthropocene and multiple other lenses. Much of this work details the pedagogical structures and aims of global citizenship education, or otherwise situates the epistemology and ontology of the Global Citizen as in tension whilst serving the agendas of multiple stakeholders. This chapter examines the limits of Ruiz-Chapman's concept of the Global Non-Citizen in relation to current trends in trans-national education and

L. Fitzwater (✉)
Business School for the Creative Industries, University for the Creative Arts, Farnham, UK
e-mail: Philip.Powell@uca.ac.uk

© The Author(s), under exclusive license to Springer Nature Switzerland AG 2022
P. Powell, B. Shankar Nayak (eds.), *Creative Business Education*,
https://doi.org/10.1007/978-3-031-10928-7_4

global citizens' lived experience. In conclusion, the global citizen will be positioned in frameworks of neo-imperialism, belonging and responsibility.

Introduction

Expanding Out from the Digital Nomad

Contemporary debates about the expanded workplace engendered by the pandemic often cite the digital nomad as the ideal entrepreneurial self, capable of navigating a globalized office space. These discussions border onto wider discourses of the global citizen.

The global citizen has been a status and an identity posited and analysed throughout the history of conceptualizing people's ability and right to move independently through nation states. This right to travel and settle, even temporarily, often rests upon the usefulness of the individual's skills, financial assets or politics to the nation state's interests, or more fundamentally the individual's representation of a federal ideal of the model, adaptable citizen. These angles on the global citizen closely relate to discourses of neoliberalism, homo economicus and cosmopolitanism.

Currently, these understandings of the global citizen are brought to bear on the trend of the '*digital nomad*'. Digital nomads can be defined as individuals who are enabled by their skills in technology-based industries to earn a living from theoretically anywhere in the world. Karsten, a practitioner and advisor, describes this as '*Complete freedom of movement while working online is the general idea*' (2022). Thereby the digital nomad can enjoy the climate, culture, and living costs of their physical location, whilst simultaneously benefitting from the professional status and remuneration rates associated with the ultimate location of the usefulness of their work output. This expansion of the scope of possibilities in living is of course highly delimited to certain forms of work, but more importantly is additionally restricted to workers who can guarantee their income will top certain thresholds monthly or yearly long term, as well as being holders of assets. Ultimately, radical financial independence and healthy local spending power positions a sub-set of people whose work can be remotely carried out productively as eligible to take advantage of the growing digital nomad schemes launched by cities and states during the Covid-19 pandemic. There are several other key considerations that complicate entry into this privileged sphere. Continuity of experience and education for the would-be digital nomad's child is a complex problem; the long history of paradigmatic curricula in international schools globally may be a solution (this is a fascinating attendant discourse pertinent but outside the remit of the present context's exploration of the global citizen). Similarly, the digital nomad's need for specialised healthcare for pre-existing conditions can be a barrier. Additionally, the digital nomad may need to travel and settle '*as a package*' with their family, which presents a very different profile of demands and local consumerism opportunities for the host location.

So, what are the parallels between the digital nomad and the global citizen? The digital nomad is the contemporary practical incarnation of the global citizen, with a particular focus on professional productivity. But the global citizen has been theorised as a status with much more wide-ranging interpretations related to consciousness, spirituality, education and privilege. Later, we will examine the pedagogic structures and aims of global citizenship education. Now let us consider the wider discourses of the global citizen.

Who Is the Global Citizen?

Who is the Global Citizen? At the core of understandings of the *personhood* of the global citizen, we will repeatedly find the concepts of self-awareness and responsibility. The behaviour of the global citizen is responsible, involving caring for, and promoting '*social justice and sustainability*'. More specifically '*[an]other character and value recommended for global citizens is socioscientific accountability*'.

There are tensions in this identity of a person attempting to behave in conscientious, evidence-based ways towards an imagined international greater good, but who is inevitably somewhat rooted in their own state's current dynamics. As Baker and Shulsky argue '*the reality is that we, as citizens of our individual nations, do have a stake in the actions and reactions*' *of others*'. These understandings foreground socially-oriented responsibility.

How does the Global Citizen attain that status or way of being in the world? Much of the literature claims the Global Citizen as a state of mind, an attitude or set of interrelated attitudes. Mat'ova et al. interpret '*conscious and transformative learning*' as the process of becoming a global citizen (2020). The aspirations of the global citizen are to carry out their agency towards a greater global purpose, responding to others and being self-critical (Papastephanou 2003). Empathetic critical thinking is required for global citizenship '*the willingness to see and hear ideas removed from one's personal paradigm [...] deep reflection as a natural, initial instinct [...] deep-seated belief that one is open to analytical exploration and possible evolution*'. De Costa argues that living as a global citizen requires an openness towards cultural diversity, and directing oneself to actively develop relationships with others (2016). Cosmopolitanism has been a framework for understanding the global citizen's inter-relationships which prioritize human diversity (Appiah 2006).

As we have seen in relation to the digital nomad, becoming a Global Citizen could also be predicated on less *other*-directed intentionalities. The right to travel, and the freedom and right to cross borders is a part of thinking about one's future as a global citizen—for example Park's investigation of North Korean migrants' aspiration to become a '*global citizen*' by emigrating to a third country after entering South Korea.

Indeed, the Global Citizen can be defined in contradistinction to the '*National*' Citizen. We might associate feelings of citizenship with close proximity to people and places engendering our sense of responsibility. Puncheva-Michelotti et al. explored the impact of global and national identity combined with distance upon the moral decision-making processes of corporate social responsibility. They concluded that '*it is important to emphasize that national and global identities are not mutually exclusive constructs, as they define one's sense of moral responsibility toward national and/or global welfare*'. It is clear that global citizen discourses shift with successive generations' sense of responsibility for equality and inter-cultural communication.

Longevity of the Global Citizen Narrative

The global citizen narrative has endured across successive educational paradigms and philosophies. We can chart and explain this through the broad possibilities of adapting the basic tenets of the right to move from nation state to nation state in search of improvements.

Currently, the Global Citizen may connect their identity to the anthropocene and to *'flight shame'*. To add some detail on the implications of the Anthropocene for global citizenship, we could say that this mindset of framework emphasises the permanent impacts and global consequences of individual's consumption choices. This is the perspective taken by Loy et al. who argue that: *'Global crises such as the climate crisis require fast concerted action, but individual and structural barriers prevent a socio-ecological transformation in crucial areas such as the mobility sector. An identification with people all over the world (i.e., global identity) and an openness toward less consumption (i.e., sufficiency orientation) may represent psychological drivers of a socio-ecological transformation'.* This provides us a very timely understanding of the self-questioning element of the global citizen. We can chart the highlights of how the global citizen narrative adapts to successive educational philosophies and frameworks.

A pertinent observation with which to begin is the development of the modern proposal of global citizenship out of the principles of cosmopolitanism, which Jefferess traces back to the Stoics (2008). This can usefully remind us of the harmony between the longer global citizen discourse and the rediscovery of humanism as a project in political philosophy, critical and cultural theory (2008). When it comes to pedagogy, it is worth noting that states' and eras' implementations of citizenship education have faced criticism for their limitations and exclusionary potentials as well as appreciation for optimistic features. The connections between citizenship, education and democracy in the infancy of the United States of America are the starting point for Barber's investigation of citizenship education as axiomatic to nation founding (2002). He goes as far as exclaiming: *'Colleges and universities had to be committed above all to the constituting of citizens. That's what education was about.'* The limitation of the status of citizen to white men of means thereby confirms subjects the nation included, protected and served. Sun (2020) provides a fascinating account of the development of the concepts of belonging and citizenship across western and Asian political philosophy. This helps us contextualise the educationally specific reinventions of global citizenship education within the longevity of broader understandings of how humans obtain knowledge of and sensitivity to their unseen surroundings beyond touching distance.

Sienfield and Kapoor (2019) and Gies and Wall (2019) chart the development of the concept of global citizenship between the 1800s and twentieth century, similarly focusing on which subjects are included (property-owning men) and who is excluded (women and children). Further, Sienfield and Kapoor call for an expanded contemporary understanding of global citizenship to encompass diverse geo-political artifacts including human rights to trade blocks.

When it comes to education, in the lead up to the millennium, global citizenship programmes faced criticisms of the limited scope of their impact because students were not offered meaningful opportunities to engage pro-actively with community projects, which could lead to a growth in political awareness (Sax 2000). Bourke et al. identify that a primary stumbling block for citizenship education at higher education level '*is to take account of the personal characteristics and attitudes*' of students (2012). These, and other criticisms levelled at the impact of citizenship programmes, have led to the development of models of learning that extend the notion of volunteerism (2012). However, a reliance upon transformative learning via volunteerism has in turned faced critique, as we shall see. The 1990s also saw claims for the importance of the development of students' values and commitment to the ethical goals of living as a global citizen, including moral responsibility (linking back to this chapter's earlier discussions about the work involved in attaining the status of the global citizen). Another angle of analysis came from Byron on the features of faith-based HE successfully creating continuity for students from their experience of citizenship education at secondary curricular level. Experiential citizenship education developed in the 1980s and 90s was in decline in the later 90s and early 2000s (Barber 2002). A proposed solution was community-service programmes with a focus on recognition of interdependence (Zett Keith 2005), and even international service learning (Annette 2002).

The role of uses of technology in global citizenship education is a thorny issue. Drache's deeply enthusiastic approach in his 2008 book *Defiant Publics*, has been critiqued as '*techno-deterministic*' and overly utopian (Werbin 2010). Indeed, publics (in the sense of reallocation of '*power and authority downwards from the élite few towards the many*' Drache 2008), and the role of global citizenship instruction in their creation, are key questions for the continued validity of these pedagogic programmes in terms of co-constructing learning environments which inspire and motivate students to enact their global identity after their formalised education has finished. In contradistinction to a *collective* mobilisation of technology to pedagogically foster global citizenship, we can look at the figure of the young "*cyberflaneur*" (Kenway and Bullen 2008) who learns as much from '*mediascapes*' (Appadurai 1995) as from curricula, providing resources for identity construction and understanding ' "*imagined lives*" *of others living elsewhere*' (Kenway and Bullen 2008). Kenway and Bullen critique the effects of global consumer culture since the 1990s and the normalisation of consumerism as the defining characteristic of a culturally-homogenized aspirational lifestyle. Within this context, global citizenship education can allow young people to navigate the desires and feelings associated with consumerism to develop agency as a reflexive cyberflaneur who can critically observe, participate in and produce culture (2008). The authors hope such curricula help young people to discover alternative codes and values to consumerism which can afford satisfying subjectivities (2008). These insights can link back to Barber's assertions that potentially impactful young global citizens are detrimentally exposed to casual education through popular opinion, advertising and entertainment (Barber 2002). As economies become globally connected there is pressure for higher education to develop student intercultural awareness and global citizenship (Brooks and Waters 2011; Waters et al. 2011).

A Contested and Fractured Subject Position

The politically motivated construction of the figure of the global citizen as a national identity can be interpreted from many pertinent angles for deepening understandings of globalized lifestyles and citizenship pedagogy. The promotion of '*neoliberal global governance*' has been seen as an underlying driver behind the production of the global citizen as a hero capable of countering accusations of federalism and Euro-American paternalism. Biccum argues that '*Live 8*' benefit concerts taking place in the mid-noughties centred on the global citizen as an aspirational subjecthood, functions as PR for G8 member states. These events produced a discourse about a new generation of globally oriented citizens capable of continuing globalisation agendas and deflecting popular criticism of post-colonial exploitation (Biccum 2007). in a similar vein, Ruland interprets the mobilization and projection of the '*good global citizen*' collective role conception by the Association of Southeast Asian Nations (ASEAN— Brunei Darussalam, Cambodia, Indonesia, Lao PDR, Malaysia, Myanmar, Philippines, Singapore, Thailand and Viet Nam). This study calls attention to the functions performed by this collective identity in this regional organisation's assiduous agenda-setting and security management (Ruland 2019). These analyses posit global citizenship discourses' usefulness for propping up national and federal agendas, so it is especially interesting to consider the potential for transnational global citizenship advocacy to bolster nation citizens' claim to enact rights which are being nationally negated and denied (Cauoette 2006). The domestic arena can be a hostile environment for '*knowledge and discourse production*' which aims for a globalized standard of rights and freedoms; this is where global citizenship identity can be a fruitful tool for citizens to circumvent local limitations, traditions and expectations (Cauoette 2006).

Pedagogical Structures and Aims of Global Citizenship Education

Much of the literature details the pedagogical structures and aims of global citizenship education, or otherwise situates the epistemology and ontology of the Global Citizen as in tension whilst serving the agendas of multiple stakeholders. Upon examination of the pedagogic agenda of Global Citizenship, one finds that the 2002 Maastricht Declaration is often pinpointed as highly influential for defining Global Citizenship Education (O'Loughlin and Wegimont 2003; Lehtomäki and Rajala 2020; Sun 2020). This declaration emerged out of a Europe-wide congress about promoting global education, attempting to develop a strategy for improving and increasing this practice in Europe up to the Year 2015. It has been seen as successfully influencing policies and practices throughout Europe (Bourn 2016). Global citizenship education was described in this declaration as an '*education that opens people's eyes and minds to the realities of the world, and awakens them to bring about a world of greater justice, equity and human rights for all*' (Europe-Wide Global Education Congress 2002: 3). This inspiring vision pushed European states, international organisations and NGOs to design and deliver Global Education initiatives, incorporated into national curricula.

The declaration (also known as '*European Strategy Framework For Improving and Increasing Global Education In Europe to the Year 2015*') repeatedly acknowledges the tensions, inequalities and conflicts that contemporary Europeans were engaged in. And it makes specific reference to global citizenship education as the keystone of transformations in sustainability, trans-border problems, inequality and democratic empowerment. It posits that with robust global citizenship education government spending on international development will gain public support. Concomitantly, these pedagogies will address and ameliorate perceived downturns in public confidence in state and regional institutions.

The declaration, or framework, delineates what, or who, an agenda of Global Education in Europe aims to *produce*. Studying the wording and allusions of the document suggests that this programme attempted to rapidly forge a universal pedagogy for transforming future generations of learners into '*global citizens*' committed to solving global, human rights and climate problems. These aspirations for global citizenship education might strike us as highly ambitious and utopian, especially after the critical considerations of the present context regarding the status of citizenship itself.

The Global Non-Citizen

Finally, this chapter examines the relevance of Ruiz-Chapman's concept of the Global Non-Citizen in relation to current critiques of worker-oriented global citizenship education.

This chapter's previous conceptions of the Global Citizen are thrown into relief by Ruiz-Chapman's argument for recognition of the Global non-citizen represented by the undocumented Latinx migrant attempting to cross the border from Mexico to USA (2020) and in so doing, attempting to save their life and that of their family. Chapman sets out to prove that '*global citizenship ultimately aids in the re-staging of some bodies, specifically Latinx ones (though not confined to them), as non-human or less than human, which in turn borders them out of any form of citizenship, including global citizenship*' (2020).

The status of *citizen* itself must be confronted as a highly contingent and exclusionary system for movement, security and wellbeing that globally delimits the opportunities for a globalized and '*nomadic*' forms of pedagogy and career. In this regard, Ruiz-Chapman's concept of the Global Non-Citizen is a framework through which to consider current trends in trans-national education and global citizens' lived experience. By looking at global citizenship as an '*ideological expression*' Ruiz-Chapman effects a dismantling of much of the literature's focus upon the meritocratic dimensions of aiming to live life as a global citizen. This characterization throws into relief the unique contours of an existence between statuses, and without the security afforded by recognition as a member of a national territory. This approach focuses upon the barriers faced by Latinx migrants, but can equally be applied to the understanding of the impossibility of crossing borders for anyone globally if they are '*undocumented*'. Ruiz-Chapman argues that the status and practice of global citizenship relies upon the maintenance of the global non-citizen. From this perspective, global citizenship combines the right to seek and attain a more secure life or employment for yourself and your family with the optimistic, altruistic, *'socioscientific accountability'* that we saw earlier.

Political Death

This line of argumentation implicates the promotion of an agenda of individual philanthropic responsibility under the auspices of global stewardship. In particular, the organisation *'Global Citizen'* comes in for criticism due to its concerts which market this agenda to young people. Ruiz-Chapman argues that this conception masks the reality of the relationship between cartography and subjectivity. True global citizenship would leverage authentic identification with a global community and this would motivate resistance to neoliberal corporate culture and encourage activism towards social justice. The challenge is to incorporate this understanding of solidarity into pedagogic programmes enabling students to learn to see themselves as global citizens and follow through with the decisions and actions that flow from that status.

Ruiz-Chapman cites the various physical traps and risks strategized by border authorities that produce Lantinx migrants as non-citizens. These *'spaces that kill'* (2020) produce a lived experience of attempting to exercise transnational citizenship by choosing checkpoints which deliver you into the hands of government officials, a *'political death'* via the non-route of deportation.

Conclusion

Ruiz-Chapman's perspective underlines the critical approach necessary to make use of the Global Citizen discourse in a meaningful manner for pedagogy. We could finally ask, how does the Global Citizen engaged in education view themselves?:

Braskamp surveyed undergraduates' identification with certain pre-provided statements (2008). In the results, the item: '*I see myself as a global citizen*' correlated strongly with these items:

I prefer complex rather than straightforward interpretations of debatable issues.

I am informed of current issues that impact international relations.

I understand how various cultures of this world interact socially.

I can discuss cultural differences from an informed perspective.

I am aware of how other cultures consider '*fairness*' differently from my own culture.

I currently feel that I am developing a meaningful philosophy of life.

I intentionally involve people from many cultural backgrounds in my life.

I enjoy when my friends from other cultures teach me about our cultural differences.

People from other cultures tell me that I am successful at navigating their cultures.

I am open to people who strive to live lives very different from my own life style.

I work for the rights of others.

I consciously behave in terms of making a difference.

I think of my life in terms of giving back to society.

At this point, to inspire continued reflection on this chapter's themes, we invite readers to complete the global citizen scale (Reysen and Katzarska-Miller 2013) https://sites.google.com/site/stephenreysen/psychology-scales/globalcitizen. A similar instrument (developed by Morais and Ogden 2011) was used by Kishino and Takahashi to discover that degree students undertaking a '*study abroad*' programme scored significantly lower for global citizenship than domestic students.

Overall, it has emerged that global citizenship education is an enigmatic phenomenon fractured by internal and external conflicts. Despite the lofty ideals, it sometimes operates as a '*technocratic pedagogical endeavour*'. The global citizen has been positioned in frameworks of neo-imperialism, belonging and responsibility.

References

Annette, J. (2002). Service Learning in an International Context. *Frontiers: The Interdisciplinary Journal of Study Abroad.* Vol: 8. No: 1.

Appadurai, A. (1995). Disjuncture and difference in the global cultural economy. In ed. M. Featherstone *Global Culture: Nationalism, Globalization, and Modernity.* Pp. 295–310. London and Thousand Oaks, CA: Sage Publications.

Appiah, K. (2006). *Cosmopolitanism: ethics in a world of strangers.* New York: W.W. Norton.

Barber, B. R. (2002). The Educated Student: Global Citizen or Global Consumer? Liberal Education. Washington DC. Available at: http://jonsenglishsite.info/Class%20Docs%205/5_The%20Educated%20Student.pdf

Biccum, A. (2007). Marketing Development: Live 8 and the Production of the Global Citizen. *Development & Change.* Vol: 38 Iss: 6. Pp. 1111–1126

Bourke, L., Bamber, P. & Lyons, M. (2012). Global Citizens: Who Are They? *Education, Citizenship and Social Justice.* Vol: 7. Iss: 2. Pp: 161–174

Bourn, D. (2016). *Global citizenship and youth participation in Europe.* DERC research. London: IOE

Braskamp, L. A. (2008) Developing Global Citizens. *Journal of College and Character.* Vol: X. No: 1.

Brooks, R. & Waters, J. (2011) *Student Mobilities, Migration and the Internationalization of Higher Education.* Basingstoke: Palgrave Macmillan

Cauoette, D., (2006). Thinking and Nurturing Transnational Activism: Global Citizen Advocacy in Southeast Asia. *Kasarinlan: Philippine Journal of Third World Studies.* Vol: 21. Iss: 2. Pp. 3–33

De Costa, P. I. (2016). Constructing the Global Citizen. *Journal of Asian Pacific Communication* 26:2, Pp. 238–259

Drache, D. (2008). *Defiant Publics: The Unprecedented Reach of the Global Citizen.* Cambridge (UK) & Malden (MA): Polity Press. ISBN: 9780745631790.

Europe-Wide Global Education Congress (2002) 'Achieving the Millennium Goals Learning for Sustainability Increased commitment to global education for increased critical public support: "The Maastricht Global Education Declaration"' In: *Europe-wide Global Education Congress.* Maastricht, The Netherlands, 15-17/11/2002. At: https://static1.squarespace.com/static/5f6decace4ff425352eddb4a/t/60b71a8b93d11c66edf21149/1622612619511/Maastricht+Congress.pdf (Accessed 21/01/2022)

Jefferess, D. (2008) Global citizenship and the cultural politics of benevolence. *Critical Literacy: Theories and Practices.* Vol: 2. Iss. 1.

Gies, W.T. and Wall, C. (2019) "The Eighteenth Centuries: Global Networks of Enlightenment", *Journal of Global Intellectual History.* Vol. 10. Iss: 2. Pp. 3. https://doi.org/10.2307/j.ctt201mnwq

Karsten, M. (2022). How To Become A Digital Nomad (Work Online From Anywhere!) https://expertvagabond.com/digital-nomad-tips/ accessed: 5/1/2022

Kenway, J., & Bullen, E. (2008). The global corporate curriculum and the young cyberflâneur as global citizen. In *Youth moves: identities and education in global perspective,* Routledge: London, England, Pp. 17–32.

Lehtomäki, E., & Rajala, A. (2020). Global Education Research in Finland. In D. Bourn (Eds.), *The Bloomsbury Handbook of Global Education and Learning.* Bloomsbury Academic.

Morais, D. B., & Ogden, A. C. (2011). Initial development and validation of the Global Citizenship Scale. Journal of Studies in International Education, 15(5), 445–466. https://doi.org/10.1177/1028315310375308

O'Loughlin, E. & Wegimont, L. (eds.) (2003), Global Education in Europe to 2015: Strategy, policies, and perspectives. Maastricht Global Education Congress 15-17.11.2002. Lisbon: North-South Centre of the Council of Europe

Papastephanou, M. (2003). Education, Subjectivity and Community: Towards a democratic pedagogical ideal of symmetrical reciprocity. *Educational Philosophy and Theory.* Vol: 35. Iss: 4. Pp. 395–406.

Reysen, S., & Katzarska-Miller, I. (2013). A model of global citizenship: Antecedents and outcomes. *International Journal of Psychology.* Vol: 48, Pp. 858–870.

Ruiz-Chapman, T. (2020) The Cartesian subject as Global Citizen, the migrant as non-human. In: Chapman, D. D., Ruiz-Chapman, T. & Eglin, P. (eds) *The Global Citizenship Nexus: Critical Studies.* Routledge

Ruland, J. (2019). Good global citizen? ASEAN's image building in the United Nations. *Asia Pacific Business Review.* https://doi.org/10.1080/1360238 1.2019.1652983

Sax, L. J. (2000). Citizen development and the American college student. In: Ehrlich T (ed.) *Civic Responsibility in Higher Education.* Phoenix, AZ: The American Council on Education/The Oryx Press, Pp. 3–18.

Sienfield, R. & Kapoor, U. (2019). The Role of a Responsible Global Citizen *(Gitizen)* in the 21st Century: The Need, the Challenges and the Future.

Journal of Technology Management for Growing Economies. Vol. 10. Iss. 1. Pp. 7–17.

Sun, X. (2020). Towards a Common Framework for Global Citizenship Education: A Critical Review of UNESCO's Conceptual Framework of Global Citizenship Education. In Zhu, X. et al (eds). *Education and Mobilities: Ideas, People and Technologies. Proceedings of the 6th BNU/UCL IOE International Conference in Education.* Springer.

Waters, J., Brooks, R. & Pimlott-Wilson, H. (2011) Youthful escapes? British students, overseas education and the pursuit of happiness. *Social & Cultural Geography*, Vol. 12. No. 5. Pp. 455–69.

Werbin, K. C. (2010). Book Review: Defiant Publics: The Unprecedented Reach of the Global Citizen. *Canadian Journal of Communication.* Vol 35.

Zett Keith, N. (2005). Community Service Learning in the Face of Globalization: Rethinking Theory and Practice. *Michigan Journal of Community Service Learning.* Spring. Pp. 5–24.

5

Storytelling and Ethics: Understanding Ethical Storytelling for the Purpose of Business Education

Kathleen Hinwood

Abstract This chapter examines the role of ethics in the context of storytelling. It is part of a wider research project about how integrated storytelling can be used to teach in business education. Throughout history, we have constructed meaning through stories. It is a way for us to understand and make sense of the world. As such a powerful tool, industries have recognised the significance of storytelling, adopting it to their own needs. Despite the ubiquity and impact of storytelling in businesses and consumers alike, it has not been fully realised as a tool that could benefit business education. Storytelling is imbued with meaning, it represents values and ideas, which raises questions of ethicality. Politics in particular has been in the spotlight with reports of political interventions on social media and the rise of '*fake news*'. Questions of ethics, therefore, are not only directed at the story but also the storyteller, who has an obligation to consider the ethical standpoint of their story. It is a fundamental

K. Hinwood (✉)
Business School for the Creative Industries, University for the Creative Arts, Farnham, UK
e-mail: Philip.Powell@uca.ac.uk

© The Author(s), under exclusive license to Springer Nature Switzerland AG 2022
P. Powell, B. Shankar Nayak (eds.), *Creative Business Education*,
https://doi.org/10.1007/978-3-031-10928-7_5

question that needs to be considered when thinking about storytelling in relation to business education. In questioning ethics, brand management is an important area to examine. Brand management is a sophisticated enterprise that relies on the familiarity of archetypal stories and characters to engage with their audiences, winning loyalty and customer retention. Key to this success, is the ability to tell stories authentically. Inauthentic stories do not resonate or connect with people, so it is important that there is a perceived truth within a story, whether that relates to a company or a specific brand. We can learn much from the archetypal stories that brands tell us, how these stories imprint in the mind through our empathy and connect with us on a neurological level. Therein lies the potential risk, where more questionable ethics may be at play. It is, therefore, important to have a clear understanding of what the motivations of the storyteller are, and where problems of self-interest may lie. It is the purpose of the storytelling that is key to understanding the ethics behind it and the storyteller.

Introduction

The chapter focuses on the ubiquity of storytelling in recent years and the potential implications of its use in business education. It has been noted that there are problems with business pedagogy, where the primary focus has been data driven, with little opportunity to apply creative thinking to decision making. However, before implementing useful tools, such as storytelling that are already used across a number of disciplines, it is important to consider the ethics of storytelling and learn from others how to tell stories.

Marketing is the master discipline of telling stories, where singular stories are created, that align the brand's collateral, giving it an identity and consistent story for its audience, its habitus. However, there is a question about the ethicality of a singular story and questions then need to be raised about the truth and ethical perception of a given narrative. Therefore, by examining the use of storytelling in different contexts, greater understanding of developing an ethical framework for business education can be developed.

Over the last decade, it has been noted that there is an inadequacy in business graduates that is in part due to the lack of cohesive and integrated learning strategies (Seethamraju et al. 2006), despite the growing recognition that there is a need '*for a holistic transformation of educational systems*' (Ferrari et al. 2009). Not only is there a lack of cohesion across disciplines but there has been a focus on models, frameworks and mathematics, rather than humanistic elements which has created a '*quality deficit within leadership across organisations*' (Ready 2002).

Therefore, introducing storytelling as an educational tool, with the qualitative aspects that appear to be fundamental and lacking in many current business school programmes, will enhance the educational experience, provide the psychological, neurological, philosophical and educational benefits that storytelling offers, enabling cohesion and collaboration across different specialisations. Pertinent to that end, is ensuring there is an understanding of how stories are told, what stories are told and to whom and why. Despite the proliferation of stories in mainstream media and society at large espousing the benefits storytelling, there is little reference to it or research on it in relation to business education. There are still gaps in understanding the impact of using storytelling within businesses and business schools, particularly in relation to the wider implications of ethics, authenticity and perceived truth (Poulton 2005), with some students acknowledging that '*they actually become less confident during their time in business school that they will be able to resolve ethical quandaries in the workplace*' (Holland 2009).

Why Storytelling?

Storytelling has proliferated in the last 20 years, infiltrating every industry, from journalism to politics and beyond, but has remained limited in use within educational settings, and particularly so in relation to business pedagogy. In order for us to understand how to utilise it in education it is important to see how it is utilised elsewhere and in what context. A critical aspect to the approach of narrative and storytelling across so many different industries raises the question of ethics and how storytelling is used and to what effect, particularly when we are witness to '*managers [...] still experiencing ethical lapses*' with significant ramifications (Lopez et al. 2005). Storytelling is elastic, flexible and adaptable to different forms and permutations—offering potential to students in many ways, providing scope for critical and creative thinking, however, it is also vulnerable to manipulation and unethical practices.

The use of universal archetypes and singular narratives deployed by brand management, for example, tell curated stories that often work unilaterally with questionable motives and outcomes, begging questions about truth and authenticity, which has become the mainstay of ethical thinking, '*as an individual relative and distinctly modern concept*' (Shuttleworth 2020).

Constructing Meaning

When watching television, most of us recognize the category that's being advertised within seconds of the start of a thirty-second commercial. This is true even on occasions when we watch a commercial for the very first time. We know when we're about to see an automobile pitch. We anticipate the humour of a beer ad. We sense a feature demonstration when a gadget is being marketed.
(Vincent 2012)

From early folk tales, myths and legends we have always constructed meaning through stories, providing us with clues that we piece together to create understanding and sense. We look for stories through metaphors and signs, but this is where the inherent risk lies. There is the opportunity for misinterpretation, misleading or manipulative stories that change our perceptions of the world around us. Not only that, but there is also a deep ethical question about the reliability of storytelling. If storytelling is a construct, then it is by its very nature, fictitious. Therefore, to harness the power of storytelling within business education, it is important to take into account the ethical considerations, thereby gaining greater understanding of the types of stories that should be told, how they should be told and why they should be told.

'*Story can change you, your perceptions*' (Storr 2019), which is why storytelling has become so powerful as a marketing and advertising tool, enabling brands to refine and define their identities that align with their consumers' ideals, aspirations and values. By personifying products and giving them particular personality traits provides consumers with their own personal avatars (Vincent 2012) The connection of the consumer to their preferred brand echoes the tribal stories and propaganda of our ancestors, anecdotes and stories which connect with our identity and understanding of the world (Storr 2019).

Brand Management and Storytelling

McElroy of Procter and Gamble is believed to have initiated the discipline of brand management in the early 1930s. Following on from a memo he wrote which described the role that a '*brand man*' should take on to build a successful brand, which included being responsible for their brand, the brand development, as well as, understanding the brand's consumers through research (Mitchell 2012). This prescient beginning has in recent decades evolved into a sophisticated enterprise where brand essence, personality and image are analysed to develop a single story, usually based on archetypes from Jungian psychology. The use of those universal models, coupled with classic stories, provides a platform redolent of childhood stories, myths, legends and fairy tales, providing relatability for consumers. Brand managers are concerned with aligning their collateral with the notion of a single story that is reflected across all their marketing and communications. This kind of storytelling resonates with the audience as it allows us to construct meaning through the metaphors, both visual and written and from the signified cues of semiotics.

We love stories because of their logic. They have a beginning, a middle, and an end, which magically satisfies our need to understand cause-and-effect relationships. That's why brands thrive when they wrap their promise in a story. They become more accessible, more easily understood, and far more familiar to us. In fact, neurological research has proven that stories actually affect our brains;

stories cause our "mirror neurons" to fire, creating a stronger sense of a relationship with the storyteller. (Vincent 2012)

Managing a brand image requires a precise level of detail and research to ensure that a unified singular story across many channels and platforms in different formats is shared with its audience. It is a narrative that we, as an audience, participate in. This is why the singular tone of voice is so successful and resonating. However, creating a single story means that other stories are left behind. Stories that companies do not want us to hear, stories that do not align with the brand image, narratives that we feel are inauthentic.

Differing Narratives

Nike is one such example, where many narratives exist, those externally portrayed and the hidden stories of sweatshops and child labour, as well as their own internal narratives, of discrimination against employees from minority ethnicities, with a complete lack of representation at board level. Our perception of the brand's authenticity may be that they champion inclusivity and diversity, supporting the Black Lives Matter movement and featuring NFL footballer Colin Kaepernick in their advertisements (Germano 2020). However, where is the authenticity when it is not reflected in the operations of the organisation?

If brand stories themselves are an artifice (Morgan 2015), what do we actual mean by authenticity and how can that be implemented in an ethical way in terms of education? Authenticity is used frequently and misused even more so as an ethical consideration, does authenticity relate to the story being told, or is it intrinsic to the company story or to the perceived truth?

As Trilling argues, '*the decline of sincerity as an ethical ideal and the emergence of authenticity as a more prevalent ideal,*' (Trilling 2009) in today's society means that there has been a shift in the ethical ideals of society. The shift from sincerity and integrity, which '*is an attribute that one possesses*' to an ethicality of authenticity that one obtains,' through rejection of externally imposed values which ones does not consciously endorse." However, authenticity is used with such ubiquity now and the notion of its true sense, and more particularly, the romantic sense which '*requires one to be free from manipulation and self-distorting influences, in order to reflect and choose, and act from desires in some sense one's own*' (Trilling 2009), has in some senses being hijacked by marketing and management responding to the demands of consumers.

Discovering this essential self through introspection, could be argued what some companies and brands do when finding their essence, meaning, identity and brand personality. The demand from consumers for companies to not only indicate but incorporate moral and ethical principles into the very fabric of their being suggests that there is manipulation and intervention in a concept that '*should be determined by the self-governing individual as opposed to social or cultural influences*' (Trilling 2009).

When we look at many narratives in society now, the stories are simple, the message is consistent, voiced from several representatives but this kind of narrative does not allow room for deviation from the given script. However, the singular story brings cohesion to a brand narrative so, is it possible to bring that kind of cohesion across functions within business education through a singular voice of shared values? Or, do we need several distinct voices to make storytelling, integrated and, of ethical value? (Larsen et al. 2020).

Authentic vs. Inauthentic

Gillette's purpose-driven attempt to revitalise its slogan, "The best a man can get", isn't just a waste of ad budget but an expensive exercise in destroying its dominant market share. (Ritson 2019)

Gillette, one of the '*hero*' brands of P&G, the world's largest FMCG (fast-moving consumer goods) companies, has had an enduring and successful tagline for some 30 years which has relied on an image of masculinity reflected in society, '*the best a man could apparently get was a hot wife, a sports victory and (this is true) a career as a space shuttle pilot. Such were the dreams of the '80s*' (Ritson 2019). However, during recent years, the changing narrative of Gillette reflected the change in society's attitudes, whilst retaining an idealised version of masculinity.

Then, in 2019 on the back of the #metoo movement, the company changed its narrative, it was responding to the rejection of toxic masculinity and the outcries over the sexual offences by high profile figures, such as, Harvey Weinstein, as well as the pervasive nature of misogyny within society. The response to the change in their narrative was palpable, 10% of viewers on youtube responded with thumbs down when the ad debuted (Ritson 2019) indicating that the narrative was false, not aligned with the brand identity as was known to its audience and therefore inauthentic. Changing their tagline to '*We Believe: The Best Men Can Be*', was deemed patronising and ill-conceived. As Mark Ritson explains:

Gillette's ad feels like a tedious, politically correct public health video—the kind of film we were forced to watch in school about road safety before they invented the internet. Never mind making me hate Gillette, it makes me feel bad about pretty much everything. (Ritson 2019)

Not only did their execution misfire but alongside their sales of USD6 bn in 2018, they donated USD1 million to various charities '*intent on improving men*' (Ritson 2019), a seemingly paltry and tokenistic act in comparison to the wealth of the brand, and the parent company, P&G.

What Gillette aimed to present in their ad was a beautiful uplifting message executed in a dreadfully disempowering way. They missed the mark by overestimating the brand's own importance in people's lives. It sounded arrogant and patronizing, talking to men as if all of them were predators-in-the-making, victimizing them the same way that toxic males victimize both women and other men. […] it is the very approach that will only make things worse because men will now feel collectively guilty and ashamed by default over some men's actions, which is a recipe for a social disaster, as the anger clearly has to be channelled somewhere. (Olbertova 2019)

Changing a successful narrative and adopting it to the demands of the consumer is therefore not a superficial undertaking. Gillette swiftly learnt its mistake and followed in 2020 with '*Made of What Matters*', engaging its audience with positive aspirations of masculinity with the use of footballers such as Raheem Sterling, thus echoing its most successful tagline, '*The best a man can get*,' without the *traditional* masculine overtones. Thereby, bringing the brand back into line with its original identity and purpose and demonstrating the notion that '*authenticity is determined in relation to inauthentic existence which is not chosen by ourselves*' (Shuttleworth 2020).

It is important to understand authenticity in the context of brand story as it is such a powerful medium. It is easy to see how something that is perceived to be inauthentic can damage reputations and also cost companies lots of money. This notion of authenticity is part of a wider framework of ethical considerations for storytelling in education. What we can understand from this example is that the audience responds negatively to messaging and stories if they feel that they are being misled or told stories that are inauthentic to the brand's narrative. '*Telling stories is a discursive action which functions as a medium for manipulation*' (Auvinen et al. 2012). Such manipulation can be construed as either inauthentic or authentic to the narrative.

Truth in Storytelling

Storytelling is typically overseen by adults who tell children what's fair and not fair, what's of value and not, and how we should behave, punishing and rewarding when we act in accordance, or not, to the models of our culture. (Storr 2019, p. 79)

In the same way that marketers and advertisers relate their brand's activities to an authentic story that resonates with their audiences, actors look for the '*truth*' in a story or character. '*Truth is inseparable from belief, and belief from truth. They cannot exist without each other and without both there can be no experiencing or creative work. 'Everything onstage must be convincing for the actor himself, for his fellow actors and for the audience. Everything should inspire belief in the possible existence in real life of feelings analogous to the actor's own. Every moment onstage must be endorsed by belief in the truth of the feelings being experienced and in the truth of the action taking place*' (Stanislavski 2017).

'*Stories are tribal propaganda. They control their group, manipulating its members into behaving in ways that benefit it. And it works*' (Storr 2019). Therefore, it can be argued that the truth within the story is particular and relevant within specific groups. '*A nation has a story it tells about itself, in which values are encoded, as does a corporation [and so on]*' (Storr 2019). Such truths are not then universal but are specific to different groups, such as political or religious. '*Influencing someone is a social action that has meaning*' (Auvinen et al., p. 4). It manifested in modern times, through gossip, anecdotal stories, word of mouth and more recently and more pervasively through social media, a conduit for curated stories for their users. Algorithms have transformed and at the same time, curtailed the availability of information by providing stories that the user will respond to, tracing their internet use, their particular activities, their likes and dislikes to provide a singular outlook on their social media, which is why one user's feed will be very different from the next persons. Stories, therefore become one's habitus, defining the '*link not only between past, present and future, but also between the social and the individual*' (Maton 2014).

In the political arena in the last few years, there have been a number of questions raised about ethics and storytelling and how the use of social media has led to a rise in political interventions, '*fake news*' and nostalgic stories that resonate with audiences. In Polleta et al.'s insightful paper on storytelling during the Trump era, she argues that those who supported him were not just '*duped by Fox News*'—a somewhat lazy and patronising response to all of those voters. They argue that there were many more layers at play, that which echoes Storr's notion of tribal propaganda or Bordieu's notion of habitus that binds the individual, where '*every human group that has a shared purpose is held together by such stories*' (Storr 2019). The disconnect that many of these people felt from Capitol Hill, from the language of the left, that could be capitalised upon and exploited through '*stories told, retold, referenced, and alluded to*' (Polletta and Callahan 2017).

The strength of Trump came in the archetype of a hero, playing to the nostalgic tropes of the American dream, engaging in anecdotal stories relating to his audience, creating a divide.

between Us and Them, further perpetuated by the '*Conservative media commentators often styled a personal relationship with the viewer or listener, in which allusive stories reinforced the bond between speaker and audience*' (Polletta and Callahan 2017).

Such stories '*have revealed another dynamic: that people's sense of personal experience may encompass experiences that are not their own [where the] narrators used the personal pronouns "we" or "you" in relating such accounts. The implication was that the personal story was a collective one. Sometimes narrators recounted events using the term "we", but the events were not ones they had actually experienced*' (Polletta et al.).

Ethics and Business

The previous examples serve to demonstrate how '*stories can serve many purposes…*' (Auvinen et al.), how storytelling can be manipulated, manipulative and incredibly powerful and influential to those groups who engage with their specific narratives. At the very heart of this is a question of ethics. By its very nature storytelling has an agenda so how is it possible to utilise it in a way that is ethically sound? Notions of authenticity and truth abound, and these are perhaps the most contentious and relevant ethical considerations of current thinking. Therefore, it is also important to consider the ethics of business organisations. As business school graduates are our future business leaders, what can we learn from current practices? How can we implement a more ethical framework into the curriculum with the use of storytelling?

Ethical Perceptions Within Business Education

Given the heightened criticism of the ethicality of managerial behaviour, it is encouraging to note that individuals are, in fact, positively affected by formal ethics training, even as adults.

Ethical perceptions vary across the different disciplines within business education (Lopez 2005) where there is a noted difference between the qualitative and quantitative functions, where the former, representing the more humanistic elements is perceived to be more ethical than their mathematically minded counterpart (Lopez 2005). It is another indicator of how there is need for improvement in the education of future industry leaders where ethical considerations are paramount, particularly in a capitalist society which adheres its own principles and self-regulation. Therefore, the use of storytelling is not just about the ethicality of the story but also of the storyteller.

The work of psychologist, Bruner focused on the learning and cultural environment of children in different educational settings, espousing the use of narratives '*to question accepted knowledge, reason and make sense of the world*' (Aubrey and Riley 2019). Narratives both '*written and spoken*' could be formed in many ways, including, '*discussions and observations of life*' (Aubrey and Riley 2019), enabling students to become involved in the narratives themselves. Stories work on different levels, providing different ways of learning. Bruner relates this idea of '*one a landscape of action in the mind*' and '*the other a landscape of the mind*' (Storr 2019) reflecting our own conscious and subconscious processes.

Applying this theory to adult students within business education offers scope for a framework within the context of the learning and cultural environment. It encourages students to reflect on their ethics as they participate in narratives—as storyteller, listener or performer. It begs the question of what type of stories should then be told. Do we align ourselves to have a singular voice or is that in itself unethical or '*inauthentic*'? If determining the truth of the story, then to bring cohesion across functions and cultures, it must be a participatory exercise but that does not mean that several strands cannot create a singular story that meets a certain reality (Larsen et al. 2020). The notion of adding to a story or creating a story through participant and user providing content, providing potentially unverified stories which may add or detract reputationally is relevant to the activities of social media in particular. Engaging in such activity allows anyone to participate which bring relevance back to the impact of storytelling on education, and the implications of the ethical framework to ensure that there is a veracity and validity to the stories being told.

How Are Stories Told?

From a Western perspective, we are primed for the three Act play, the beginning, middle and end. We have learned this from fiction, from folk talks and from plays—the set-up, confrontation and resolution (Yorke 2013), it is a way for us '*to order everything outside ourselves*' (Yorke 2013), which provides ample scope within business education for greater understanding of the roles people play, the ethos and problems within organisations, the ability to develop stories, collaboration and ability to build creative thinking skills. It echoes the principles of Bruner and the '*importance of culture and environment in learning*' (Aubrey and Riley 2019).

Storytelling brings with it values and ideas, it manifests in many guises, through role-play, case studies, anecdotal conversations and more. At its heart an authentic story has truth! In engaging students with storytelling we are encouraging them to develop their own stories, with '*the idea of valuing those intrinsic reasons—doing something worthwhile, pride in achievement, joy in learning—perception of what is more socially acceptable*' (Storr 2019).

Collaboration and internationalism in both education and industry means that we need to explore a wider understanding of story, not only following the Greek myths but engaging with students (and staff) from different regions of the world, understanding their stories, along with it, their values and ideals.

Conclusion: What Do We Want to Learn from Stories?

Storytelling is a powerful tool that can be used to manipulate, motivate and engage its audience. The storyteller, therefore, has an obligation to consider the ethical standpoint of their story. Advertising and marketing materials abound with stories, stories that rely on the humanistic response to the familiar shape and form, leaning on archetypal characters that we relate to or aspire to be. There is a perceived '*truth*' and '*authenticity*' to these stories, when aligned and executed in accordance with the precepts of the brand or organisation. Any discordance is perceived to be '*inauthentic*'. Such truth is expounded upon in Storr's view of the tribal story and the propaganda (Storr 2019) that is inherent within it. Such propaganda can be associated with the rise of '*fake news*' and the narrowing of the field of information that individuals receive on their social media feeds.

Ethics is therefore a fundamental question that needs to be considered when thinking about storytelling in relation to business education. It is not just a question about the '*ethical lapses*' in recent times of large organisations—we only need to look to the collapse of Lehman Brothers, as a result of irregularities in the banking sector and the subprime mortgage crisis which led to a global recession to understand that leadership quality is in deficit and we need to consider how we want not only the leaders of tomorrow to be but also how we want businesses to function in the future. Building an ethical framework of storytelling is part of the evolution for a more cohesive and integrated business education experience and better for future practice.

Storytelling therefore needs to be challenged, where questions of ethics are posed and where ethicality in terms of truth and authenticity is clearly defined. We need to understand what kind of stories we want to tell, how we want to tell them and why. There are examples of where storytelling has been used in limited capacity in different business schools, primarily for personal development and for the understanding of moral dilemmas and questions that arise in management and leadership. This is one aspect of cross-function use of storytelling, fostering the development of individuals to develop their own ethical code but there can be a much broader use of storytelling in the way that we have witnessed brands do this so successfully, for example.

Key, to this, is the ability to tell stories through a lens of authenticity, with a clear understanding of what motivations may be at play, and where problems of self-interest may lie. In ascertaining that certain specialisms are more prone to risk, and therefore, potentially, more questionable ethics, then it is important that there is an understanding of the purpose of stories and '*Our choice is whether we use values and stories ethically and strategically or ignore them*' (Larsen et al. 2020).

References

Aubrey K. & Riley A. (2019), *Understanding & Using Educational Theories*, SAGE, 2nd Edition

Auvinen T., Sintonen A-M. & Takala T. (2012) *Leadership Manipulation and Ethics in Storytelling*, Published online: 6 September 2012, Springer Science+Business Media B.V. 2012 [Accessed Saturday 4th September 2021]

Ferrari A., Cachia R. and Punie Y. (2009) Innovation and Creativity in Education and Training in the EU Member States: Fostering Creative Learning and Supporting Innovative Teaching—Literature review on Innovation and Creativity in E&T in the EU Member States (ICEAC), Luxembourg: Office for Official Publications of the European Communities © European Communities, 2009 [Accessed Saturday 30th January 2021]

Germano S. (2020) "Nike Diversity Chief Leaves after two years in role," *Financial Times*, July 28th 2020, Financial Times Limited [Accessed Saturday 4th September 2021]

Holland K. (2009) *"Is It Time to Retrain B-Schools?"* *The New York Times*, 12th March 2009 [Accessed 12th December 2021]

Larsen J. , Boje D. and Bruun L. (2020) *True Storytelling, Seven Principles for an Ethical and Sustainable Change-Management Strategy*, Taylor and Francis

Lopez Y., Rechner P. & Olson-Buchanan J. (2005) Shaping Ethical Perceptions: An Empirical Assessment of the Influence of Business Education, Culture, and Demographic Factors, *Journal of Business Ethics* (2005) 60: 341–358 _ Springer 2005 [Accessed Saturday 4th September 2021]

Maton K. (2014) *"Chapter 3: Habitus,"* *Pierre Bourdieu, Key Concepts*, Edited by Michael Grenfell, Routledge, 2nd Edition

Mitchell A. (2012) From 1930s 'Brand Man' to today: the evolution of the brand manager, The role of the brand manager has changed beyond recognition; today's practitioners are more akin to magazine editors, Campaign, April 12, 2012 [Accessed Sunday 12th September 2021]

Morgan, N. (2015) Authenticity and Artifice, Forbes, forbes.com [Accessed Sunday 12th September 2021]

Olbertova M. (2019) Why global brands fall into the gap of meaning, Research on WARC, March 2019, [Accessed on Thursday 9th September 2021]

Polletta F. and Callahan J. (2017) Deep stories, nostalgia narratives, and fake news: Storytelling in the Trump era, Macmillan Publishers Ltd. 2049-7113 American Journal of Cultural Sociology, www.palgrave.com/journals

Poulton M.S. (2005) Organizational Storytelling, ethics and morality; How stories frame limits of behaviour in organizations, EJBO—Electronic Journal of Business Ethics and Organization Studies, Vol. 10 (2). [Retrieved from http://ejbo.jyu.fi on Thursday 9th September 2021]

Ready D.A. (2002) How Storytelling builds next-generation leaders, MIT Sloan Management Review (Vol 43, Issue 4), Sloan Management Review [Accessed Saturday 30th January 2021].

Ritson M. (2019) Gillette's new ad will trash its sales and be the year's worst marketing move, Marketing Week, 15th January 2021 [Accessed Friday 10th September 2021]

Seethamraju, R. & Leonard, J. & Razeed, A. (2006) Development of integrated learning in business curriculum, HERDSA Review of Higher Education [Accessed Monday 8th February 2021]

Shuttleworth K. (2020) *The History and Ethics of Authenticity, Meaning, Freedom & Modernity*, Bloomsbury

Stanislavski K. (2017) *An Actor's Work*, Translated and edited by Jean Benedetti, Routledge

Storr W. (2019) *The Science of Storytelling*, William Collins, London

Trilling L. (2009) *Sincerity and Authenticity*, Harvard University Press

Vincent L. (2012) *Brand Real—How Smart Companies Live Their Brand Promise and Inspire Fierce Customer Loyalty*, Amacom, American Management Association

Yorke J. (2013) *Into the Woods, How Stories Work and Why We Tell Them*, Penguin Random House UK.

6

'My God I'm Wearing Tesco!': Fashion, Pre-Teen Femininity and the Commercialisation of Childhood

Julie Blanchard

Abstract '*My God I'm wearing Tesco!*', exclaims 10-year-old Georgia, in exaggerated horror, as she realises that she has admitted to wearing a piece of clothing from a supermarket chain, in a focus group with friends. Her comments imply young girls' awareness of the branding of fashion and its commercial source. Edwards (Living dolls? The role of clothing and fashion in 'sexualisation'. *Sexualities*, Vol. 23 (5–6), 702–716, 2020), examining children's clothing, addresses continuing popular concern in the UK about fashion being part of both the sexualising and commercialising of childhood, suggesting that there is little research about children's relationship with dress. This chapter focusses on what commercialisation might involve and what part it may play in girls' understanding of fashion, particularly examining notions of consumerism and economic activity in relation to how girls talk about their consumption of clothing.

J. Blanchard (✉)
Business School for the Creative Industries, University for the Creative Arts, Farnham, UK
e-mail: Philip.Powell@uca.ac.uk

© The Author(s), under exclusive license to Springer Nature Switzerland AG 2022
P. Powell, B. Shankar Nayak (eds.), *Creative Business Education*,
https://doi.org/10.1007/978-3-031-10928-7_6

Introduction

Teaching history and theory in a creative arts institution for over twenty years, I have sometimes been challenged to justify what I teach—for instance, why are dry theoretical concepts relevant to the everyday work of a fashion journalist? Because good journalists should offer new perspectives, and I help students to learn how to research, using academic ideas to help explore and critique the fashion industry and the wider world, debating movements such as #metoo, #blacklivesmatter and challenging the ethically and environmentally unsustainable status quo. My teaching practice is informed by my own research, which keeps me up to date with the latest fashion studies. Partly inspired by debates with students about the fashion business and links with commercialisation, sexualisation and children's fashion consumption, I outlined and explored these issues and argued against such trends in this chapter.

Gap in Our Knowledge

'*My God I'm wearing Tesco!*', exclaims 10-year-old Georgia, [1] in exaggerated horror, as she realises that she has admitted to wearing a piece of clothing from a supermarket chain, in a focus group with friends. Her comments, further discussed below, imply young girls' awareness of the branding of fashion and its commercial source. Edwards (2020), in a recent academic article about children's clothing, addresses continuing popular concern in the UK about fashion being part of both the sexualising and commercialising of childhood, suggesting that there is little research about children's relationship with dress. This chapter focusses on what commercialisation might involve and what part it may play in girls' understanding of fashion, particularly examining notions of consumerism and economic activity in relation to how girls talk about their consumption of clothing.

---

[1] All names of people and places are pseudonyms to maintain anonymity

Childhood in a Commercial World

In British newspaper articles addressing the commercialisation of childhood, fashion is presented as a significant part of a contemporary world ensuring that '*the boundaries between adulthood and childhood have become dangerously blurred*' (Lichtenstein, *MailOnline* 2010). Here childhood and adulthood are constituted as fixed life stages associated with separate identity positions of child and adult, distinctions that are considered to be under threat from social change. Children are seen as increasingly targeted by '*greedy retailers*' (Daily Mail 2010) who are part of a '*marketing culture that now targets young girls relentlessly*' (McCartney, *Telegraph* 2010). The supposition is that advertisers are manipulative and that children are incapable of negotiating or resisting their marketing ploys. Children are assumed to be more conformist than adults and are '*under pressure to keep up with trends*' (Cochrane, *Guardian* 2010) and the result is children who have become '*more materialistic*' (Taylor, *Guardian* 2010) and now have '*false*' needs, newly created wants and desires that corrupt their innocence.

From this popular discussion it can be seen that childhood is perceived as a stable period when children are passive, innocent and vulnerable (MacDonald 2003: 110). Hence, children are frequently presented in the media as particularly in need of protection. It is argued that we are currently living in what can be characterized as a '*risk society*' (Giddens 1991; Beck 1992, 1999). The claim is that British society has been profoundly transformed since the 1970s, with economic rationalism, reduced welfare state, de-industrialisation and increased globalism meaning politics and decision-making are conducted at an international rather than local level; these changes mean that there is sense of insecurity, fragmentation and a breakdown of social networks. Global and technological change is thought to have eroded all that was secure, unchanging and natural (Giddens 2000, p. 51).Yet, the construction of childhood has come to symbolise all that is natural and traditional (Jenks 1996), so the constant concern about childhood being at an end reflects wider fears about change in contemporary life. As Prout (2000) explains, in a world increasingly seen as shifting and uncertain, children, because they are regarded as unfinished, are considered good target for attempts to control the future. Critics of the emotive language and unsubstantiated claims used in contemporary debates about the commercialisation and sexualisation of childhood, such as Bragg et al. (2011), Smith and Attwood (2011) and Kehily (2012), indicate that the concern about young girls is linked to wider anxiety about what is considered an increasingly consumerist and sexually explicit Western culture.

Paradoxically, the universalised notion of the child as fragile, at risk and in need of protection is also operating in a society in which children are also seen as individuals with increased autonomy and have more legal rights that they can assert (directgov 2008). The bestowal of civil rights suggests that children are to some extent legally invoked as citizens (Buckingham 2000). These contemporary changes to childhood also include the shift to individualisation (Christensen and Prout 2005), which is embedded in Beck's (1992, 1999) notion that people, regardless of their age, are coming to think of themselves as unique individuals who can shape their own identities. Children are increasingly aware of cultural norms and expectations and are enjoined to speak, make themselves visible, and regulate their own behaviour (James et al. 2005). This individualisation of childhood is driven not only by children gaining rights as citizens, but also because within marketing, advertising and popular culture children are increasingly being addressed as consumers (Kenway and Bullen 2001).

Marketers are progressively addressing children more directly, because with fewer children being born in Britain than in the '*baby boom*' of the mid-twentieth century (Office of National Statistics 2008a), children are likely to live in households with fewer siblings and so have a larger share of the family wealth (Gunter and Furnham 1998). Britain is also, on the whole, an increasingly affluent society (Bocock 1993; Ransome 2005: 37); therefore children are an attractive target market. [2] Other alterations in family life have also affected children's access to money and goods; marketing literature suggests that with an increase in households in which both parents work and higher levels of divorce, upheaval for children and less time spent with them by their parents sometimes results in giving

---

[2] Though the gap between the rich and the poor is growing (ONS 2008b).

children money or gifts (Key Note 2001; Kenway and Bullen 2001). Children today have more '*pester power*' than children had in the past, and as Boden (2006a) emphasises, collectively these changes mean that children's consumption is of growing importance and marketing companies are increasingly targeting them with new consumer goods. One of the commercial areas that has benefitted from this rise in children's consumption of goods is the fashion market—designer labels now do children's ranges and supermarket chains such as Asda and Tesco are offering children's fashion (Boden 2006a). In the commercial world the pre-teen is recognised as an important consumer and both the children, and their parents, are faced with an array of targeted goods. How girls respond to this commercial address, and what their everyday practices of fashion consumption might tell us, is the focus of this chapter.

Girls as Consumers

In current childhood sociology children are not seen as merely passive recipients imprinted upon by society but as agents constructing and maintaining their social and cultural worlds. Although the new paradigm in childhood studies research children as agents, few who take up this paradigm examine children's consumer lives (see Cook 2008 for a critique of this absence). The girl child as active social agent and their lived experience of consumer culture is addressed by Russell and Tyler (2002), as they ask what it means to do feminine childhood against the backdrop of contemporary consumer culture. Femininity is an aesthetic phenomenon bound up with the commodified world, one which could be seen to be commercially exploitative, however, it is a world in and through which girls become women (Russell and Tyler 2002). Russell and Tyler (2002) acknowledge the continuous nature of identity work and refer to the active doing of childhood, which '*recognizes the status of children as active social agents, yet also emphasizes the extent to which children are involved in an ongoing inter-subjective process of "becoming"*' (Russell and Tyler 2002: 622). Russell and Tyler (2002) maintain that whilst girls engage in active meaning, they have an awareness of what are frequently adult expectations about gender. Russell and Tyler (2002) conclude that whilst girls are active and knowing in their performance of gender through the consumption of make-up and accessories, they do not question the ideal of femininity that exists, thereby suggesting that there is a limit to girls' critical awareness. My intention is to draw on this notion of the complexity of girls' positions as subjects and to explore girls' active engagement with fashion and dress.

More recent research has turned its focus on to *teenage* girls' interaction with fashion as its specific interest (such as Klepp and Storm-Mathisen 2005). But it is vital to attend to the specificity of age because cultural constructions for every age group within a particular historical moment differ (Renold 2005), and if popular discussion positions children as non-agents then it is work with the specific age grouping of 8 to 11-year-olds will bring that positioning into question. Further, as those who have researched children's fashion assert, there has been little exploration of children or specifically young girls' fashion as material culture (Pilcher 2009; Boden et al. 2004; Cook and Kaiser 2004). An exception is an ethnographic study carried out by Boden et al. (2004) with children aged 6–11, which acknowledges that children's consumption is affected by social structures and parental concerns; it describes how children use their consumption to demonstrate an increased autonomy from their parents and develop notions about what suits them and signifies their self-image (Boden et al. 2004: 11). Children also exert considerable power in the family, influencing parental consumption in terms of clothing both for themselves and their parents.

Pilcher (2013) posits that children's consumption is significantly different to adult consumption in that there are specific discourses and cultural determinants of childhood that structure both the production and consumption of children's clothes. These discourses explored in Boden et al. (2004) and Pilcher's (2009) earlier work, frame childhood as a time of innocence, or as Renold (2005) more explicitly states—assexuality. As well as these discourses of childhood, there are other frameworks shaping children's consumption of clothing such as the production-market of children's clothing (what is available to be worn) and their '*life world*' (Pilcher 2013: 92) involving many social and cultural influences such a gender, age, family and peers. Pilcher (2013) argues that children's consumption is shaped, not only by the frameworks and discourses listed here but also by their own determination and sense of self. Determinativity is a useful concept for thinking through many of the factors that shape young girls' consumption of fashion and suggests that research with girls must acknowledge social and cultural, family and peers but also girls' own reflexivity and ability in using dress to present the self (Pilcher 2013). These ideas will be engaged with in relation to my own findings.

Researching with Girls About Fashion: A Methodology

In order to do qualitative research with young girls, one of the most straightforward ways is to get access through schools; I sent letters to head-teachers of primary schools in the predominantly white, middle-class, city of Bridworth in the South of England. The two that responded positively, passed on information about my research and asked the girls to register their interest. Information sheets and consent forms were then sent to both parents, and to the girls, in keeping with my methodological perspective of treating children as social actors. Once agreements were in place, empirical research was carried out in 2011 and 2013 with thirty-two girls aged 8 to 9 and 10 to 11-years-old. Six focus groups of between three and eight participants were undertaken to investigate the negotiation of fashionability, as fashion is a social phenomenon and inter-subjective practice (Bottero 2010).

Focus groups or group interviews are group discussions conducted with typically six to eight participants, focussing on debating a set of questions (Morgan 1998). My groups ranged from as few as three participants, to as many as eight girls. The girls were in groups in which they were familiar with everyone, and were friends with some of the participants, which helped to foster a comfortable and non-threatening atmosphere (Renold 2005) in which they discussed going round to each other's houses, family members the others knew of and friends that they had common. The group debated the questions amongst themselves with minimal intervention from me, the researcher (Gibbs 1997), for between forty minutes and an hour. Although I provided some direction for the groups, the intention was that in their interaction the girls shaped the discussion and raised topics that were of interest to them. Their familiarity with each other also allowed their shared interests to come to the fore. Focus groups can help to redress the power imbalance between the researcher and participants, as they are '*particularly useful for allowing participants to generate their own questions, frames and concepts and to pursue their own priorities on their own terms and in their own vocabulary*' (Barbour and Kitzenger 1999, p. 5). The intention was that because the researcher's power was also reduced in terms of simply being outnumbered, the girls did not just tell me what they thought I wanted to hear (Punch 2002).

My interest was in fashion worn outside of the official school context and in girls' interaction with fashion and their clothes. Therefore, as the girls usually wore a uniform in school time, I conducted these focus groups on special dress-down days at the schools. Girls' clothing choices were to be the starting point for the discussion, so that the girls' own wardrobes influenced their interaction. The aim was not to suggest that there is any '*neutral*' or '*natural*' setting (Barbour and Kitzinger 1999) but that on special days, wearing their own clothes at least freed the girls from some of the usual official school constraints on dress, if not from parental ones. This chapter focusses on data collected from two groups of girls, one of each age range, as they are representative of many of the key issues related to retail and purchasing fashion that arose in the focus groups.

Girls' Consumption of Fashion and Their Engagements with Consumer Culture

Knowledge of Fashion Retailers

All the girls that took part in this study were knowledgeable about names of many fashion retailers and explained where their clothes came from, therefore are conscious of the production-market for children's clothes (Pilcher 2013). For example, in response to being asked where they went to buy clothing, Focus Group 4 replied:

Focus Group 4 (Aged 8–9)
Lucie: Primark, Next
Sara: Debenhams
Ella: Primark, Gap, Debenhams, I love
Sara: Next
Ella: I like Next definitely
Lucie: Hollister
Ella: Hollister, Abercrombie, except that nothing at Hollister fits me
Leah: George
Lucie: Monsoon

Here, even in the younger age group, familiarity with a whole range of fashion retailers of girls' clothes is shown, ranging from the cheapest such as Primark and supermarket brands like George at Asda, to the more expensive High Street stores like Gap. This group, like all in my study, and in the work of others (Boden 2006b; Rysst 2010), could identify which brands they liked and ones that fitted them too (Rysst 2010).

In Focus Group 2 there was lots of discussion about the shops that the girls bought their clothes in and some evaluation of what these stores were like.

Focus Group 2 (Aged 10–11)
Lauren: New Look, Primark
Jessica: Primark, Primark, I get everything from Primark
Georgia: I hadn't been to Primark until it first came to Bridworth
Lauren: Yeah like the first day it opened I quickly got on the bus
Georgia: I would never go into a cheap shop but then my mum started going in the charity shops in Bridworth
JB: Yeah
Georgia: Cos she likes it in there … so ever since then she keeps going in the charity shops so it got me into going into places like Primark
JB: Hmm
Georgia: These are from Primark ((pointing at boots)), New Look ((pointing at leggings)) New Look ((pointing at skirt))
…
Georgia: Tesco ((pulling at t-shirt))
Lauren: Tesco?

Georgia: My God I'm wearing Tesco!
Lauren: I got this from Primark ((pulling at sweatshirt)), no, no Debenhams…I
quite like Debenhams it's quite fashionable
Georgia: Yeah
Lauren: I got these from Primark ((pulling at jeans)) and my plimsolls from
New Look…
Georgia: Debenhams can be a bit babyish

The girls knew where each item of clothing they were wearing was purchased from, so they clearly played an active role in choosing the clothes or paid attention to the labels that were in their clothes, as Boden (2006a) also found. Much of what the girls were wearing was from cheap, but up-to-date, fashion chains such as New Look and Primark. Georgia described how originally, she was disdainful of shopping in cheap shops like Primark, however once her mum began to think that shopping in charity shops was acceptable, then going to Primark was alright. She also expressed some mock horror that her t-shirt came from Tesco, so even within a group of friends who shop in stores such as Primark, the wearing of very cheap clothes from a supermarket chain was a matter of some unease. This kind of evaluation suggests the cultural capital to differentiate between store types was evident (Bourdieu 2010). In this extract the problem is also raised, acknowledged in all bar Group 1, of ensuring that you were dressed appropriately for your age; here the concern is about clothes that might be too young for your age. Engagement with or rejection of certain goods from popular culture can be used to express ideas about age grade, life course and growing up (Boden 2006a; Pilcher 2013).

At the other end of the age scale, commercialisation has been posited as rushing girls through their life course by encouraging the wearing of clothes thought to be too grown up for their age. However, girls also understood that just because certain clothes are aimed at them, they need not necessarily wear items that are considered to make them look too old, as seen even in the younger age group below.

Focus Group 4 (Aged 8–9)
Sara: yeah, sometimes, I love Primark but sometimes in Primark
Ella: it's a bit cheap

Sara: yeah but sometimes in Primark they're for kids but they're really like grown up clothes and say I really like them but I'm just not being me when I wear them
Lucie: what I think about Primark is that they've got like really nice clothes and they look really nice but then they're really cheap but people buy them and they're not good quality.

This excerpt demonstrates Sara's understanding of the discourses of childhood (Pilcher 2013), and the maintenance of an asexual appearance whereby girls should not look too old. These discourses were engaged with in all except one focus group, thereby showing the critical awareness of girls as social actors (James et al. 2005). Sara's reflection that to look older would be inauthentic to the construction of her current aged identity suggests a knowing interaction with the discourse of childhood; more about this relationship between pre-teen dress, age and identity construction can be found in Blanchard-Emmerson. In her wanting to '*be me*', Sara also implies the desire to be active in her constitution of subjectivity discussed further below. What is also evident here, is that the participants are conscious of the price of goods and that cheapness is often linked with poor quality, knowledge potentially linked again to girls' cultural capital (Bourdieu 2010).

Pressure to Consume

In relation to the popular concern about commercialisation, evidence for the commercial pressure on girls to consume could also be found. Some girls competed about how much they were able to spend on clothes and how much clothing they have, as the following extract demonstrates.

Focus Group 2 (Aged 10–11)
Jessica: my mum says I can go shopping in Primark soon with 20 pound
Lauren: I spent with my old friend Nicky, I spent about £60 on clothes
Georgia: I get £20 a week on clothes cos I keep moaning 'I've got no clothes' but I've got 7 drawers full and a whole wardrobe/ and 2 drawers under that. So I've got 9 drawers and I'm still asking for more, so I get £20 a week for it

Jessica: I've got ((counts under breath with fingers)) I've got 16 drawers full of stuff
JB: Wow!
Jessica: Plus a whole cupboard full, it's about from there to there
Lauren: I've got a chest of drawers full of stuff, a wardrobe and boxes that go under the bed

Not only did the girls enjoy shopping and spending money on dress, but they were also boasting here about how much furniture was full of their clothing. However, Georgia was conscious that she had plenty of clothes, and that wanting more was unnecessary over-consumption. Conversely, she has the self-awareness to acknowledge that she still asks for additional clothing, feeling a compulsion to consume. As with Russell and Tyler's (2002) argument that girls do have some critical awareness about the social construction of gender, but did not critique the existence of the ideal, here the limit of criticality is reached in the refusal to consume. However, over-consumption of fashionable goods is a huge social and environmental issue that many adults are only beginning to recognise, let alone reach sustainable conclusions to (Bly et al. 2015).

Also, despite this exuberant discussion of consumption, when I asked Georgia about whether she was allowed to go out and spend the £20 clothes allowance, the following exchange took place:

Georgia: Yes, I'm getting £62 because I sold one of those biscuit dogs I've got that does all those commands
Lauren: Oh no
Georgia: I sold him on eBay. My step-dad bought it for me and he didn't know and he was pretty upset. So I was a bit annoyed and then, well, he was annoyed anyway. So I had £62 and £20 so I had £82
JB: And so you are just allowed to go and buy whatever you like with that?
Jessica: Yeah
Lauren: Yeah
Georgia: No. My mum won't give me £62 because I'll go out and spend it on rubbish.
Lauren: Basically I
Jessica: That's what my mum said

Lauren: Basically I save up all year and then at the end of the year I do a big shop of clothes
Georgia: I save up, but even when I say I'm going out, my mum says 'no you're not'

Regardless of their seeming embracement of consumerism, there was recognition that money for shopping trips may not be unlimited or automatically forthcoming, demonstrating that girls are agents capable of reflecting on their social worlds (James et al. 2005). Whilst, again, there was no suggestion that you might not want to spend at all, there was awareness that in order to have more money to spend, you might have to sell some of your own goods or save up. And although at first there was the intimation that the girls could spend money on whatever clothes they like, there was a shift to acknowledge that spending would be a matter of negotiation with mothers. Parents, particularly mothers, are '*life world*' influences (Pilcher 2013) shaping children's consumption.

Further, economics are understood to play a part in their family's ability to spend; financial constraints and the expense of consumption were discussed in all the Focus Groups, thereby suggesting girls' agency involves some monetary sense. Children's economic agency is an area recognised by Xolocotzin and Jay (2020) as in need of further research. What can be seen above, is that as well as some understanding of monetary cost of fashion goods, girls in the study were predominately happy to buy in cheap shops, and several other groups talked positively about buying clothes from Ebay, charity shops (Focus Groups 3, 5 and 6) and receiving hand-me-downs (Focus Group 4 and 6). Therefore, girls are not always the rampant consumers of the latest trends that popular discussion might have us believe. However, many girls were certainly interested in what was currently in fashion and this chapter turns to their engagement with trends next.

Pressure to Keep Up with Trends

When asked about how they knew what was in fashion, the younger group answered:

Focus Group 4 (Aged 8–9)
Ella: magazines, I do lots of Girl Talk which has quite a lot of pages about what styles there are, what celebrities wear and they have loads
Sara: my mum's magazines
Millie: I usually just check what my friends
Ella: in my mum's magazine there was a 10-page spread about fashion so I tore it out and put it in my room
Sara: I normally just get all the fashion magazines
Ella: normally on a dress as you please day like today… if I like something someone else is wearing I just get the style
Sara: not exactly the same but
Leah: (inaudible) like what celebrities wear and fashion in Girl Talk
Ella: cos I always have my own look I don't copy anybody else's so I'm normally being my own person with my style and stuff so I kind of
Sara: it's like basically it's a coincidence that me and Millie wore all this
Ella: cos they were discussing wearing dresses and high heels they were discussing it together
Sara: yeah
Millie: so we just added to each other and stuff

In this extract there are several sources of fashion knowledge: girls' magazines, adult fashion magazines, what celebrities are wearing and friends. (The rejection of what celebrities' wear as being appropriate for young girls to wear is discussed in Blanchard-Emmerson 2017). Yet, despite their interest in other people's style and what is fashionable, the girls also discuss notions of individuality and self-expression, or in Pilcher's (2013) words '*determinative me-making*'. This determinativity is an interactive process and here can be seen to take place in relation to peers, as well as within commercialised popular culture. This evaluation and collaborative dialogue between friends, of their knowledge base and fashion practice, is an example of engagement with fashion being an '*intersubjective practice*' (Bottero 2010).

Indeed, ideas about what was fashionable were also a matter of negotiation between friends. In Focus Group 2 everyone stated that pink was fashionable, and I then asked what else was '*in*':

Focus Group 2 (Aged 10–11)

Jessica: Black
Georgia: Fluorescent colours
Lauren: Yeah mostly bright colours
Georgia: Hi Tops are in (0.1) sometimes ((says tentatively looking at Lauren)).
Lauren: Yeah sometimes
Georgia: Some girls wear/
Lauren: Boob tubes are in
Georgia: Yeah but I wouldn't want to wear them in winter, even though I am personally
Jessica: Jumpers because like everyone else wears them like boys and stuff
Georgia: Mm ((wrinkles up her nose))
Lauren: Mm kind of
Georgia: But I don't really care about boys' fashion.
Jessica: Shirts, like girl shirts
((Georgia and Lauren look at each other, Lauren pulls face))
Georgia: yeah/
Jessica: I've got a couple of them

Here we see different suggestions being made and either confirmed, qualified or covertly denied or ignored by the other participants. Lauren confirmed that it was bright colours and not black that was in, Georgia paused after her proposal of Hi Tops and looked to Lauren to corroborate, a confirmation she only receives when qualified with a '*sometimes*'. Lauren and Georgia sought to endorse each other's ideas of fashionability at every turn. Yet they were at odds with Jessica, whose suggestions remain unsupported or were skirted round with replies such as '*But I don't really care about boys' fashion*'. At one point Jessica's suggestion was verbally endorsed with a '*yeah*' from Georgia, but this assent was undermined by the look exchanged between Georgia and Lauren and by Lauren's face-pulling; thus, girls were disagreeing whilst avoiding open conflict (Underwood 2004). What was in fashion was clearly not defined just by what was available in retail outlets or about straightforward following of prevailing styles but instead was a matter of debate and negotiation between girls themselves. The negotiation demonstrates the inter-subjectivity (Bottero 2010) of determining fashionability and suggests some sense of agency on the part of the girls to sometimes take up only the fashion trends that they either individually or collectively, in friendship groups, agree upon or decide to pick up (as Woodward 2007 suggests happens with adults).

Conclusions

The data arising from this research suggests that girls as young as eight are aware of the commercial nature of fashion, its retailers and trends, and the pressure to consume. Therefore, in many respects the participants are living commercialised lives. However, what is missing from the popular debate about this commercialisation, is the nuance and complexity of girls' engagements with the discourses of childhood and fashion. These engagements have brought to light girls' understanding of how they are meant to dress in relation to age, their disagreements about fashion, their negotiations about what to consume and where from. Evidence presented here suggests that girls are sometimes thoughtful consumers of cheap and second-hand clothing and are often conscious of financial constraints. Overall, young girls' relationship with fashion is, as Pilcher proposes, mindful of a whole range of influences that shape their consumption, including self-determination—their desire to be themselves.

As the research was based on predominately white, middle-class girls, there would be merit in examining other races, classes, and the experiences of boys, of the commercial call of fashion. Additionally, the acknowledgement of consumerism by the participants, combined with the recent rise of youth-based environmental activism, suggests a future study could consider how growing awareness of fashion's negative impact influences girls' current fashion consumption.

References

Barbour, R.S. and Kitzenger, J. (eds) (1999) *Developing Focus Group Research: Politics, Theory and Practice*, London: Sage.

Beck, U. (1992) *Risk Society*, London: Sage.

Beck, U. (1999) *World Risk Society*, Cambridge: Polity Press.

Bly, S., Gwozdz, W. and Reisch, L. (2015) 'Exit from the high street: an exploratory study of sustainable fashion consumption pioneers' in *International Journal of Consumer Studies*, Vol. 39, pp. 125–135.

Bocock, R. (1993) *Consumption*, London: Routledge.

Boden, S., Pole, C., Pilcher, J. and Edwards, T., (2004) 'New Consumers? The Social and Cultural Significance of Children's Fashion Consumption', *Cultures of Consumption Working Paper*, No. 16.

Boden, S. (2006a) '"Another Day, Another Demand": How Parents and Children Negotiate Consumption Matters', *Sociological Research Online*, Volume 11, Issue 2. Available at: http://www.socresonline.org.uk/11/2/boden.html.

Boden, S. (2006b) 'Dedicated followers of fashion? The influence of popular culture on children's social identities', *Media Culture Society*, Vol. 28, No. 2. pp. 289–298.

Bottero, W. (2010) 'Intersubjectivity and Bourdieusian Approaches to "Identity"' *Cultural Sociology*, Vol. 4, No. 1, pp. 3–22.

Bourdieu, P. (2010) *Distinction*, Oxford: Routledge (1st published in translation to English 1985).

Bragg, S., Buckingham, S., Russell, R. and Willett, R. (2011) 'Too much, too soon? Children, "sexualization" and consumer culture', *Sex Education: Sexuality, Society and Learning*, Vol. 11, No. 3, pp. 279–292.

Buckingham, D. (2000) *After the Death of Childhood: Growing up in the Age of Electronic Media*, Cambridge: Polity Press.

Christensen, P. and Prout, A. (2005) 'Anthropological and Sociological Perspectives on Childhood' in S. Greene and D. Hogan (eds) *Researching Children's Experience: Approaches and Methods*, London: Sage.

Cochrane, K. (2010) 'The padded kids' bikini that should never have existed', *Guardian*, [online] April 14th, http://www.theguardian.co.uk [Accessed 6th August 2010].

Cook, D. and Kaiser, S. (2004) 'Betwixt and Be Tween: Age Ambiguity and the Sexualization of the Female Consuming Subject', *Journal of Consumer Culture*, Vol. 4, No. 2, pp. 203–227.

Cook, D. (2008) 'Missing Child in Consumption Theory', *Journal of Consumer Culture*, Vol. 8, No. 2, pp. 219–243.

Daily Mail (2010) 'Primark withdraws padded bikinis for 7-year-olds after being accused of exploiting "paedophile pound"', *Mail Online*, April 14th, Available at: http://www.dailymail.co.uk [Accessed 20th August 2010].

DirectGov. (2008) Children's Human Rights, Available at: http://www.direct. gov.uk/en/Parents/ParentsRights/DG_4003313 [Accessed 12th February 2008].

Edwards, T. (2020) Living dolls? The role of clothing and fashion in 'sexualisation'. *Sexualities*. Vol. 23 (5–6) 702–716.

Gibbs, A. (1997) 'Focus Groups', *Social Research Update*, Issue 19, December, Available at: http://sru.soc.surrey.ac.uk/SRU19.html [Accessed 5th January 2009].

Giddens, A. (1991) *Modernity and Self Identity*, Cambridge: Polity.

Giddens, A. (2000) *Runaway World*, London: Routledge (1st published 1999).

Gunter, B. and Furnham, A. (1998) *Children as Consumers: A Psychological Analysis of the Young People's Market*, London: Routledge.

James, A., Jenks, C. and Prout, A. (2005) *Theorizing Childhood*. Oxford: Polity Press and Blackwell Publishers Ltd. (1st published in 1998).

Jenks, C. (1996) *Childhood*. London: Routledge.

Kehily, M. J. (2012) 'Contextualising the sexualisation of girls debate: innocence, experience and young female sexuality', *Gender and Education*, Vol. 24, Issue 3, pp. 255–268.

Kenway, J. and Bullen, E. (2001) *Consuming Children*, Buckingham: Open University Press.

Key Note (2001) *Tweenagers: 2001 Market Assessment*, Hampton: Key Note Ltd.

Klepp, I. and Storm-Mathisen, A. (2005) 'Reading Fashion as Age: Teenage Girls' and Grown Women's Accounts of Clothing as Body and Social Status', *Fashion Theory*, Vol. 9, Issue 3, pp. 323–342.

Lichtenstein, O. (2010) 'What a sick world when women yearn to look like girls... and little girls are dressed to look like women', *Femail: Mail Online*, 19th April, Available at: http://www.dailymail.co.uk [Accessed 7th August 2010].

Macdonald, M. (2003) 'Children "at risk"' in *Exploring Media Discourse*, Oxford: Arnold Publishers.

McCartney, J. (2010) 'Primark padded bikini row: Leave our kids alone', *Telegraph*, April 18th, Available at: http://www.thetelegraph.co.uk [Accessed 5th August 2010].

Morgan, D. (1998) *The Focus Group Guidebook*, London: Sage.

Office of National Statistics (2008a) 'Live Births', Dec 9th, Available at: http://www.statistics.gov.uk/cci/nugget.asp?id=369 [Accessed 13th May 2009].

Office of National Statistics (2008b) 'Income Inequality', Dec 16th, Available at: http://www.statistics.gov.uk/cci/nugget.asp?id=332 [Accessed 13th May 2009].

Pilcher, J. (2009) 'What not to Wear? Girls, Clothing and "Showing" the Body', *Children and Society*, 5th June, published online, https://doi.org/10.1111/j.1099-0860.2009.00239.x.

Pilcher, J. (2013) '"Small, but very determined": A Novel Theorization of Children's Consumption of Clothing', *Cultural Sociology*, Vol. 7, No. 1, pp. 86–100.

Prout, A. (2000) 'Children's Participation: Control and Self-realisation in British Late Modernity', *Children & Society*, Vol. 14, pp. 304–315.

Punch, S. (2002) 'Research with Children: The Same or Different from Research with Adults?' *Childhood*, Vol. 9, No. 3, pp. 321–341.

Ransome, P. (2005) *Work, Consumption and Culture: Affluence and Social Change in the Twenty-First Century*, London: Sage.

Russell, R. and Tyler, M. (2002) 'Thank Heaven for Little Girls: "Girl Heaven" and the Commercial Context of Feminine Childhood', *Sociology*, Vol. 36, No. 3, pp. 613–637.

Rysst, M. (2010) '"I am only Ten Years Old": Femininities, clothing-fashion codes and the intergenerational gap of interpretation of young girls' clothes', *Childhood*, Vol. 17, pp. 76–93.

Smith, C. and Attwood, F. (2011) 'Lamenting sexualization: research, rhetoric and the story of young people's "sexualization" in the UK Home Office review', *Sex Education: Sexuality, Society and Learning*, Vol. 11, No. 3, pp. 327–337.

Taylor, M. (2010) Primark to stop selling children's padded bikini tops', *Guardian*, April 14th, Available at: http://www.theguardian.co.uk [Accessed 7th August 2010].

Underwood, M. (2004) 'Glares of Contempt, Eye Rolls of Disgust and Turning Away to Exclude: Non-verbal Forms of Social Aggression among Girls', *Feminism & Psychology*, Vol. 14, No. 3, pp. 371–375.

Woodward, S. (2007) *Why Women Wear What They Wear*, Oxford: Berg.

Xolocotzin, U. and Jay, T. (2020) 'Children's perspectives on their economic activity—Diversity, motivations and parental awareness' in *Children & Society*, Vol. 34, pp. 424–442.

7

Inclusive Teaching Strategy in Creative Industry Education

Yue Wang

Abstract Creative industry development has become a new trend world-wide. Many universities have created such courses and there are more international students who prefer to study in English. As diverse characters in creative industries and students with multiple cultural backgrounds, there is a requirement to adopt an inclusive teaching method in creative industries units. There is prior research about the relationship between education and creative city policy, and limited research about the relationship in terms of creative industries, higher education and international students. This research employs critical thinking to explore the topic and finds that the academic experience is founded on connections and discourse. Therefore, inclusive teaching is effective and will help improve creative industry education, especially for international students.

Y. Wang (✉)
Business School for the Creative Industries, University for the Creative Arts, Farnham, UK
e-mail: Philip.Powell@uca.ac.uk

107
P. Powell, B. Shankar Nayak (eds.), *Creative Business Education*,
https://doi.org/10.1007/978-3-031-10928-7_7

Introduction

Creative industry development has become a new trend worldwide. Many higher education institutions (HEIs) have created this major or unit to follow this trend and there are more and more international students who prefer to study in English. As diverse characters in creative industries and students with multiple cultural backgrounds, there is a requirement to adopt an inclusive teaching method in any relevant units in creative industries. As for previous research, there is some research about the relationship between education and creative city policy, while there is limited research about the relationship in a creative industry, higher education and international students. This research uses critical thinking to explore this topic and find that the academic experience is founded on connections and discourse. Therefore, inclusive teaching is most effective in helping to improve creative industry education, especially for international students.

The term 'creative industries' was first used to refer to a wide range of industries, including design, advertising, cinema, fashion, interactive technology, popular music, and various other fields. However, cultural theorists have argued that these professions promote more than just economic progress and social and cultural development in recent years. In this perspective, the creative industries are located within civic and commercial life.

With globalisation, many international students with different cultural backgrounds are studying aspects of creative industries in the UK. This results in students with diverse cultural and educational backgrounds studting together. This necessitates the use of non-traditional teaching strategies. 'Inclusive education' tries to explore a new way to address the needs of multicultural students in higher education.

Salamanca presents inclusive education as having multiple meanings (Liasidou 2016). It has been utilised in England for learners with disabilities or special needs. Many universities that adopted it no longer associated it with special requirements. Slee (2013) believes that the inclusiveness and globalisation shown by the concept of inclusive education are increasingly being applied to understanding and perceiving different things.

Accordingly, all creative industry units must have different content to help students get additional skills and create their own value to enhance their competitiveness after graduation (Shulman 2005). This study explores inclusive strategies in creative industry education.

Inclusive Teaching Strategy Definition

The inclusive education system that requires adopting specific teaching strategies stems from traditional teaching methods guided by behaviourist pedagogy. This method of teaching focuses on changing the learner's behaviour to achieve goals. Florian and Black-Hawkins (2011) present that two different inclusive teaching strategies need more attention. First, the teaching methods are modified to incorporate various methodologies and be discussed by other tutors, such as using a different layout for a classroom. At the same time, it is important is to set multiple learning tasks and provide appropriate methods even for students with specific learning requirements. Second, teaching is a process that satisfies the need to impart knowledge and facilitate the learning process.

While different learners are at different learning experiences and levels, the students' learning experience must be measured in order to adjust and modify the teaching methods to match different students' status in the teaching process. A multi-level approach becomes a strategy used by teachers to respond to different level's students. This form of teaching leads to students learning at their level (Vayrynen 2003). According to Gardner's (2011) theory in multiple intelligence, this is expressed in nine different dimensions: verbal-linguistic, mathematical-logical, musical, visual-spatial, bodily-kinaesthetic, interpersonal intrapersonal, naturalistic and existential (Bartolo et al. 2007; Vayrynen 2003). Meanwhile, inclusive teaching is defined as a kind of instruction that incorporates all of the senses. It encompasses various senses, including sight, hearing, taste, touch, and smell. Base on previous research, Molbaek (2018) has established four dimensions of inclusivity thinking: a framing dimension, a relational dimension, a didactic dimension, and an organisational dimension.

As in much of the previous research, this study is based on the four dimensions from Molbaek. For example, first, it explores a tutor adoption of the four dimensions into teaching approaches to encourage inclusivity in the teaching and learning process. Second, it analyses students use of the different dimensions in the learning process as tutors construct educational programmes that allow students to get more inclusivity support. Finally, it compares this with the traditional education approach to explore inclusive teaching strategies that suit all learners' learning requirements flexibly.

Inclusive Teaching Strategies Play an Essential Role in the Creative Industries

Learning is considered a process by which students acquire new knowledge and are facilitated in different ways (Schmidt et al. 2011). Therefore, in order to enhance inclusiveness in the learning process, teachers must be aware of learners' preferences for learning styles. Inclusive teaching strategies provide this diversity of teaching styles and enable students to live a more active and selective life in learning. In addition, inclusive teaching strategies promote a collaborative relationship between tutor and learner, allowing them to exercise creativity.

Murphy (1999) presents three levels of the learning process, the first stage is reception, which is the acquisition of knowledge. The second stage is construction, which is the acquisition of meaning primarily from knowledge. The third stage is reconstruction, i.e. exploring the structure of knowledge more deeply, mainly through interaction with others, while the views of others influence perspectives. Finally, collaborative learning is defined as a learning style that identifies and shares common reference points and patterns in the learning process.

Sebba and Ainscow (1996) suggest that different teaching strategies will lead to more inclusive elements. It could refer to social constructivism theory, which divides teaching into three steps in reality: knowledge and learning (Kim 2001). For example, co-teaching is considered an essential prerequisite for inclusivity (Boyle et al. 2012; Loreman et al.

2005; Walsh 2012). Tutors can adopt different pedagogical approaches to enhance interaction with learners. Teachers can choose specific teaching strategies depending on the subject, such as the classroom climate, the learning material, assessments, language and cultural references.

Further, participation and interaction are considered central to inclusive teaching strategies (Tetler 2007; WHO, 2002), emphasising the teacher's job to support the learning process for all students. Dreier (2008) suggests an understanding of the cultural background and diversity of the participants, focusing on self-awareness can support student learning through new insights and possibilities. If teachers gain feedback on student satisfaction through research, new practice opportunities can engage all students (DuFour and Marzano 2011; Fullan and Hargreaves 2012). This may hinder more in-depth research into inclusive teaching strategies if they are only seen as the work of teachers and not associated with students with special requirements (for example, international students) (Barton 1997; Booth and Ainscow 2002; Booth 2011).

Meanwhile, many universities have established programmes worldwide focussed on the global rise of the creative industries. Creative industries education is a new topic for exploring inclusive education systems for two main reasons. First, many studies have shown that exploration is imaginative and insightful, in contrast to unravelling traditionalist and stable social relationships. Creative industry workers are seen as skilled and creative. As a result, the educational process is seen as worth exploring. Second, creative industries research has not adequately considered teaching and learning strategies in higher education; in particular, it has not examined the links between academia and industry.

Comunian and Gilmore's (2014, 2016) studies express the importance of the relationship between creative industries research, higher education institutions and public policy. Bridgstock and Cunningham's (2016) study focuses on promoting learning in the context of economic growth policies. Florida (2002) proposes strategies and approaches for adapting higher education in Hong Kong, Singapore and other Asian cities (Yue 2006; Kong and O'Connor 2009; Comunian and Ooi 2016). However, there are research limitations regarding the relationship between the creative industries and higher education, such as inclusive teaching and learning strategies in creative industry-related applications. Also, research on how to help international students in creative industries education is limited. This study seeks to address these issues.

In conclusion, an inclusive teaching strategy could help tutors and students teach, and learn relevant knowledge in the creative industry. Further, an inclusive teaching strategy could help students with special learning requirements.

Four Dimensions in Inclusive Teaching Method in Creative Industry

As creative industry education has become global, more international students prefer international learning experience. Inclusive teaching strategies could help international students adapt to their environment and improve their learning. As Molbaek (2018) has established four dimensions of inclusivity thinking into a framing dimension, a relational dimension, a didactic dimension, and an organisational dimension, this could relate to a different category in inclusive teaching methods.

Framing Dimension: Classroom Climate and Learning Materials

The framing dimension focuses on traditional classroom strategies and tries to create more flexible methods of learning materials management. It is represented by classroom climate and learning materials revision.

Classroom Climate

One of the inclusive teaching strategies is to focus on classroom management. A tutor needs to propose teaching methods that positively impact student learning and help students get great outcomes and academic and social engagement (Hattie 2009; Lingard 2007; Meyer 2004). Under an inclusive teaching strategy, students are more inclusive in informal classroom layouts. It encourages students to communicate with their group members, especially for international students who are shy to speak in class, helping them engage in learning activities.

Bergmann et al. (2013) and Stone (2012) list several advantages of '*flipping the classroom*.' First, developing lifelong learners, increasing engagement with the material and increasing interaction between students and teachers. And it is clear from the research that smaller classes lead to more positive learning outcomes.

Meanwhile, modern classrooms are often equipped with the necessary technological devices to aid teaching and learning. Teachers must use these devices to ensure that all learners have access to the instructional materials. For example, two technologies that dominate the inclusive research literature are computer-assisted instruction (CAI) and information communication technology (ICT). The former uses computers to deliver lessons, capture learners' performance and provides feedback on learners' progress. In contrast, ICT such as web queries, spreadsheets and graphical presentations also support teaching and learning.

However, there are times when large lectures are classroom-based. Sometimes this will interfere with student learning and create barriers. For example, someone who lacks concentration in a large room and does not see the screen clearly because of equipment problems or myopia and astigmatism. Therefore, if lecturers have a large lecture room, it needs to be assessed for inclusive teaching strategies. First, equipment needs to function. Second, the students can choose their room layout before they start. Finally, the tutor can use techniques such as group discussions or questions to enhance learning. For example, in modern teaching or learning environments, many institutions try to use round tables or small rooms to provide the same learning conditions for their students. Studies have shown that if the room layout is changed to round tables and divided into small groups, it helps students be more efficient and meet their learning requirements.

Learning Materials

Differentiation is an approach in the inclusive teaching strategy that tries to meet learners' needs. Thus, there is more freedom in selecting instructional materials, groupings, and teaching techniques.

The learner can use teaching materials to guide how to direct their study and the tutor can use the student to provide direction for the learner. On the other hand, it assists learners in building upon their old knowledge to acquire new knowledge (Bender 2008). For example, slides and handbooks are essential learning materials for students. Slides and handbooks need to show study aims and objectives, course syllabus, assessment, and course content clear and upload onto on-line common study areas on time. Students can check all information about the course through slides and handbooks. Students will feel confused about the course setting if the slides or handbooks are unclear and logical, especially for disable students and international students who use a second language to study. In Everett and Oswald's (2018) research, inclusive materials improve partnerships and attitudes around disability and accessibility measures. Thus, course slides need to show in the background with bullet points to clarify the layout. The slides or handbooks need be available to students in advance of the lecture to help students understand the content and prepare lecture questions. Students can highlight parts or take notes in advance. This is a basic how-to-use old knowledge to gain new knowledge before the unit starts.

Sometimes, learning materials have been ignored in traditional teaching process. While it is an essential part of inclusive teaching methods, it motivates students to learn in advance. It could help students mark the important or interesting parts before they join units.

Classroom climate changing and learning materials updating could revise the framing dimension in order to improve the teaching strategy in terms of the care and well-being aspects.

Relational Dimension: Assessment

The relational dimension responds to the instructors to foster communication and collaboration with all actors. It is an eopportunity to let students understand the global creative industry. And for the research process, all students in a study group may be involved in group work and attend group tutorials. For instance, assessment could include presentation, content and outcome. These three overlapping circles set out the components of evaluation. Outcomes are necessary with a flexible approach to allow for different ways of presenting knowledge, such as video, presentation, written essay.

Course leaders may try to make assessments more inclusive. The intention is that they collaborate with group members and improve their group working skills. Assessment method changing represent the relational dimension in order to show the outcome and the qualification in an inclusive teaching strategy.

Didactic Dimension: Language

The didactic dimension includes the instructors' topic knowledge, teaching abilities, and their understanding of the students' learning capacities. It is represented by language in an inclusive teaching strategy.

In every education system, language is an essential tool for communication between tutors and learners. Language is a tool to convey a message, information or meaning. According to Wardhaugh, language is a historical-culture tool.

In a higher education environment, international students often face language barriers. For this reason, handbooks and learning tasks and outcomes need to be clear. And lectures, workshops or tutorials, tutors must speak clearly and coherently and try to ensure non-native English speakers understand what they present. For example, academic terms need to be explained simply. Further, the tutor could suggest students join in language courses before any unit starts. International students find it easier to understand the study process from pre-session and academic studies and learn to compose essays. Course leaders can provide multiple engagements to students, such as a reading lists, discussions in class, videos and group work. Group work is essential to help improve students' communication skills, teamworking, collaboration, and language learning.

A language is a tool for communication and study, but it should not be the most significant barrier for international students. Tutors can adopt inclusive teaching strategies to reduce the impact of learning obstacles for international students. Thus, language is part of the didactic dimension and helps to improve an inclusive teaching strategy.

Organisational Dimension-Cultural References

The organisational dimension component includes culture, customs, and values and is represented by cultural references in an inclusive teaching strategy.

As more and more international students travel, there are requirements that tutors need to employ multiple cultural reference methods in their teaching. Different cultural background cases facilitate students to obtain a global version. Cultural references guide students to improve specific translation competence aspects (González Davies and Scott-Tennent 2005). It enables international students to understand the theory with cases presented with suitable cultural backgrounds. Further, it helps students learn faster and feel more at ease.

If the tutor always uses the same background example or reference to different cultural background students, it will create barriers to learning. Students will have negative feedback to a single cultural background reference. Sometimes, due to cultural background differences, it will hard to understand the case. A tutor needs to deliver cultural references to different cultural backgrounds and provide diverse cultural references. And culture reference could be a part of the organisation dimension to improve the knowledge and academic aspects of an inclusive teaching strategy.

Creative industries have their own specificity as they encompass many different industries. Moreover, many global projects work together in different countries. For this reason, all learners in the creative sectors have to learn a variety of knowledge. Therefore, universities must adopt a two-way interactive approach to teaching and learning, where learners are recipients of knowledge and need to contribute to the learning. The former can be referred to as '*direct teaching*' and the latter as an '*interactive teaching*' approach (Muijs and Reynolds 2001). Therefore, inclusive teaching and learning strategies will play an essential role in the process of creative industries education.

Conclusion

As creative industry education is a global and the creative industries are varied. Thus, it requires to tutor to adopt inclusive teaching strategies for students. When the academic experience is founded on connections and discourse, inclusive teaching is most effective. An inclusive teaching method can have four dimensions, which could present in different teaching methods such as cultural references, classroom environment, language, learning resources, and evaluation.

References

Bartolo, P.A., Janik, I., Janikova, V., Hofsass, T., Koinzer, P., Vilkiene, V., Calleja, C., Cefai, C., Chetcuti, D.A., Ale, P. and Lous, A.M., 2007. *Responding to student diversity: teacher's handbook*. University of Malta. Faculty of Education.

Barton, L., 1997. Inclusive education: romantic, subversive or realistic?. *International Journal of Inclusive Education*, *1*(3), pp. 231–242.

Bender, W.N., 2008. *Differentiating instruction for students with learning disabilities: Best teaching practices for general and special educators*. Corwin Press.

Bergmann, J., Overmyer, J. and Wilie, B., 2013. The Flipped Class: What it is and what itis not. *The Daily Riff*. Retrieved July 11, 2014.

Boyle, C., Topping, K., Jindal-Snape, D. and Norwich, B., 2012. The importance of peer-support for teaching staff when including children with special educational needs. *School Psychology International*, *33*(2), pp. 167–184.

Booth, T. and Ainscow, M., 2002. *Index for inclusion: Developing learning and participation in schools*. Centre for Studies on Inclusive Education (CSIE), United Kingdom.

Booth, T., 2011. The name of the rose: Inclusive values into action in teacher education. *Prospects*, *41*(3), pp. 303–318.

Bridgstock, R. and Cunningham, S., 2016. Creative labour and graduate outcomes: Implications for higher education and cultural policy. *International Journal of Cultural Policy*, *22*(1), pp. 10–26.

Comunian, R. and Gilmore, A., 2016. Higher education and the creative economy: introduction to a new academic and policy field. In *Higher Education and the Creative Economy* (pp. 35–50). Routledge.

Comunian, R. and Gilmore, A., 2014. From knowledge sharing to co-creation: paths and spaces for engagement between higher education and the creative and cultural industries. *Beyond Frames Dynamics: Between The Creative Industries, Knowledge Institutions and the Urban Context*, pp. 174–85.

Comunian, R. and Ooi, C.S., 2016. Global aspirations and local talent: The development of creative higher education in Singapore. *International Journal of Cultural Policy*, *22*(1), pp. 58–79.

Dreier, O., 2008. Learning in structures of social practice. *A qualitative stance: Essays in honor of Steinar Kvale*, pp. 85–96.

DuFour, R. and Marzano, R.J., 2011. *Leaders of learning: How district, school, and classroom leaders improve student achievement*. Solution Tree Press.

Everett, S. and Oswald, G., 2018. Engaging and training students in the development of inclusive learning materials for their peers. *Teaching in Higher Education*, *23*(7), pp. 802–817.

Florian, L. and Black-Hawkins, K., 2011. Exploring inclusive pedagogy. *British Educational Research Journal*, *37*(5), pp. 813–828.

Florida, R., 2002. The learning region. In *Innovation and social learning* (pp. 159–176). Palgrave Macmillan, London.

Hattie, J., 2009. The black box of tertiary Assessment: An impending revolution. *Tertiary Assessment & Higher Education Student Outcomes: Policy, Practice & Research*, *259*, p. 275.

Fullan, M. and Hargreaves, A., 2012. Reviving teaching with 'professional capital'. *Education Week*, *31*(33), pp. 30–36.

Gardner, H.E., 2011. *Frames of mind: The theory of multiple intelligences*. Hachette UK.

González Davies, M. and Scott-Tennent, C., 2005. A problem-solving and student-centred approach to the translation of cultural references. *Meta: journal des traducteurs/Meta: Translators' Journal*, *50*(1), pp. 160–179.

Kim, B., 2001. Social constructivism. *Emerging perspectives on learning, teaching, and technology*, *1*(1), p. 16.

Kong, L. and O'Connor, J., 2009. *Creative economies, creative cities: Asian-European perspectives* (Vol. 98). New York, NY.

Liasidou, A., 2016. Inclusive education twenty years after Salamanca.

Lingard, B., 2007. Pedagogies of indifference. *International Journal of Inclusive Education, 11*(3), pp. 245–266.

Loreman, T., Deppeler, J. and Harvey, D., 2005. *Inclusive education: A practical guide to supporting diversity in the classroom.* Psychology Press.

Meyer, D.S., 2004. Protest and political opportunities. *Annu. Rev. Sociol., 30,* pp. 125–145.

Molbaek, M., 2018. Inclusive teaching strategies–dimensions and agendas. *International Journal of Inclusive Education, 22*(10), pp. 1048–1061.

Muijs, D. and Reynolds, D., 2001, April. Being or doing: The role of teacher behaviors and beliefs in school and teacher effectiveness in mathematics, a SEM analysis. In *Annual meeting of the American Educational Research Association*, Seattle, WA (pp. 10–14).

Murphy, P. ed., 1999. *Learners, learning & assessment* (Vol. 2). Sage.

Schmidt, H.G., Rotgans, J.I. and Yew, E.H., 2011. The process of problem-based learning: what works and why. *Medical Education, 45*(8), pp. 792–806.

Sebba, J. and Ainscow, M., 1996. International developments in inclusive schooling: mapping the issues. *Cambridge Journal of Education, 26*(1), pp. 5–18.

Stone, B.B., 2012, May. Flip your classroom to increase active learning and student engagement. In *Proceedings from 28th Annual Conference on Distance Teaching & Learning*, Madison, Wisconsin, USA.

Slee, R., 2013. How do we make inclusive education happen when exclusion is a political predisposition?. *International Journal of Inclusive Education, 17*(8), pp. 895–907.

Shulman, L.S., 2005. Signature pedagogies in the professions. *Daedalus, 134*(3), pp. 52–59.

Tetler, W.G., 2007. *A collaborative filtering prediction algorithm for ClassRank subject recommendations* (Doctoral dissertation, Massachusetts Institute of Technology).

Vayrynen, S., 2003. *Observations from South African classrooms.* Kimberly: National Institute of Higher Education.

Walsh, J.M., 2012. Co-teaching as a school system strategy for continuous improvement. *Preventing School Failure: Alternative Education for Children and Youth, 56*(1), pp. 29–36.

World Health Organization, 2002. *The world health report 2002: reducing risks, promoting healthy life.* World Health Organization.

Yue, A., 2006. Cultural governance and creative industries in Singapore. *International Journal of Cultural Policy, 12*(1), pp. 17–33.

8

Implications of Pedagogical Disassociation in U.K. Higher Education Business Schools: A Culturally Responsive Outlook

Abdul Jabbar and Shajara Ul-Durar

Abstract This chapter explores the pedagogical approaches of business school academics in the north of England. We investigate the role of UK tutors who are increasingly teaching ethnically diverse international student cohorts whose educational and cultural backgrounds can be very different to tutors' past experiences. As part of this investigation, we propose the development of an academic cultural consciousness, by highlighting the notion of pedagogical disassociation. We argue that this should be a pre-requisite to improving the academic success of international students. Our findings demonstrate an inconsistent approach to pedagogy creation for ethnically diverse students; it is within this

A. Jabbar (✉)
School of Business, The University of Leicester, Leicester, UK
e-mail: Philip.Powell@uca.ac.uk

S. Ul-Durar
Business School for the Creative Industries, University for the Creative Arts, Farnham, UK

© The Author(s), under exclusive license to Springer Nature Switzerland AG 2022
P. Powell, B. Shankar Nayak (eds.), *Creative Business Education*,
https://doi.org/10.1007/978-3-031-10928-7_8

uncertain environment that the phenomenon of '*pedagogical disassociation*' emerges. It is important to highlight that it is not a premeditated phenomenon, rather it is typified by a lack of cultural understanding, under-developed student awareness, and assumptions based on racial stereotypes. We identify the need for educators and institutions to have an awakening of consciousness. As part of this awakening, academics must first articulate a vision of teaching and learning which acknowledges the diverse nature of UK HE Business Schools.

Introduction

This chapter explores the pedagogical approaches of business school academics in the north of England. We investigate the role of UK tutors who are increasingly teaching ethnically diverse international student cohorts whose educational and cultural backgrounds can be very different to tutors' past experiences. As part of this investigation, we propose the development of an academic cultural consciousness, by highlighting the notion of pedagogical disassociation. We argue that this should be a pre-requisite to improving the academic success of international students. Our findings demonstrate an inconsistent approach to pedagogy creation for ethnically diverse students; it is within this uncertain environment that the phenomenon of '*pedagogical disassociation*' emerges. It is important to highlight that it is not a premeditated phenomenon, rather it is typified by a lack of cultural understanding, under-developed student awareness, and assumptions based on racial stereotypes. We identify the need for educators and institutions to have an awakening of consciousness. As part of this awakening, academics must first articulate a vision of teaching and learning which acknowledges the diverse nature of UK HE Business Schools.

This chapter investigates the cultural consciousness of academic tutors in three universities in the north of England. The study is focused on each university's business school where the increasing internationalisation of student cohorts is particularly concentrated due to the popularity of business courses globally. This has led to predominantly Western-educated, UK tutors increasingly teaching ethnically diverse international student cohorts whose educational and cultural backgrounds can be different to tutors' past experiences.

As well as being Northern English universities, the three universities in this study have a common ethos as part of the University Alliance group which describes itself as *'Britain's universities for cities and regions'*. The University Alliance accounts for 25% of all students in the UK and is more likely to contain universities that focus more on teaching and learning, albeit with growing research activities. All three have substantial business schools attracting international students. Nonetheless, there is insufficient attention being paid to the impact of business school academic tutors' ability to be responsive to international student cohorts as part of the student experience in UK Business Schools (Lumby and Foskett 2015; Rienties et al. 2012). This study aims to address this gap through an empirical investigation of business school tutors' views on teaching international cohorts of students in the UK.

In order to frame this study, we propose the development of an academic cultural consciousness, as a pre-requisite to improving the academic success of international students. This cultural consciousness needs to take into consideration two key factors; first, each individual's sociocultural consciousness; this is the understanding that people's ways of thinking, behaving and being are deeply influenced by factors such as race, ethnicity, social class, culture, and language (McGee Banks and Banks 1995; Villegas and Lucas 2002), and second, that academics possess a cultural knowledge base about their ethnically diverse international students. Gay (2002) defines a cultural knowledge base as understanding the cultural characteristics and contributions of different ethnic groups, and further, implies that educators are inadequately prepared to teach international students (Gay 2002; Jabbar and Hardaker 2013).

This study focuses on business schools as students from an international background are increasingly viewing UK higher education (HE) Business Schools as a destination of choice (Beddall-Hill et al. 2011; Hardy and Tolhurst 2014; Jabbar and Analoui 2018; Joy and Poonamallee 2013) and, for many Business Schools, these students are an important source of revenue to facilitate institutional financial health (Humfrey 1999; Molesworth et al. 2009; Schapper and Mayson 2004; Tomalin 2007). However, while institutions achieve this financial goal by recruiting international students, achievement and attainment is poor in comparison to a mainstream non-ethnically diverse student (Richardson 2008; Turner 2006).

Different educational theorists (Modood 2006; Richardson 2008; Tomalin 2007; Turner 2006) propose divergent reasons as to this lack of achievement. Some are of the view that UK HE places emphasis on the dominant Western learner at the expense of the international student (Tomalin 2007; Turner 2006), while others articulate the controversial perception that internationally diverse students are lacking in the conviction, motivation and skills to succeed (Tomlinson 2005; Villegas and Lucas 2002). These poor perceptions highlight a lack of cultural consciousness that can impact on the international student in a negative way, leading to issues of poor pedagogy development (Gay 2000, 2002), inappropriate institutional policies and procedures (Irvine 1990; Jabbar and Mirza 2017; Turner 2006), and out-dated, or insensitive academic staff training strategies (Sabry and Bruna 2007).

In developing this work, the authors discussed the notion of cultural consciousness with Business School academics and how they impact on the creation of pedagogy. The key methodological issues are then defined and articulated alongside our data collection and data analysis approach. We then highlight our key findings which define the critical components of cultural consciousness, the themes of '*Background and Heritage*', '*Academic Confidence & Skills*' and '*Student understanding*' all contribute to the pedagogy creation process. From these themes, we unearth a significant contribution to this paper by identifying the phenomenon of "*pedagogical disassociation*", a disturbing trend which can have negative ramifications for UK HE stakeholders.

Cultural Consciousness Within Business Education

Cultural consciousness is underpinned by a body of literature within culturally responsive teaching (Gay 2000, 2002; Ladson-Billings 1995b; Villegas and Lucas 2002), and, as a concept, has featured prominently in the development of frameworks by multiple researchers. Examples include the six salient characteristics (Villegas and Lucas 2002); the essential elements (Gay 2000, 2002); and the Five-pillar framework (Jabbar and Hardaker 2013). Each of these frameworks contains an implicit argument that educators need to have a wider, holistic view of the students they teach, and a confidence in how they communicate and interact with students from backgrounds that are different to their own. There is a view that educators from a non-diverse background struggle to widen their world view and may have low expectations and negative attitudes towards students from an international background, these conclusions are based on empirical data provided by a very few in-depth case studies highly situated in US teacher education for schools (Durden et al. 2014; Durden and Truscott 2013). Consequently, there are few messages from these studies relevant to UK HE Business Schools and for educators in the context for this study.

In order to widen the world view of educators and to expand their knowledge horizons and experiences, Gay and Kirkland (2003), alongside Joy and Poonamallee (2013), propose the need for critical self-reflection in questioning dominant Western narratives and academic literature, to equip educators with the skills to communicate with students from other cultures. In order to achieve this, self-reflection is a key tenet of multicultural education, which includes raising awareness of student background and experiences, and how these backgrounds can be used in the classroom (Foster 1995; Irvine 1990; McAllister and Irvine 2002). In addition, there exist practical mechanisms that can help build cultural consciousness as part of HE teaching. For example, Cummins (1996) discusses developing pedagogy that acknowledges the wealth of languages that may be spoken within the classroom, and Gay (2002) advocates the need to embed culture and native languages as part of the teaching and learning curriculum.

In the creation of these pedagogical approaches, cultural consciousness acknowledges that the role of the educator is to mould the beliefs and behaviours of the student into meaningful and validating pedagogy, unhindered by Western dominated academic attitudes, languages and expectations (Giroux 2004; Nieto 1999: 135). This is '*risky*' pedagogy, taking educators out of their comfort zones and asking them to develop pedagogy which recognises the international diversity of UK HE Business Schools (Banks 2008; Jabbar and Analoui 2018; Oikonomidoy 2010).

Methods

This research seeks to understand the cultural consciousness of Business school academics and how these experiences could influence academic perceptions, student engagement and pedagogy development for international students. In developing this discussion, we take the view that culturally responsive teaching pedagogy is a conversation between educator and student (Orbe 2000; Tomalin 2007) and this conversation is enriched by meaning that is generated by the academics understanding how students engage with the realities of the world (Crotty 1998; Papert and Harel 1991).

To understand this concept of cultural consciousness, we interviewed Lecturers and Senior Lecturers who had a minimum of three years' experience of teaching within UK HE Business Schools. The criteria for the interview sample were kept simple in order to capture the main Business subjects and to maximise the amount of respondents we could potentially interview (Ritchie et al. 2003). In adopting a purposeful sampling strategy, we conducted a total of 22 interviews (nine male and thirteen 13 female academics) across three different Business Schools in the North of England. A description of the participants is provided below (Table 8.1):

Data Collection

Each interview lasted between 50–90 minutes, with informed consent being acquired at the start of each interview. The interviews were conducted in a private, quiet and comfortable room, or a setting deemed to be neutral, for example, a meeting space, a coffee area or a respondent's office (Oppenheim 1992). All interviews were recorded using a smart phone as opposed to a traditional Dictaphone; this served a dual purpose allowing high quality audio recording as well as instant backup of data to the Cloud (Beddall-Hill et al. 2011). For further anonymity and security, all devices on which the data resided were password protected.

In addition, the collection method was supplemented with the maintenance of a reflexive diary. Within qualitative research it is not possible

Table 8.1 Description of the participants

Name	Role	Experience (years)
Academic 1	Senior lecturer	30
Academic 2	Senior lecturer	6
Academic 3	Senior lecturer	8
Academic 4	Director of education	12
Academic 5	Senior lecturer	20
Academic 6	Lecturer	4
Academic 7	Senior lecturer	7
Academic 8	Lecturer	8
Academic 9	Lecturer	4
Academic 10	Senior lecturer	7
Academic 11	Course leader	15
Academic 12	Course leader	7
Academic 13	Senior lecturer	6
Academic 14	Director of education	25
Academic 15	Lecturer	3
Academic 16	Principal lecturer	7
Academic 17	Lecturer	3
Academic 18	Principal lecturer	30
Academic 19	Principal lecturer	35
Academic 20	Senior lecturer	4
Academic 21	Lecturer	27
Academic 22	Course leader	9

for researchers to be totally objective because total objectivity is not humanly possible (Crotty 1996, 1998). We can never know with certainty that an account is true because we have no independent and completely reliable access to reality. We must, therefore, judge validity on the basis of the adequacy of the evidence offered in support of the phenomena being described (Hammersley 1992). Hence, in order to be objective and to create a certain level of validation within the research, a reflexive diary served as a tool to minimise our influence on the participant (Finlay 2002). This diary opens up the researcher's account to public scrutiny, and while it may not prove anything definitively, it does allow the researcher's thought processes to be probed and demonstrates a level of integrity (Ahern 1999; Finlay 2002; King and Horrocks 2010). Integrity is not solely defined by the methods that are used but also the '*moral integrity*' of the researcher (Kvale and Brinkmann 2009).

Data Analysis

The researchers independently read and transcribed each interview over a period of five months while comparing notes on a weekly basis. The use of multiple coders shows some measure of inter-rater reliability (Pratt 2009). To help organise and sort the collected data, the analytical approach of template analysis was employed (Brooks et al. 2015; King 2004, 2012). This is a relatively new approach and while it may not be as well-known as other qualitative analytical methods such as Interpretive phenomenological analysis (IPA), it is regarded in qualitative circles as providing similar analytical rigour and findings (Langdridge 2007). Template analysis was selected because it is a flexible approach that is not associated with a single delineated method. It refers to multiple, but related, techniques for thematically organising and analysing codes and can be applied across multiple methodological and epistemological approaches, and in particular in situations where an interpretative approach is used, as in this study (King 2004, 2012).

In preparing the data, we first manually transcribed all the interviews, memoing data and reflective diaries into a Word document, which was then imported into a computer-based data management tool NVivo (QSR international, version 10). The initial process of coding mapped the transcribed interviews, reflexive notes and memos onto the a priori code set, which was used to inform template A. At this stage, the researchers cross referenced the data and, subsequently, through the use of a parallel coding approach (axial coding), created template B (King 2012; Saldaña 2012). Parallel coding within template analysis allowed for segments of text to be classified within two or more different codes at the same level and allowed for the placement of data into multiple codes as well as identifying any relationships across clusters and themes (Crabtree and Miller 1999; King 2004). In order to ensure data validity and consistency between researchers, the data was read for a final time, notes were compared, parallel coding was undertaken, and template C was developed. From this template we identified a key higher-level code from the four-step process (Cultural Consciousness). To further investigate this in step 1 we defined an *a priori* template, which is a key aspect of template analysis; this is based on the Five Essential Elements (Gay 2002), the Six

Salient Characteristics (Villegas and Lucas 2002) and the Five Pillars (Jabbar and Hardaker 2013), which are all culturally responsive teaching frameworks.

In step 2 Template A echoes the continuing work of the researchers by giving additional context to each of the higher-level codes. During this step the researchers identified the importance of '*affirming cultural heritage*' and '*pedagogy that is validating*' to understanding student background and culture. We also added a new higher-level code that recognise the importance of academics who are transformative by nature, due to their expectations, perspectives and views of their international students.

In step 3 Template B, the researchers identified additional depth and context to the '*affirming cultural heritage*' and '*pedagogy that is validating*' codes. The cross referencing of data via the parallel approach (Axial coding) identified data which fits into more than one subheading, this additional data validation identified an additional higher-level code that acknowledged the importance of '*student motivation*' in UK HE.

In step 4 Template C, the researchers identified additional sub-level codes for '*affirming cultural heritage*', but no further higher-level codes. The additional sub-level codes identify academic perceptions on previous student experience and how this governs interactions in the classroom. Template C is an output of the previous three steps and highlights the five main higher-level codes. Based on the above process Table 8.2 outlines the key nodes which form part of cultural consciousness:

This is the basis for the three themes which emerged as illustrated in Fig. 8.1 below:

The first theme acknowledges the importance of *background and heritage* and '*pedagogy that is validating*' (Durden and Truscott 2013; Tisdell 2009) with the onus on academic tutors to have a cultural and background knowledge of students. In the second theme we highlight the importance of *academics having the confidence* and skills to motivate and empower students from an international background (Durden 2008; Jabbar and Mirza 2017; Villegas and Lucas 2002). For the third theme we identify *student understanding* and culture as an important aspect of building learning relationships between academic tutors and students.

It was at this stage, that the researchers identified that academics subconsciously lay success and failure in UK HE at the feet of their

Table 8.2 Final coding template for Cultural consciousness

Background and heritage	Student understanding	Academic confidence and skills
Parental influence	Engagement	Attitude
Language	Poor skills	Passion
Previous educational experience	Selfish pedagogy	Status
	Student expectations	Freedom
	Fear of failure	
	Student attainment	
	Patronising pedagogy	
	Independence	

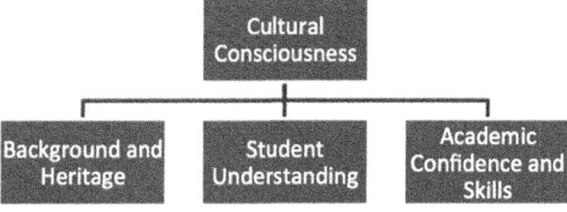

Fig. 8.1 The three themes of cultural consciousness

international students by making sweeping assumptions about their language skills, their attitudes to learning and questioning their thinking skills. This is highlighted in template B and template C, we refer to this disturbing phenomenon as *'pedagogical disassociation'*, a significant contribution of this paper to Business School education. We define this phenomenon as a *'subconscious reflex which comes to the fore when academics struggle to identify shortcomings within their own pedagogy'*, and speculate that this is a defence mechanism used to protect the academics' own personal pedagogical shortcomings.

Findings

Pedagogical engagement and student motivation are critical elements in the learning process, which require academics to view students as capable learners (Leese 2010). The awakening of academic cultural consciousness recognises the need for academics to understand that cultural under-standing and positive affirming attitudes are fundamental for teaching successfully in a multi-ethnic society (Giroux 2004; Higbee, Lundell, et al. 2007a; Villegas and Lucas 2002).

Theme 1: Background and Heritage

We defined Background and Heritage as pedagogical components that exist when educators modify their teaching in ways that will facilitate the academic experience of students from diverse, racial, ethnic, cultural and in this case international backgrounds (Gay 1995; Schmeichel 2011). Our findings indicated a tension between academic perceptions of '*main-stream*' Western students and the '*non-mainstream*' students from a non-Western background (Durden and Truscott 2013; Ngambi 2008). This tension stems from two elements: first, educational theory, which dis-cusses Western-dominated contexts of learning as superior to non-Western contexts of learning (Ghere et al. 2007; Giroux 2004; Joy and Poonamallee 2013). Second, educators who struggle to relate to students from an international background pedagogically, view these students as lacking in academic skills (Giroux 2004). These perceptions disadvantage ethnically diverse students at the very start of their academic lifecycle and entrenches the attitudes that international student background and cul-ture is deficient and inferior, reaffirming the dominance and superiority of the culture of the Western education system (Joy and Poonamallee 2013; Turner 2006). This dominance leads some academics to reject issues of Background and Heritage:

> *In a world of no racial discrimination then you treat everyone the same. I don't even agree, personally, with all this crap about what's your ethnic background, well, if we are not discriminating then what does it matter what the person's background is.* (Academic 1)

Another academic described how her Western background influenced the way she designed and developed her pedagogy, when faced with dif-ferent cultures she describes her shock and shame:

One year during the Christmas period, I designed an activity around Jesus and the Nativity. However, I vividly remember one girl, I'm not sure where she was from asked, what is Christmas and who is Christ? I was surprised and ashamed, I took it for granted, everybody knows Christmas. (Academic 6)

The topic of Christmas was also discussed by another female academic:

As a tutor, I am very sensitive to different cultures and ensuring that I don't offend somebody, and something that I did at Christmas I realised that actually it did not work at all because it was so culture related and around Christmas. (Academic 2)

The use of Western holidays and festivities as part of pedagogy can be a source of frustration, as it so clearly defines the cultural divide between Western and non-Western students (Sabry and Bruna 2007). As a way of crossing this cultural divide one academic commented on the importance of developing different perspectives as part of teaching:

From a personal perspective everybody deserves the same opportunities and the same help. It might be different, and I can accept different groups, no matter who they are or where they've come from, will need different help, different support, different encouragement. (Academic 3)

The onus is on academics to create support structures that provide a platform of achievement and attainment, while allowing students to maintain a sense of identity and connection with their communities (Banks 1995; McGee Banks and Banks 1995; Tisdell 2009).

In summarising this theme, student Background and Heritage should be built on positive social learning relationships that support student growth:

You need to create relationships that help to overcome the hurdles that they must get over, or a flipping gate that they've got to get through. It's about giving them something that they can succeed at, and it isn't just about the mark that they get at the end of it. (Academic 3)

Although a minority view, this outlined the opportunity to develop growth and create relationships, but this requires time, trust and, crucially, student interactions based on cultural influences and differences (Rubie-Davies et al. 2006).

Theme 2: Academic Confidence and Skills

We found that current pedagogical strategies employed by academic staff are heavily reliant on confidence and skills. In this research respondents felt they lacked the confidence to engage (Tomalin 2007) and motivate their students in the classroom (Monroe and Obidah 2004). The lack of confidence and skills we argue are related to the notion that current teaching practices are too insular with little focus on plurality and difference with an emphasis on traditional pedagogy; invariably this is Western dominated and favours the Western learner. In order to illustrate this phenomenon, we identified three response types academics display when they develop pedagogy: '*oblivious to difference*' (Housee 2011; Schapper and Mayson 2004); '*resistance to difference*' (D'Souza 1991, 1995) and 'acceptance of difference' (Jabbar et al. 2019; Santoro 2013). These responses govern how pedagogy and student engagement is developed.

Oblivious to Difference

Within this behaviour we found that some of our respondents preferred their students to leave their culture at the classroom door. This is an example of accommodation without acculturation (Gibson 1987; Jabbar et al. 2017), and we link this behaviour type very closely to '*pedagogical disassociation*'.

> *I don't make any allowances for specific ethnic groups. It is the same for everybody.* (Academic 13)

> *I accept exactly what the culture is, but with me in this room you can pretend that.*
>> *that doesn't exist.* (Academic 11)

This behaviour culture is not seen as something to be developed or as a vehicle for learning (Ladson-Billings 1995b) but is viewed as an obstacle in teaching and learning (Joy and Poonamallee 2013). This obliviousness also questions student motivation and accepts that these students are lacking in academic skills and context; this is evidenced by academic 14 who fails to recognise the issue of motivation when students are disengaged in the classroom.

Resistance to Cultural Difference

When academics resist difference, they view culture as a non-entity, a factor to be eradicated from the teaching and learning process (D'Souza 1995). While exploring this phenomenon some of the respondents became quite animated, and in two specific instances were quite aggressive with their tone, speech and body language. During the interview there were subtle indications that some academics felt uncomfortable discussing these issues; eye contact was reduced, the tone of voice changed, and body language became defensive with the crossing of arms and legs. This body language highlighted issues of discomfort, on a subconscious level, which can lead to the creation of pedagogy that is very single minded to the detriment of all other approaches (academic number 7 who talks about pedagogy within military terms.)

Acceptance of Cultural Difference

There are elements of good practice and our research highlights academics who are comfortable with their cultural consciousness. Some academic tutors we interviewed attempted to develop relationships with ethnically diverse students and they encouraged their students to bring culture into the classroom (Lipka 1991; Vita 2001) and to use their own skills to achieve and attain (Beverly 2003). Hence, the acceptance of difference reflects academics' values and the values of their institution (Meyer 2002).

Theme 3: Student Understanding

Business Management is a functional and practical subject (Joy and Poonamallee 2013), which can thrive when cultural characteristics and contributions of international student backgrounds are recognised within the classroom (Houser 2008; Raelin 2007). This approach allows a conducive space where academics can create student understanding and engagement with international students. Based on our initial research and the data we collected, this manifests itself in two ways; first '*Expectations of educators*' towards their students (Hardy and Tolhurst 2014) and second '*Classroom support*' (Choo 2007; Hardy and Tolhurst 2014). '*Expectations of educators*' and '*Classroom support*' are key elements for building relationships with ethnically diverse students to support student understanding. Student understanding can blossom when approached in the correct manner. However, if these two forms (Expectations of educators; Classroom support) are not treated equally there is a danger that student support and understanding can become too pastoral, with the focus on compensation for the student, to the detriment of expectations and achievements (Jenks et al. 2001). This suggests that there is a lack of expectation in international students being able to think about certain abstract concepts within an academic environment, and requiring constant support (Hurtado et al. 1999):

> *They expect me to give them work that they can then jumble up and give it back to me and get a good grade because that's what they've been taught to do.* (Academic 1)

These low expectations manifest themselves in students requiring additional pastoral support to the detriment of academic structured opportunities to bridge the gap towards HE standard work (Hultberg et al. 2008). This focus on pastoral elements is inappropriate and can lead to narrow pedagogy development (Jenks et al. 2001), creating an environment where international students fail to engage if they feel the subject does not provide value and they are not given appropriate opportunities to demonstrate what they know (Higbee, Siaka, et al. 2007b).

Many Chinese students don't understand the concept of continuous assessment. If I say this is not assessed they just switch off, no assessment, no reward, off! (Academic 7)

Academics persevere with a dogmatic pedagogical approach even though it may become clear that this approach to pedagogy is not resonating with international students. Rather than reflect on their own practice to make sense of culture (Zhu and Bargiela-Chiappini 2013), our findings indicate that educators '*pedagogically disassociated*' themselves from their students.

Pedagogical Disassociation

Our key contribution to this work, is the notion that a lack of academic cultural consciousness feeds into 'pedagogical disassociation'. This particular phenomenon was observed and identified as an output of academics who struggle to accept cultural consciousness as part of their teaching. Educators whose own academic background and experience is insufficient to overcome these shortcomings instinctively look for the fault in the student and fail to reflect on personal pedagogy. To illustrate, the placement of 'pedagogical disassociation' within our research, Fig. 8.2 below highlights the phenomenon as a negative construct arising from the emerging three themes.

If unchallenged '*pedagogical disassociation*' can have a negative impact on cultural awareness and student experience, achievement and attainment. To highlight the prevalent nature of this phenomenon and the impact it has had on the pedagogy creation process, our research findings were mapped onto the framework of Kumaravadivelu (2003).

Many academics have been struggling to resolve internal conflicts between dialectically opposed modes of instruction and adaptation (Kolb and Kolb 2005). This conflict is underpinned by staff who are worried that they cannot work effectively because they do not have sufficient knowledge about different cultures and religions (Tomalin 2007). When this process of conflict resolution breaks down, this research has suggested that the phenomenon of '*pedagogical disassociation*' emerges.

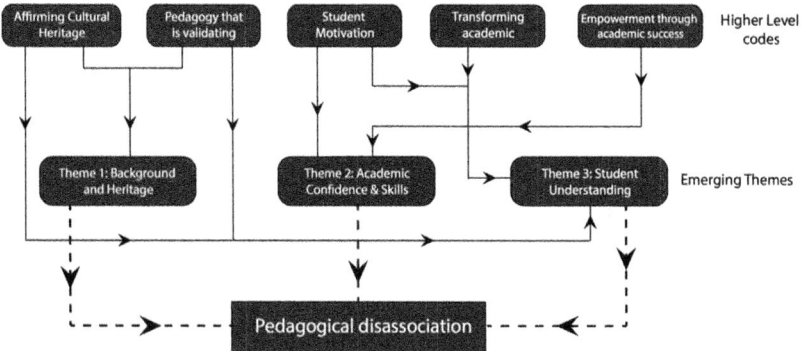

Fig. 8.2 Pedagogical disassociation here

Discussion

What's the Impact?

Our findings demonstrate a very inconsistent approach to pedagogy creation for ethnically diverse students; it is within this uncertain environment that the phenomenon of '*pedagogical disassociation*' emerges. It is important to highlight that it is not a premeditated phenomenon, rather it is typified by a lack of cultural understanding, under-developed student awareness, and assumptions based on racial stereotypes (Hardy and Tolhurst 2014; Modood 2006). This research proposes that a large part of this phenomenon is borne out of academic frustration and helplessness due to a lack of understanding, knowledge, under-developed student awareness and in many scenarios, a lack of skills and confidence (Howard 2003; Oikonomidoy 2010; Vita 2001). This becomes a hurdle to educators as they respond to cultural diversity in the educational field where they feel as a '*fish out of water*' (Bourdieu and Wacquant 1992, p. 127). However, this could be addressed through the design of holistic critical reflection and structured academic training which takes into consideration the development of pedagogical strategies that go beyond generic Western teaching methods (Jenks et al. 2001).

It may, therefore, take some time to create a healthy, culturally diverse educational field, which will be dependent on the academic tutors being sufficient to understand how to support students, and also to overcome established practices. A further area of potential future research is the impact of technology. The use of technology within HE can allow students to build their own knowledge representations and meanings at their own pace within an environment where they feel comfortable (Traxler 2009), allowing for the building of consciousness across a variety of channels and modes (Stein 2000). The deployment of technology can become a neutral and interactive ground to develop engagement and meaning within HE.

Potential for Change

Training Strategies and Resources

It is clear that current training and teaching strategies for educators who teach International students have been reported as lacking in content and criticality (Coulson and Harvey 2013; Gay 2000, 2002; Gay and Kirkland 2003; Goodman and Cirecie 2009; Howard 2003). The development of cultural consciousness requires that academics create environments of learning which support students of ethnic diversity (Gay 2002). The creation of any such teaching and training strategies should encompass two key characteristics; first it should embrace multiple teaching perspectives (Durden 2008; Vita 2001) and, second, these perspectives should make explicit connections between culture and learning (Howard 2003). Any such programme of training and reflection should imbue academics with the analytical skills and confidence (Bajunid 1996; Gay 2002) to not only to have mastery of the subject matter, but also to identify the needs of culturally diverse students and how best to support them.

A structured training programme may also be useful in addressing the misconception that Western pedagogy is superior to other cultural forms of learning (Joy and Poonamallee 2013; Ngambi 2008). This may require academics to widen their reading and research in order to expose students to curriculum material that is multicultural by nature (Banks 1995; Howard 2003; McGee Banks and Banks 1995; Ngambi 2008; Swartz 1996).

The development of multicultural resources and assessment is stage one; engaging students in the classroom is significantly more challenging, with many students often reluctant to participate in classroom discussion (Beekes 2006). In order to overcome this challenge, good pedagogical practice dictates that there should be a greater focus on self-directed study and group work. In addition, academics should be sensitive to the notion that many international students are not comfortable with responding in class and, therefore, are often reluctant to contribute in class for fear of '*losing face*' (Beekes 2006; Tomalin 2007; Turner 2006).

Policies and Procedures

The creation of multicultural resources and assessment is the responsibility of the academic. In addition to this, the institution has a role to play in the development of a multicultural curriculum, and the implementation of institutional policies and procedures which acknowledge difference (Gay 2002; Nieto 2005: 7). One such policy that has been mooted is the recruitment of educators who share a heritage with their students. Research (Dee 2005; Ladson-Billings 1995a) suggests that this produces attentive students who are more likely to complete their work, work harder and succeed. However, this is a controversial policy which has been criticised by the opponents of multicultural education as one of the types of '*leftist policies*' which, continue to serve the victim mentality, which is prevalent in many ethnically diverse students (D'Souza 1991, 1995).

What is clear is that such a recruitment strategy cannot be implemented in isolation; it needs to be embedded as part of a comprehensive approach to policies and procedures (Gay 2002). In addition, any programme of recruitment must run in parallel with educator training that makes a commitment to developing transformative learning (Jenks et al. 2001).

Students as Producers of Knowledge

While the discussion and implementation of policies and procedures are done at senior manager level, academic training and confidence are still key factors in the creation of a curriculum that is open and conducive to learning. Hence, there are differing techniques that academics can employ to develop the curriculum; one such approach is allowing students to become producers of knowledge, which is directly related to their lived experiences (Gatimu 2009), and another pedagogical approach is the need for an emancipatory pedagogy to break the cycle of privilege (David and Kienzler 1999; Sleeter 2001; Swartz 1996). In order to break this cycle, emancipatory pedagogy aims to encourage more open-ended approaches; looks at course material from multiple perspectives; and has a focus on critical reflection, not on what is right or wrong (David and Kienzler 1999; Schapper and Mayson 2004).

A balance needs to be struck between these two techniques, and the potential for a partnership emerges with students as producers of knowledge and academics as facilitators of knowledge. However, in this balance lies the concern that academics, in combatting these issues, are facing a *'fear of the unknown'* (Gay 2000, 2002; Sabry and Bruna 2007). Educators need to have more than just mastery of content knowledge but also knowledge of the student population (Gay 2002; Raelin 2007).

Conclusion

In conclusion, we identify the need for educators and institutions to have an awakening of consciousness. As part of this awakening, academics must first articulate a vision of teaching and learning which acknowledges the diverse nature of UK HE Business Schools. This research is intended to support academics in reflecting on the revision of curriculum approaches, training needs, policies, procedures towards the creation of a cultural consciousness and the reduction of *'pedagogical disassociation'*.

Annexure

Table 8.3 Pedagogical disassociation perceptions

Typical stereotypes (Kumaravadivelu 2003)	Illustration of academic views
Non-Western learners are obedient to authority	'We have a lot of Chinese students, you really notice that with these people the lecturer is the big boss and you don't question what they say. They are so obedient.' (Academic 1)
	'In Chinese and Asian cultures teachers are second to their parents, there has to be a great respect for the teachers.' (Academic 5)
	'It's like that with Chinese when I teach in Hong Kong, if I told them the sky is green and the grass is blue and the water's yellow, they'll have it because that's what the teacher says it is, they don't know any better.' (Academic 5)
	'They tend to think that you are the lecturer and you know it all you are right. Whereas British students will challenge you, they will disagree with you, they can be rude and all that and you find that the foreign students tend not to be that way.' (Academic 10)
Non-Western learners lack critical thinking skills	'It's a completely different learning style, they are regurgitating, not expecting me to ask them questions and for them to have an opinion.' (Academic 7)'I'm not sure what goes on in China, but quite a number of them repeat anything they come across.' (Academic 1)
	'The Chinese students they have no real creativity; they like being boxed in; UK students don't like being boxed in.' (Academic 7)
	'The Chinese seem semi-comfortable with regurgitating theory because they can memorise it. When you memorise stuff you don't have to understand it.' (Academic 4)
	'I am now basically telling them what to do, whereas I'm of the opinion that you need to develop as an independent thinker.' (Academic 21)
	'A lot of Chinese and Indians for example, I have noticed that for them it is normal to say follow one book and say reading and possibly reporting from that book.' (Academic 13)

(continued)

Table 8.3 (continued)

Typical stereotypes (Kumaravadivelu 2003)	Illustration of academic views
Non-Western learners do not participate in classroom interaction	'Chinese students are never ever encouraged to speak, to give an opinion, but they expect me to give them the answers.' (Academic 7) 'With Chinese students I have noticed that they are really afraid to speak.' (Academic 6) 'The problem that I do have, and again this is potentially with the international students is that they won't actually ask you if they don't understand what you are asking them to do.' (Academic 12) 'Most of my international students, they don't question, they don't challenge.' (Academic 2)
Non-Western students have severe language issues	'Give out a sizable case study and you get well I can't do it, the Chinese, Nigerian, Middle eastern students will say well this is too long, I can't read it' (Academic 1) 'Language right now is the barrier but I haven't noticed any major problems after the transition. Obviously, they have problems with understanding this casual relationship with the tutors and students.' (Academic 6) 'How many hours in the day do you speak English? You can speak Arabic when you go back home.' (Academic 14) 'There are several issues, one of their issues is about their reading, their speaking and their writing. A lot of the African students write extremely well, they understand English because English is the official language in Ghana and Nigeria, so no problem understanding, but reading and speaking that is a major battle for a lot of them, for the Chinese is it a major problem.' (Academic 10)
Non-Western students have motivational issues	'It's all about status, and the students that come over to the UK from China are always sold the dream.' (Academic 7) 'I find the Asian girls more difficult to deal with than the boys, the girls are just very hard work, a bit precious.' (Academic 8) 'Some of my Asian students have the attitude that I only want a degree so I can marry a better girl.' (Academic 5) 'An enormous amount of my students have no real passion for the subject [...] so now I just send students away because nobody's done any work.' (Academic 1)

(continued)

Table 8.3 (continued)

Typical stereotypes (Kumaravadivelu 2003)	Illustration of academic views
Non-Western learners are obedient to authority	*'We have a lot of Chinese students, you really notice that with these people the lecturer is the big boss and you don't question what they say. They are so obedient.'* (Academic 1)
	'In Chinese and Asian cultures teachers are second to their parents, there has to be a great respect for the teachers.' (Academic 5)
	'It's like that with Chinese when I teach in Hong Kong, if I told them the sky is green and the grass is blue and the water's yellow, they'll have it because that's what the teacher says it is, they don't know any better.' (Academic 5)
	'They tend to think that you are the lecturer and you know it all you are right. Whereas British students will challenge you, they will disagree with you, they can be rude and all that and you find that the foreign students tend not to be that way.' (Academic 10)
Non-Western learners lack critical thinking skills	*'It's a completely different learning style, they are regurgitating, not expecting me to ask them questions and for them to have an opinion.'* (Academic 7)
	'I'm not sure what goes on in China, but quite a number of them repeat anything they come across.' (Academic 1)
	'The Chinese students they have no real creativity; they like being boxed in; UK students don't like being boxed in.' (Academic 7)
	'The Chinese seem semi-comfortable with regurgitating theory because they can memorise it. When you memorise stuff you don't have to understand it.' (Academic 4)
	'I am now basically telling them what to do, whereas I'm of the opinion that you need to develop as an independent thinker.' (Academic 21)
	'A lot of Chinese and Indians for example, I have noticed that for them it is normal to say follow one book and say reading and possibly reporting from that book.' (Academic 13)

(continued)

Table 8.3 (continued)

Typical stereotypes (Kumaravadivelu 2003)	Illustration of academic views
Non-Western learners do not participate in classroom interaction	*'Chinese students are never ever encouraged to speak, to give an opinion, but they expect me to give them the answers.'* (academic 7) *'With Chinese students I have noticed that they are really afraid to speak.'* (Academic 6) *'The problem that I do have, and again this is potentially with the international students is that they won't actually ask you if they don't understand what you are asking them to do.'* (Academic 12) *'Most of my international students, they don't question, they don't challenge.'* (Academic 2)
Non-Western students have severe language issues	*'Give out a sizable case study and you get well I can't do it, the Chinese, Nigerian, Middle eastern students will say well this is too long, I can't read it,'* (Academic 1) *'Language right now is the barrier but I haven't noticed any major problems after the transition. Obviously, they have problems with understanding this casual relationship with the tutors and students.'* (Academic 6) *'How many hours in the day do you speak English? You can speak Arabic when you go back home.'* (Academic 14) *'There are several issues, one of their issues is about their reading, their speaking and their writing. A lot of the African students write extremely well, they understand English because English is the official language in Ghana and Nigeria, so no problem understanding, but reading and speaking that is a major battle for a lot of them, for the Chinese is it a major problem.'* (Academic 10)
Non-Western students have motivational issues	*'It's all about status, and the students that come over to the UK from China are always sold the dream.'* (Academic 7) *'I find the Asian girls more difficult to deal with than the boys, the girls are just very hard work, a bit precious.'* (Academic 8) *'Some of my Asian students have the attitude that I only want a degree so I can marry a better girl'* (Academic 5) *'An enormous amount of my students have no real passion for the subject [...] so now I just send students away because nobody's done any work.'* (Academic 1)

References

Ahern, K. J. (1999). Ten Tips for Reflexive Bracketing. In *Qualitative health research* (Vol. 9, Issue 3, pp. 407–411). https://doi.org/10.1177/104973239900900309

Bajunid, I. A. (1996). Preliminary explorations of indigenous perspectives of educational management: The evolving Malaysian experience. *Journal of Educational Administration, 34*(5), 50–73. https://doi.org/10.1108/09578239610148278

Banks, J. A. (1995). Multicultural Education and Curriculum Transformation. *The Journal of Negro Education, 64*(4), 390–400. https://doi.org/10.2307/2967262

Banks, J. A. (2008). *Teaching Strategies for Ethnic Studies* (8th, illustr ed.). Pearson/Allyn & Bacon. http://books.google.co.uk/books?id=1jYOnwEACAAJ

Beddall-Hill, N., Jabbar, A., & Shehri, S. (2011). Social Mobile Devices as Tools for Qualitative Research in Education: iPhones and iPads in Ethnography, Interviewing, and Design-Based Research. *Journal of the Research Center for Educational Technology, 7*(1), 67–89. http://eprints.hud.ac.uk/10507/

Beekes, W. (2006). The "Millionaire" method for encouraging participation. *Active Learning in Higher Education, 7*(1), 25.

Beverly, E. C. (2003). Learning or Unlearning Racism: Transferring Teacher Education Curriculum to Classroom Practices. *Theory into Practice, 42*(3), 203–207.

Bourdieu, P., & Passeron, J. C. (1990). *Reproduction in education, society and culture* (Vol. 4). Sage.

Bourdieu, P., & Wacquant, L. J. D. (1992). *An invitation to reflexive sociology.* University of Chicago Press.

Brooks, J., McCluskey, S., Turley, E., & King, N. (2015). Qualitative Research in Psychology The Utility of Template Analysis in Qualitative Psychology Research. *Qualitative Research in Psychology, 12*(2), 202–222. https://doi.org/10.1080/14780887.2014.955224

Choo, K. L. (2007). Can critical management education be critical in a formal higher educational setting? *Teaching in Higher Education, 12*(4), 485–497. https://doi.org/10.1080/13562510701415524

Coulson, D., & Harvey, M. (2013). Scaffolding student reflection for experience-based learning: a framework. *Teaching in Higher Education, 18*(4), 401–413.

Crabtree, B. F., & Miller, W. L. (1999). *Doing Qualitative Research.* SAGE Publications. http://books.google.com/books?hl=en&lr=&id=MEd2AwAAQBAJ&pgis=1

Crotty, M. (1996). *Phenomenology and nursing research.* Churchill Livingstone.

Crotty, M. (1998). The foundations of social research. In *Meaning and perspective in the research process*. Sage Publications. http://library.hud.ac.uk/catlink/bib/314610

Cummins, J. (1996). *Negotiating identities: education for empowerment in a diverse society*. California Association for Bilingual Education. https://books.google.co.uk/books?id=NlQlAQAAIAAJ

D'Souza, D. (1991). *Illiberal education: The politics of race and sex on campus*. Simon and Schuster.

D'Souza, D. (1995). *The end of racism: Principles for a multiracial society*. Free Press.

David, C., & Kienzler, D. (1999). Towards an emancipatory pedagogy in service courses and user departments. *Technical Communication Quarterly*, *8*(3), 269–283.

Dee, T. S. (2005). A teacher like me: Does race, ethnicity, or gender matter? *American Economic Review*, 158–165.

Durden, T. (2008). Do Your Homework! Investigating the Role of Culturally Relevant Pedagogy in Comprehensive School Reform Models Serving Diverse Student Populations. *The Urban Review*, *40*(4), 403–419.

Durden, T., Dooley, C. M., & Truscott, D. (2014). Race still matters: preparing culturally relevant teachers. *Race Ethnicity and Education*, ahead-of-print, 1–22.

Durden, T., & Truscott, D. (2013). Critical Reflectivity and the Development of New Culturally Relevant Teachers. *Multicultural Perspectives*, *15*(2), 73–80.

Finlay, L. (2002). "Outing" the Researcher: The Provenance, Process, and Practice of Reflexivity. *Qualitative Health Research*, *12*(4), 531–545. https://doi.org/10.1177/104973202129120052

Foster, M. (1995). African American Teachers and Culturally Relevant Pedagogy. In J. A. Banks & C. A. M. Banks (Eds.), *Handbook of research on multicultural education* (pp. 570–581). Macmillan New York.

Gatimu, M. W. (2009). Undermining critical consciousness unconsciously: Restoring hope in the multicultural education idea. *Journal of Educational Change*, *10*(1), 47.

Gay, G. (1995). Making School multicultural: Campus and Classroom. In C. A. Grant & M. Gomez (Eds.), *Making School multicultural: Campus and classroom* (pp. 37–54). Merrill/Prentice Hall.

Gay, G. (2000). *Culturally Responsive Teaching: Theory, Research, & Practice*. Teachers College Press.

Gay, G. (2002). Preparing for culturally responsive teaching. *Journal of Teacher Education*, *53*(2), 106–116.

Gay, G., & Kirkland, K. (2003). Developing cultural critical consciousness and self-reflection in preservice teacher education. *Theory into Practice*, *42*(3), 181–187.

Ghere, D. L., Kampsen, A., Duranczyk, I. M., & Christensen, L. L. (2007). Adopting and integrating multiculturalism: a closing assessment of general college. *CRDEUL*, 25.

Gibson, M. A. (1987). The school performance of immigrant minorities: A comparative view. *Anthropology & Education Quarterly*, *18*(4), 262–275.

Giroux, H. A. (2004). Cultural Studies and the Politics of Public Pedagogy: Making the Political More Pedagogical. *Parallax, 10*(2), 73–89. https://doi.org/10.1080/1353464042000208530

Goodman, R. D., & Cirecie, A. W.-O. (2009). Applying Critical Consciousness: Culturally Competent Disaster Response Outcomes. *Journal of Counseling & Development, 87*. http://web.ebscohost.com/ehost/pdf?vid=2&hid=107&sid=9676df33-1de0-443f-ab7a-0e119356cabb@sessionmgr4

Groenewald, T. (2004). A phenomenological research design illustrated. *International Journal of Qualitative Methods*, *3*(1), 42–55. http://journals.sagepub.com/doi/full/10.1177/160940690400300104

Hammersley, M. (1992). The generalisability of ethnography. *What's Wrong with Ethnography*, 85–95.

Hardy, C., & Tolhurst, D. (2014). Epistemological beliefs and cultural diversity matters in management education and learning: A critical review and future directions. *Academy of Management Learning & Education*, *13*(2), 265–289.

Higbee, J. L., Lundell, D. B., & Duranczyk, I. M. (2007a). *Diversity and the Postsecondary Experience*. Center for Research on Developmental Education and Urban Literacy, University of Minnesota.

Higbee, J. L., Siaka, K., & Bruch, P. L. (2007b). Student perceptions of their multicultural learning environment: A closer look. *Diversity and the Postsecondary Experience*, 3–23.

Housee, S. (2011). What Difference Does "Difference" Make? A Discussion with Ethnic Minority Students about Their Learning Experience in Higher Education. *Learning and Teaching: The International Journal of Higher Education in the Social Sciences*, *4*(1), 70–91. https://doi.org/10.3167/latiss.2011.040105

Houser, N. O. (2008). Cultural plunge: a critical approach for multicultural development in teacher education . *Race Ethnicity and Education*, *11*(4), 465–482. https://doi.org/10.1080/13613320802479034

Howard, T. C. (2003). Culturally Relevant Pedagogy: Ingredients for Critical Teacher Reflection. *Theory into Practice, 42*(3), 195–202. https://doi.org/10.1207/s15430421tip4203_5

Hultberg, J., Plos, K., Hendry, G. D., & Kjellgren, K. I. (2008). Scaffolding students' transition to higher education: parallel introductory courses for students and teachers. *Journal of Further and Higher Education, 32*(1), 47–57. https://doi.org/10.1080/03098770701781440

Humfrey, C. (1999). *Managing international students: Recruitment to graduation.* Open University Press.

Hurtado, S., Milem, J., Clayton-Pedersen, A., & Allen, W. (1999). Enacting Diverses Learning Environments: Improving the Climate for Racial/Ethnic Diversity in Higher Education. *ASHE-ERIC Higher Education Report, 26*, 8.

Irvine, J. J. (1990). *Black students and school failure. Policies, practices, and prescriptions.* Greenwood Press.

Jabbar, A. (2013). Characterising features of culturally responsive teaching in UK Higher Education Business Schools. *10th ALDinHE Conference 2013: Celebrating Learning Development, 25th–27th March 2013.* http://eprints.hud.ac.uk/17059/

Jabbar, A., & Analoui, B. (2018). Academics ' Perspectives on the Impact of Managerialism on Teaching International Students. *Journal of International Business Education, 13*, 55–78.

Jabbar, A., Analoui, B., Kong, K., & Mirza, M. (2017). Consumerisation in UK higher education business schools: higher fees, greater stress and debatable outcomes. *Higher Education.* https://doi.org/10.1007/s10734-017-0196-z

Jabbar, A., & Hardaker, G. (2013). The role of culturally responsive teaching for supporting ethnic diversity in British University Business Schools. *Teaching in Higher Education, 1–13.* https://doi.org/10.1080/13562517.2012.725221

Jabbar, A., & Mirza, M. (2017). Managing diversity: academic's perspective on culture and teaching. *Race Ethnicity and Education, 3324*(November), 1–20. https://doi.org/10.1080/13613324.2017.1395325

Jabbar, A., Teviotdale, W., Mirza, M., & Mswaka, W. (2019). Academics' perspectives of international students in UK higher education. *Journal of Further and Higher Education, 00*(00), 1–15. https://doi.org/10.1080/0309877X.2018.1541974

Jenks, C., Lee, J. O., & Kanpol, B. (2001). *Approaches to multicultural education in preservice teacher education: Philosophical frameworks and models for teaching* (Vol. 33, Issue 2, pp. 87–105). Springer.

Joy, S., & Poonamallee, L. (2013). *Cross-cultural teaching in globalized management classrooms: Time to move from functionalist to post-colonial approaches?* Academy of Management Learning & Education.

King, N. (2004). Using templates in the thematic analysis of texts. In C. Cassell & G. Symon (Eds.), *Essential guide to qualitative methods in organizational research* (pp. 256–270). Sage Publications.

King, N. (2012). Doing template analysis. In G. Symon & C. Cassell (Eds.), *Qualitative organizational research: Core methods and current challenges* (pp. 426–450). Sage.

King, N., & Horrocks, C. (2010). *Interviews in qualitative research.* SAGE Publications Limited.

Kolb, A. Y., & Kolb, D. A. (2005). Learning styles and learning spaces: Enhancing experiential learning in higher education. *Academy of Management Learning & Education, 4*(2), 193–212.

Kumaravadivelu, B. (2003). Problematizing cultural stereotypes in TESOL. *Tesol Quarterly, 37*(4), 709–719.

Kvale, S., & Brinkmann, S. (2009). *InterViews: learning the craft of qualitative research interviewing.* Sage Publications. http://library.hud.ac.uk/catlink/bib/590440

Ladson-Billings, G. (1995a). But that's just good teaching! The case for culturally relevant pedagogy. *Theory into Practice, 34*(3), 159–165.

Ladson-Billings, G. (1995b). Toward a theory of culturally relevant pedagogy. *American Educational Research Journal, 32*(3), 465–491.

Langdridge, D. (2007). *Phenomenological psychology: Theory, research and method.* Pearson/Prentice Hall, 2007.

Leese, M. (2010). Bridging the gap: supporting student transitions into higher education. *Journal of Further and Higher Education, 34*(2), 239–251. https://doi.org/10.1080/03098771003695494

Lipka, J. (1991). Toward a Culturally Based Pedagogy: A Case Study of One Yup'ik Eskimo Teacher. *Anthropology & Education Quarterly, 22*(3), 203–223. https://doi.org/10.1525/aeq.1991.22.3.05x1050j

Lumby, J., & Foskett, N. (2015). Internationalization and Culture in Higher Education. *Educational Management Administration & Leadership, 44*(1), 95–111. https://doi.org/10.1177/1741143214549978

McAllister, G., & Irvine, J. J. (2002). The Role of Empathy in Teaching Culturally Diverse Students: A Qualitative Study of Teachers' Beliefs. *Journal of Teacher Education, 53*(5), 433–443. https://doi.org/10.1177/002248702237397

McGee Banks, C. A., & Banks, J. A. (1995). Equity pedagogy: An essential component of multicultural education. *Theory into Practice, 34*(3), 152–158.

Meyer, H.-D. (2002). The new managerialism in education management: corporatization or organizational learning? . *Journal of Educational Administration, 40*(6), 534–551. https://doi.org/10.1108/09578230210446027

Modood, T. (2006). Ethnicity, Muslims and higher education entry in Britain. *Teaching in Higher Education, 11*(2), 247–250. https://doi.org/10.1080/13562510500527826

Molesworth, M., Nixon, E., & Scullion, R. (2009). Having, being and higher education: the marketisation of the university and the transformation of the student into consumer. *Teaching in Higher Education, 14*(3), 277–287. https://doi.org/10.1080/13562510902898841

Monroe, C. R., & Obidah, J. E. (2004). The Influence of Cultural Synchronization on a Teacher's Perceptions of Disruption: A Case Study of an African American Middle-School Classroom. *Journal of Teacher Education, 55*(3), 256–268. https://doi.org/10.1177/0022487104263977

Ngambi, H. (2008). Diversity Dynamics in Teaching. In M. B. Par Martensson Kristina Nilsson (Ed.), *Teaching and Learning at Business Schools: Transforming Business Education* (pp. 101–110). Gower.

Nieto, S. (1999). *The Light in Their Eyes: Creating Multicultural Learning Communities. Multicultural Education Series* (1st ed.). Teachers College Press.

Nieto, S. (2005). *Why we teach*. Teachers College Press.

Oikonomidoy, E. (2010). Zooming Into the School Narratives of Refugee Students. *Multicultural Perspectives, 12*(2), 74–80.

Oppenheim, A. N. (1992). *Questionnaire design, interviewing and attitude measurement.* Continuum. http://books.google.co.uk/books?hl=en&lr=&id=6V4Gn ZS7TO4C&oi=fnd&pg=PA1&dq=questionnaire+design,+interviewing+and +attitude+management&ots=szL98n_MiG&sig=SQMVFU88puNNPBr7_ vPys0j-lyc#v=onepage&q&f=false

Orbe, M. P. (2000). Centralizing diverse racial/ethnic voices in scholarly research: the value of phenomenological inquiry. *International Journal of Intercultural Relations, 24*(5), 603. https://doi.org/10.1016/S0147-1767(00)00019-5

Papert, S., & Harel, I. (1991). Situating constructionism. *Constructionism, 36*, 1–11.

Pratt, M. (2009). From the Editors: for the Lack of a Boilerplate : Tips on Writing Up (and Reviewing) Qualitative Research. *Academy of Management Journal, 52*(5), 856–862. https://doi.org/10.5465/AMJ.2009.44632557

Raelin, J. A. (2007). Toward an epistemology of practice. *Academy of Management Learning & Education, 6*(4), 495–519.

Richardson, J. (2008). The attainment of ethnic minority students in UK higher education. *Studies in Higher Education, 33*(1), 33–48.

Rienties, B., Beausaert, S., Grohnert, T., Niemantsverdriet, S., & Kommers, P. (2012). Understanding academic performance of international students: the role of ethnicity, academic and social integration. *Higher Education, 63*(6), 685–700.

Ritchie, J., Lewis, J., & Elam, G. (2003). Designing and selecting samples. In J. Ritchie & J. Lewis (Eds.), *Qualitative research practice: A guide for social science students and researchers* (pp. 77–108). Sage.

Rubie-Davies, C., Hattie, J., & Hamilton, R. (2006). Expecting the best for students: Teacher expectations and academic outcomes. *British Journal of Educational Psychology, 76*(3), 429–444. https://doi.org/10.1348/000709905X53589

Sabry, N. S., & Bruna, K. R. (2007). Learning from the experience of Muslim students in American schools: Towards a proactive model of school-community cooperation. *Multicultural Perspectives, 9*(3), 44–50. https://doi.org/10.1080/15210960701443730

Saldaña, J. (2012). *The coding manual for qualitative researchers* (Issue 14). Sage.

Santoro, N. (2013). 'If I'm going to teach about the world, I need to know the world': developing Australian pre-service teachers' intercultural competence through international trips. *Race Ethnicity and Education, 17*(3), 429–444. https://doi.org/10.1080/13613324.2013.832938

Schapper, J. M., & Mayson, S. E. (2004). Internationalisation of curricula: an alternative to the Taylorisation of academic work. *Journal of Higher Education Policy and Management, 26*(2), 189–205. https://doi.org/10.1080/1360080042000218258

Schmeichel, M. (2011). Good Teaching? An examination of culturally relevant pedagogy as an equity practice. *Journal of Curriculum Studies, 44*(2), 211–231. https://doi.org/10.1080/00220272.2011.591434

Sleeter, C. E. (2001). Preparing teachers for culturally diverse schools research and the overwhelming presence of whiteness. *Journal of Teacher Education, 52*(2), 94–106.

Stein, P. (2000). Rethinking resources in the ESL classroom: Rethinking resources: Multimodal pedagogies in the ESL classroom. *Tesol Quarterly, 34*(2), 333–336.

Swartz, E. (1996). Emancipatory pedagogy: a postcritical response to 'standard' school knowledge. *Journal of Curriculum Studies, 28*(4), 397–418. https://doi.org/10.1080/0022027980280402

Tisdell, E. J. (2009). Spirituality, Cultural Identity, and Epistemology in Culturally Responsive Teaching in Higher Education. *Multicultural Perspectives, 8*(3), 19–25. https://doi.org/10.1207/s15327892mcp0803_4

Tomalin, E. (2007). Supporting cultural and religious diversity in higher education: pedagogy and beyond. *Teaching in Higher Education, 12*(5–6), 621–634. https://doi.org/10.1080/13562510701595283

Tomlinson, S. (2005). Race, ethnicity and education under New Labour. *Oxford Review of Education, 31*(1), 153–171. https://doi.org/10.1080/0305498042000337246

Traxler, J. (2009). Current State of Mobile Learning1. *Mobile Learning*, 9.

Turner, Y. (2006). Chinese Students in a UK Business School: Hearing the Student Voice in Reflective Teaching and Learning Practice. *Higher Education Quarterly, 60*(1), 27–51. https://doi.org/10.1111/j.1468-2273.2006.00306.x

Villegas, A. M., & Lucas, T. (2002). Preparing culturally responsive teachers rethinking the curriculum. *Journal of Teacher Education, 53*(1), 20–32. https://doi.org/10.1177/0022487102053001003

Vita, G. De. (2001). Learning styles, culture and inclusive instruction in the multicultural classroom: A business and management perspective. *Innovations in Education and Teaching International, 38*(2), 165–174.

Zhu, Y., & Bargiela-Chiappini, F. (2013). Balancing emic and etic: Situated learning and ethnography of communication in cross-cultural management education. *Academy of Management Learning & Education, 12*(3), 380–395.

9

Understanding Trends of Collaboration and Creative Practice in the Fashion Industry: A Critical Approach Towards Curriculum Development in Higher Education

Terry Newman

Abstract This chapter explores the necessity of collaboration within a creative and dynamic business workplace and highlights areas within the fashion industry where co-operation and teamwork build results. This kind of collective working environment can be rewarding within a creative business school and can be utilised effectively as a learning skill in cross-course units. The chapter examines what collaborative learning might entail and how it correlates to collaborative creativity in the Fashion Industry concentrating on areas including production, sustainability, slow-fashion, authenticity, art, activism, NFTs and gaming. Collaboration is fundamental to an innovative workplace and as such should be mirrored within as much as possible within the boundaries of higher

T. Newman (✉)
Business School for the Creative Industries, University for the Creative Arts, Farnham, UK
e-mail: Philip.Powell@uca.ac.uk

© The Author(s), under exclusive license to Springer Nature Switzerland AG 2022
P. Powell, B. Shankar Nayak (eds.), *Creative Business Education*,
https://doi.org/10.1007/978-3-031-10928-7_9

education. Formal assessments that correspond to real-world practice support student progress post-graduation.

Introduction

Success in fashion, business and creativity has always centred around effective collaboration. The infrastructure of a brand or fashion house is like an ant colony where everyone has a common goal. A creative business school is therefore a uniquely productive student environment where a variety of disciplines network and learn through cross-taught units. It makes sense that team-work in a creative business school is embedded in curriculum and students are scaffolded to enable cluster projects to happen and thrive as a collective. Understanding how to problem solve in groups is a life-long skill and interaction and peer learning a powerful method of development. Perceiving limitations, supporting study through working with knowledgeable others and technology and tools to help produce projects that resonate and succeed is an essential element of a creative business practice. Collaborative pedagogic theory platformed by Vygotsky wires the idea of learning communities and in the twenty-first century, with the additional advantage of digital connectivity it has never been more effective. Vygotsky recognises that '*learning always occurs and cannot be separated from a social context. Consequently, instructional strategies that promote the distribution of expert knowledge where students collaboratively work together to conduct research, share their results, and perform or produce a final project, help to create a collaborative community of learners*' (Cole et al. 1978). Assignments that are formed by analysis of real-world problems and briefs that employ an inclusive methodology are most likely to foster an ability to succeed post-graduation. They enable students to think on their feet creatively and flexibly approach a job in hand. An example of this—a recent UCA fashion journalism student, fed-back to their Programme Director, saying:

> *Just wanted to reach out to you with some exciting news: after working as a freelance since December, I've now been offered a contract at RTL as a TV and radio journalist, focusing mainly on culture, art and music. I've also been writ-*

ing quite a bit of fashion-related content for the English department of RTL which has been great. So, I just wanted to say thank you, because without UCA and the tutors, I would've never had the basis to do this job and adapt this quickly to different situations and environments, which, especially during these times, has proven to be such a crucial skill. So, thank you for everything!

What Is Collaborative Learning and how Does it Correlate to Collaborative Creativity in the Fashion Industry?

Leigh Smith and MacGregor explain in their book: *What is Collaborative Learning?* that *'collaborative learning practitioners would say that all collaborative learning is about building learning communities. However, in a more specific sense, in terms of intentional reconfiguration of the curriculum. In the past 15 years, a number of colleges have recognized that deep-seated structural factors weaken the quality of undergraduate learning and inhibit the development of community. These schools have attacked the problem directly by developing learning communities, a "purposeful restructuring of the curriculum to link together courses so that students find greater coherence in what they are learning and increased interaction with faculty and fellow students'*. As such, learning communities are a delivery system and a facilitating structure for the practice of collaborative learning. This approach maps directly to the creative fashion work-place where ideas are expressed best through collective team-work.

In order to help create industry standard assignments for students to work on, it is useful to unpick the kinds of collaboration that previously existed, currently exist and look set to exist in the future within the business of fashion. In this way learning communities within higher education can be structured most usefully. It is also constructive to review how the Covid-19 global health crisis has impacted a consumer mind-set and more generally the way the fashion industry work together in order to help build a relevant and topical learning space. Reflective learning, curiosity and imaginative ways of solving problems all can come from studying the logics of collaboration within the fashion industry.

Mallevays wrote in a 2021 Business of Fashion feature how collaborations have evolved over the last 20 years within the fashion industry (2021): '*brand collaborations pairing hot designers with volume retailers to produce eye-catching, limited-edition collections at affordable prices have long served to generate media impressions and drive traffic to stores, creating powerful touchpoints with fashion customers.*' Collaboration can be a high-profile activity, to such an extent that in 2021, authenticity is a key for any new project to flourish. Politically and social aware shoppers are likely to cancel firms who step away from their brand values in an attempt to drive traffic to their online sites and stores.

Truthfulness is crucial. For example, when American designer Halston partnered with JC Penney in 1983 to create the Halston III line it was unable to match or mirror in any meaningful way the high-octane glitz of his main collection and the designer's heart was not in the project. The alliance eventually led to Halston losing the rights to use his name. He was not aware of the ramifications of the deal he made with JC Penney on many levels. Learning how contracts work, why they can be beneficial and protective are elements of a helpful arts-business education and key to any collaborative venture. Mallevays (2021) goes on to evaluate the value of collaborations that work between luxury and streetwear brands: '*Luxury labels have also used brand collaborations to go after streetwear-obsessed Gen-Zers. Dior's Nike Air Jordan 1 High OG sneakers were one of the hottest collaborations of 2020. Five million people registered on a dedicated microsite created by Dior for the launch of the shoes, which were sold for around $2,000. (You could have made a ten-fold return on your investment on the resale market if you were one of the lucky few to have secured a pair of Air Dior at launch). The product was authentically streetwear whilst being uncompromisingly luxurious, generating a halo effect on Dior's wider offering and recruiting younger customers to the brand.*'

However, confident and clever ingenuity when collaborating is something savvy shoppers endorse. This is why blue-sky thinking in a university environment, testing possibilities and assembling an experimental body of work is crucial for any arts and business institution. Thinking side-ways and inventively is what higher education is about. This is exactly the rationale behind one of the first hugely successful fashion-high street collaborations—Target and Isaac Mizrahi in 1999—La Ferla explained in an August 2019 New York Times feature (La Ferla 2019): '*Target's initiative conferred cool on designers as well, shifting the perception that they were too fancy or too haughty to care about their less affluent fans. It also made hash of old rules.*' Students should be taught to make a hash of old rules and instead consider ways of creating new and vital industry strategies.

Collaboration, Slow-Fashion and Sustainability

There are many ways in which alliances in fashion are formed—and at the very heart are the building blocks of textile mills who are transforming the fabric production industry, and petit mains craftspeople who sew together the vision of a designer. Production is fundamental and the very essence of making clothes. Frumat for example is an Italian textile company who aim for circularity in their fabric innovations and have devised a vegan leather made from 50% apple waste. Responsible production is a merit most fashion brands are now keen to adopt and collaborating with such technological fabric is one form of connecting and collaborating within industry. Frumat is just one of myriad organisations connecting with companies who aim to put a green philosophy at the core of what they do. Fashion United reported in February 2021 (Stenzel 2021) that: '*over 30 fashion brands and manufacturers have joined a new initiative to collaborate on cutting down textile waste and reusing materials to create new products in Bangladesh's garments factories. The Circular Fashion Partnership announced this week that it is bringing brands such as H&M, OVS, Marks & Spencer, Berska, Pull & Bear, C&A, Kmart Australia, and Bangladeshi recycling firms and garment manufacturers on board the movement.*'

Equally, slow-fashion is something the fashion industry has been addressing in an attempt to put the brakes on waste. At the very highest end is Chanel's Metiers D'art collection shown every December was devised by Karl Lagerfeld in 2003 as a show-case for all the artisans they work with including Lemarie, a feather and flower company which began its work during the Belle Époque. They created Chanel's signature 16 petal camellia flower. Lesage is an embroidery company, founded in 1924 whose speciality is working with diamante, beading and gems. Causse is a glove-making institution, that has created couture since 1892. Many more of these kinds of workshops have been bought by Chanel in order to maintain their longevity and heritage. Extraordinary expertise in making clothes result in pieces that aren't made to throw away quickly, but treasure, mend and hand-down the generations. Nevertheless, despite its rarefied, exclusive position within the bigger fashion industry, Chanel's Metiers D'art collection is collaboration born of necessity: an understanding how to produce a garment or accessory. Zhang writes in his fashion paper, Collective Action, for The Fashion Journal: '*That fashion is produced by large teams of people working together should be no mystery—after all, it would be impossible for one person to perform every task necessary to produce a single fashion collection in a sustainable way. At the same time, however, we still tend to conflate entire companies with a single creative genius, producing the image of the celebrity fashion designer.*'

Sustainability is an issue driving consumption in fashion this century. A July 2020 McKinsey survey (Granskog et al. 2020) reported that '*more than three in five consumers said brands' promotion of sustainability was an important factor in their purchasing decisions.*' Responsible fashion is a distinctly important element to consider when creating a collaboration. An example of a collective project is seen in Adidas' campaign to become carbon neutral as a company by 2050 and by 2024 to use only recycled polyester. Their most celebrated sneaker, The Stan Smith is now made with re-claimed material and to promote this they collaborated with Depop. Jing Daily reported in May 2021 (Ref 5): '*for the Adidas collaboration, 40 Depop sellers were invited to customize pairs of the new Stan Smith Primgreen shoes and choose a charity to receive the proceeds. Three other Depop creatives worked with upcycling designer Paolina Russo, track athlete Laviai Nielsen and British alternative R&B band Easy Life to rework items of adidas apparel, resulting in an exclusive collection of one-of-a-kind pieces intended to complement the Stan Smith shoes.*' This kind of cross-pollination of ideas evidences how a message, mission and ambition to connect with new audiences generates new ways of thinking and problem solving—all themes we foster within a creative business school. Reflecting on how industry engages with each other helps frame our teaching and the students' learning.

Authenticity and Collaboration

Authenticity and collaboration strategies that work well tell an eloquent brand story that resonates. How an idea connects with others and grows, as per the Adidas Stan Smith product is part of the seeding process of building a loyal and relatable customer. A Magazine curated by Eckhaus Latta, is a thought-provoking concept. Eckhaus Latta is an American brand that spans art, sustainability, fashion, performance and video. In October 2017, i-D Magazine wrote (Stran 2017):

> *The most exciting magazine of the season is not really a magazine at all. It's an art project that takes the form of a classic September issue, by the progressive bi-coastal brand Eckhaus Latta. As the most recent incarnation of A Magazine Curated By, which allows designers like Alessandro Michele and Proenza Schouler to live out their editing fantasies, the book takes classic Condé Nast tropes and f**ks them up a bit. Using familiar categories like "Beauty" and "Interiors," designers Mike Eckhaus and Zoe Latta opened up the issue to their friends and family. When you're one of the most authentically collaborative brands around, that includes a cover by Roe Ethridge, a home feature with Susan Cianciolo, a letter to the editor by Tim Blanks, and an advice column by Juliana Huxtable. There are "fake advertisements by real artists" including Alex Da Corte and Ryan Trecartin, and "paparazzi" photos of little-known people in the Eckhaus orbit. The "magazine" is packed with ideas, good ideas!*

Creative collaboration is one way of facilitating imaginative marketing and supporting brand identity and values. And it can work brilliantly as a niche venture, as per the Eckhaus Latta/A Magazine Curated by, but the process of collaboration is a key creative ambition for many brands. It works on many levels. In the past couplings included: Alexander Mc Queen and American Express, H&M and Comme des Garcons and Aries Arise and Havana Club. Avant garde fashion houses and block-busting house-hold names can gel. There no cap on where collaboration can go and therefore a great starting point for responsible arts-business education. How it is being realised now and tomorrow both in business and as a trend can be seen by looking at some of the more side-ways and ingenious hook-ups.

Vaquera is, as Fashionista wrote in 2018, an '*art project masquerading as a fashion line.*' However, the Vaquera X Hulu collaboration signalled surprising new directions. For the partnership, Hulu asked Vaquera to create a collection inspired by The Handmaidens Tale narrative—a show screened on the streaming channel. The result included a uniform worn by the Handmaids: a long red cape and white bonnet. '*Hulu approached us to work on this project because we discuss similar themes with our own work. The novel has been an inspiration since the beginning of Vaquera because [of] its use of visual language to discuss poignant social issues. We are excited to work on something so ground-breaking and timely,*' Vaquera told Refinery29 at the time.

Odd things can work. Counterintuitive ideas are interesting to explore, and at an art school it's a good place to experiment and be bold. In 2017 ASAP Rocky and Krispy Kremes produced a limited-edition donut and sold it exclusively in the UK at a specially re-created bodega in London's Selfridges Department Store. Collaborations are meant to be fun too. It is also a method of establishing brand values without the huge carbon footprint of a fashion collection.

Art and Fashion Collaborative Approaches

Art and fashion have a symbiotic relationship and, as described in *Legendary Artists and the Clothes they Wore* (Newman 2019): '*today more than ever, the empires of fashion and art stand shoulder to shoulder.: the fashion industry is an important patron of the art world, and at times that relationship hazes with stylish ingenuity. Miuccia Prada's pink, neon-lit Double Club installation in collaboration with Carsten Holler—first shown in London in 2008 and then in 2017 at the juggernaut melting-pot fair, Art Basel Miami, has proved that art can be quite a happy and creative bedfellow with fashion, producing new ideas and enjoying mutual benefaction.*' *Fashion United* reported in June 2021 about one of the latest and most interesting art-fashion-projects: '*Helmut Lang has launched a collection in collaboration with American conceptual artist Hank Willis Thomas, focusing on his text-based lenticular work 'It's All About You / It's Not About You'. The limited-edition collection of ready-to-wear includes hoodies, T-shirts and* dresses, which read 'It's All About You' or 'It's Not About You' depending on the viewers' vantage point. *The collection aims to address what the brand is calling a moment in time where we are all being called to examine our own privileges and biases, as the project compels people to think about how their own position literally affects what they see.*' It's one of very many art-fashion connections, from Salvador Dali's collaboration with Elsa Schiaparelli in 1930s, including most famously the painted lobster dress worn by Wallis Simpson in 1937 to Louis Vuitton's partnership with Japanese pop-artist, Takashi Murakami, to installation artist's Vanessa Beecroft's collaborations with Kanye West's Yeezy label for drops 1, 2 and 3, February 2015–2016.

In May 2021, Jing Daily reported on the LVMH brand Loewe's collaboration with auction house, Sotheby's and said it: '*offered a glimpse into the future of brand partnerships, further explaining that "the COVID-19 pandemic—along with a sea change in consumer attitudes—is enticing brands that long resisted resale to begin incorporating it into their broader retail strategies. And the Sotheby's Buy Now marketplace could very well become luxury's go-to platform for luxury brand-supported resale but also special one-off collections and collaborations. For Chinese consumers fixated on product authenticity, limited-edition items, ease of purchase, and name recognition, Sotheby's is a known and trusted entity*' (Ekstract 2021). The two created a collection of chestnut roasters, designed by Japanese artist ARKO, Chinese artist Min Chen, and Spanish artist Laia Arqueros and Sotheby's displayed them in their galleries together with pieces by Jean-Michel Basquiat, Roy Lichtenstein and Claude Monet, putting them up for sale via Sotheby's Buy Now Market Place. In the process they '*united art, commerce and luxury.*' The Buy Now Market-Place provides a credible digital space for clients to buy verified limited-edition designer collectibles, collaborations and one-off specialist art-fashion pieces. An exclusive and inestimable zone of mutual collective possibilities.

Re-Sell and Activism and Collaboration

Pre-pandemic: WGSN forecast the growth of low-impact consumerism, and re-sell is only one part of the story. On September 2019, more than four million people protested at the Youth Climate Strike—the largest mass protest for action on global warming in history. The strike, and others like it, are helping to drive this new narrative around consumption, leading consumers to question whether they need more stuff. Re-thinking business models creatively will help brands evolve as the world moves towards an economy looking for reasons not to buy. Collaboration is also about not buying too many things. Mattress company Casper partnered with CBD edibles company Plus to create sleep enhancing gummies. Clever collaborative initiatives can work within the eco-system of responsible and sustainable consumerism too if shrewd.

The value of seasonal fashion has been questioned for a long time now, and the emergence of buy now catwalk shows, gender-fluid fashion collections and avoiding the seasons altogether replacing them with special projects of drops, in the way pioneered by Supreme has become the new norm. Supreme are now owned by US based company VF Corporation, a US-based apparel and who bought the global streetwear brand for $2.1bn in December 2020. During 2020 fashion adapted to the global pandemic by skipping seasons—designers Marc Jacobs, Gucci and Michael Kors did not show during New York Fashion Week in September. Other fashion houses reduced waste by creating digital shows instead of costly catwalks: Celine's men's and womenswear collections were displayed in high-value, socially distanced films shot for Autumn/Winter 2021. All these resourceful responses to the pandemic introduced bold new ways of collaboration.

NFTs and Collaborative Approaches

Clothes have always used as a signal for others to read and a brand now has an encyclopaedia of ways of communicating their what they want to say. Today collaborative relationships within the fashion industry are not just about clothes, but also the message they send about company values, authenticity, viewpoints as well as its vision. Also, their technological status. In a recent Business of Fashion podcast (BofTeam 2021), they examined Fashion's interest in non-fungible tokens and described how a collaboration between digital artist, Fewocious and RTFKT—a virtual sneaker brand—sold 621 pairs of shoes issued as NFTS for approximately $3.1 million. '*buyers will later be sent a pair of physical shoes from the RTFKT and Fewocious collaboration, but more as a thank you note for the digital purchase. The true asset, as those with faith in the market believe, is the digital product*' they explained. As the artist himself told Jing Daily the possibilities of brand collaborations this way is huge: '*someone said, well what if a big company like Foot Locker bought an NFT, then started printing as many as they want? They could have the art in their line. It's opening up a whole new door!*' In 2019, Miu Miu revealed its Miu Miu Twist perfume in a video game. Balenciaga's entire Autumn/Winter 2021 show was a video game itself, entitled '*Afterworld: The Age of Tomorrow*.' The creative director, Demna Gvasalia told Vogue (Mower 2020): '*I hate the idea of fashion film. I find it very dated*.' These are ideas that require finding and collaborating with industries outside of the traditional areas fashion has worked with. Fashion today is often digital and in the world of gaming fabric and factories are not required, although a partnership is. Roblox, was the stage for the Web version of the Gucci Garden Archetypes, an immersive experience originally opened at the Gucci Garden in Florence, Italy, it launched in Roblox on May 17 2021, closing May 31st. The Roblox Gucci Garden invited players to appreciate Alessandro Michele's creative fashion world in a series of virtual rooms and also to try on Gucci accessories. Some were free—a wide brimmed denim logoed hat for example, or you could and buy them, including the Queen Bee Dionysus bag which initially sold for 475 Robux (around $5). As a limited edition, the bag was available for just an hour a day for two days, it began to re-selling quickly. The highest successful listing to date sold the bag for $4115. According to Statista (2021), Roblox had, in the first quarter of 2021, '*over 42.1 million active daily users world-wide*.' At first glance, the concept behind one of Italy's oldest fashion houses, founded 100 years ago, collaborating with a child's online metaverse might seem counterintuitive, however it is just one example of how creative collaboration works within fashion. Imagination is the only limitation.

Conclusion

Within the Business School at University for the Creative Arts, Epsom, many units utilise the power of collaborative learning to successful effect. The Fashion Journalism BA (soon to become Magazine Publishing to incorporate a wider academic remit) initiates collaborative practice from year 1 through to year 3 with group presentations, creative film and podcast content making, newsletter, zine, social media and website production, where skills including research, graphics, moving image, writing, marketing, promotion and people-management are all integral learning elements. Students find their feet with many of these disciplines and for those who find expertise is weighted stronger one way or another, the challenge is to find and work with like-minded creatives to get the job done. For final projects in year 3, journalism/magazine publishing students are tasked with pulling together their editorial vision and have to connect with contributors and collaborators in order to get it made. Collaboration has also been a resourceful response to pandemic restrictions in 2020–2021. The fashion communications work-placement unit was re-structured so that all the cohorts across the business school came together to build a media agency platform and magazine. Music, fashion promotion, business management and journalism students worked on a single vision and contrasting skills were used to maximum effect. Across the School, marketing, promotion, social media, event management and advertising are courses where fruitful partnerships can be and are made— often designed through learning outcomes, and sometimes arising through student initiative. Going forward, mirroring industry enterprise helps foster a can-do, confident work-ethic. A creative business integrated academic experience is a dynamic stepping stone to future productiveness. What is key for the generation of students who are studying in a pandemic and post-pandemic world is authenticity and action. Fitzwaters (2021), the critical theory senior lecturer explains the '*L4 Fashion Business and Practices Unit is really noteworthy in this discussion because it requires students to work in groups to design, source, and market a fashion brand extension. Roles that the students perform included: Head of Sourcing and Corporate Social responsibility Director, so they really had to accurately research and accommodate ethical sourcing into the pricing structure and the project's critical path.'* Industries working more closely together towards a greener, fairer, and more creative global market-place is ironically a fundamental result of enforced isolation the world over. Higher education has always softly embraced collaborative learning and its pertinence has accelerated when looking to embed a candidly creative business curriculum. The limitations of rooting efficient collaboration within a syllabus however is set with complications. Engagement across courses is difficult to implement—especially during short six week units. For example, the Foundation to Marketing and Communications unit has struggled with capturing students' willingness to work independently in groups for a project that requires them to devise a hypothetical industry collaboration.

The ideas are wonderful, but students operating as a team and producing results have been a challenge. Student engagement is key to success; if a student misses out on the first few planning sessions they often fail to catch up and contribute meaningfully to the task given. Vigilant monitoring of attendance is clearly necessary. Group tasks are also difficult to re-create when a student goes to re-take or has to re-submit a unit. UCA implements a '*Boot-Camp*' programme in advance of assessed units and it's feasible that this space could also scaffold student and tutor expectations in collaborative work and highlight the benefits up-front. Collaborations within single courses usually work efficiently and the fashion journalism programme regularly sets up cluster projects—such as a magazine or website task—with satisfying conclusions.

The value of examining how fashion and business collaborations exist in the post-pandemic, digitised, globally connected metaverse are fuel for thought when designing creative arts and business curriculum. In January 2021 Fashion Think Tank, Fashion Round-Table, took over online fashion-space Showstudio (2020) and Fashion Round-Table founder Tamara Cincik discussed with journalist Sarah Mower and fashion director and editor Karen Binns the value of creative education and importance of embedding business strategy competences within an arts education. In order for the creative industries to flourish post-pandemic diverse skills and abilities are required. Cross collaboration between business and arts students is one method of entrenching these mind-sets and the infrastructure of the Business School, University for the Creative Arts, is especially well positioned to develop these kinds of cross-study enrichment, where students in every cohort and year group are introduced to inter-disciplinary tasks and taught by doing and Socratic enquiry. Collaborative projects are key in nurturing students with varied skill-sets and rooting a rewarding and effective creative business landscape for the future.

References

Bof Team. (May 2021) *What the NFT Goldrush Means for Fashion.* Business of Fashion. https://www.businessoffashion.com/podcasts/technology/nft-fashion-podcast

Cole, M. et al. (eds.) (1978) *L.S. Vygotsky: Mind in society: the development of higher psychological processes.* London: Harvard University Press.

Ekstract, Steven. (May 2021) Jing Daily. *CollaBrands: Adidas Goes Green in Sustainability Partnerships with Disney and Depop.* https://jingdaily.com/collabrands-adidas-goes-green-in-sustainability-partnerships-with-disney-and-depop/

Fitzwaters, Lynda. (June 2021). *Business School TEAMs general meeting, reflection,* BSCI, University for the Creative Arts, UK

Granskog, Anna; Lee, Libbi; Magnus, Karl-Hendrik, Sawers, Corrine. (July 2020) *McKinsey: Survey: Consumer Sentiment on Sustainability in Fashion.* https://www.mckinsey.com/industries/retail/our-insights/survey-consumer-sentiment-on-sustainability-in-fashion

La Ferla, Ruth. (August 2019) *New York Times: You've Heard of the Drop? Target had it First.* https://www.nytimes.com/2019/08/28/style/youve-heard-of-the-drop-target-had-it-first.html

Mallevays, Pierre. (*BoF*, May 11 2021). *Are Luxury Brands Pushing too many Collaborations?* https://www.businessoffashion.com/opinions/finance/are-luxury-brands-pushing-too-many-collaborations.

Mower, Sarah. (December 2020). With Balenciaga's New Gaming App, Afterworld, Demna Gvasalia Makes the "Quantum Leap" the Industry has been Waiting For. *Vogue Magazine.* https://www.vogue.com/fashion-shows/fall-2021-ready-to-wear/

Newman, Terry. (2019) Harper Collins. *Legendary Artists and the Clothes they Wore.*

Stran, Rory. (October 2017) *Eckhaus Latta's Brilliant Parody of a September Issue Revels in Magazine Culture.* i-D Magazine. https://i-d.vice.com/en_uk/article/59y97d/eckhaus-lattas-brilliant-parody-of-a-september-issue-revels-in-magazine-culture

Stenzel, Tess. (Feb 2021). *Big Fashion Brands back Bangladesh Recycling Scheme.* Fashion United. https://fashionunited.uk/news/fashion/big-fashion-brands-back-bangladesh-recycling-scheme/2021021253569

Statista. (August 2021) https://www.statista.com/statistics/1192573/daily-active-users-global-roblox/

Showstudio. (December 2020). *Fashion Roundtable Takes over Showstudio.* https://www.showstudio.com/projects/instagram-takeover-fashion-roundtableIn January 2021

10

Student Voices: Journalism in Creative Education

Charles Lambert

Abstract The University for the Creative Arts has, since the early 1990s, taught journalism within the Schools of Film & Media, Fashion and, more recently, the Business School for the Creative Industries. There have been more than half a dozen different journalism courses from the straightforward (BA Journalism) to the highly niche (BA Automotive Journalism) and the combined (BA Journalism & Creative Writing). This overview of undergraduate journalism at UCA, 2003–2019, unpicks some of the key concerns of student writers and broadcasters during this period and, in particular, the balance between what might be termed big P political stories (such as national protests or debates) and small p personal political stories (for example relating to sexuality or mental health). It argues that student journalists have not shied away from difficult or contentious political issues, but the language used to discuss their anxieties has changed. Finally, it reflects on the role that changing institutional priorities may have on the content of student publications.

C. Lambert (✉)
University for the Creative Arts, Farnham, UK
e-mail: Philip.Powell@uca.ac.uk

P. Powell, B. Shankar Nayak (eds.), *Creative Business Education*,
https://doi.org/10.1007/978-3-031-10928-7_10

169

Introduction

The expansion of university education is one of the largest social changes in post-war British history. In 1997, Dearing's report into National Committee of Inquiry into Higher Education estimated that overall participation in higher education had increased from just over 5% of 18–19 year-olds in 1961 to 33% in 1995 (Dearing 1997); by 2019/20, using the UK government's new preferred measure of Higher Education Initial Entry Percentage, an estimated 53.4% of the population will embark on an HE course before their 30th birthday (Department for Education 2021).

This chapter is an attempt to understand the interests, concerns and motivation of students who would probably not have studied at university before 1997, using surviving pieces of published journalism.

There have been several studies in recent years looking at student protests over the post-war period (for example, Hanna 2008; Freeman 2014; Hensby 2014). Of these, Webster's (2015) thesis is of relevance to this research because it is based on analysis of student *journalism* at two institutions, the University of Manchester and the London School of Economics (LSE). She takes issue with the narrative that students since the 1960s have been largely apathetic 'pointing to student engagement in formal and informal political activity, such as political party membership, voluntary action and campaigning for NGOs and pressure groups' (ibid., p. 8).

Webster chose Manchester and the LSE because both had a consistent tradition of student journalism which enabled her to catalogue instances of student engagement with politics or protest. This is also the case at other universities; generations of students at Oxford University have worked on *Cherwell*, similarly Kingston students on *The River* and York students on *Nouse*. By contrast, UCA students have been free to develop their own publications and each cohort has been free to impose its own personality and house style on the newspapers and magazines they produce. Thus, the print titles analysed here include *The Tab, The Farnham Chronicle, Herald, Canvas, The Blackwater Bulletin, Scoop, No Idea, Scintilla* and *Emergence*. While this may have had benefits for freedom of expression, it could be argued that the continued presence of an established title enables student journalists to act as watchdogs, consistently holding university management to account and, in Matheson's words (2010) '*often spectacularly, to be carrying out the fourth estate role described in the Anglo-American liberal traditio*". (This author once worked in the press office at another university and recalls the sense of concern when a new edition of the student newspaper was due to come out.) From the point of view of a researcher, a run of publications and a rigorous system of archiving, provides a reliable set of data to analyse. As will be seen, the material available at UCA proves to be much more sporadic.

The University for the Creative Arts is a good example of a post-Dearing university. It became a university in 2008, following the merger of the Kent and Surrey Institutes of Art and Design, which were themselves amalgamations of earlier art schools stretching back to the mid nineteenth century. Many students are the first in their family to attend university or even to engage in any form of post-16 education. It is, thus, to be expected that the principal concerns of UCA students will be different to those at the longer-established and more traditionally academic institutions addressed by Webster. In the 1960s, some of the most-publicised and longest-running student protests took place at art schools and colleges such as Hornsey, Brighton and Guildford (McLoughlin 2019), the last-named being one of UCA's predecessor institutions. In the 1970s, they were breeding grounds for music scenes such as punk. For example, Viv Albertine (2014, pp. 62–86), guitarist in punk band The Slits, describes meeting members of Wire and the Clash at art colleges and first seeing the Sex Pistols perform at Chelsea School of Art. Given this tradition, it would be surprising to find that arts students have been apathetic or quiescent for the past four decades.

Since 1993, the University for the Creative Arts (UCA) has offered a range of journalism provision including BA Journalism, BA Automotive Journalism, BA Fashion Journalism, BA Journalism & Creative Writing, BA Lifestyle Journalism, BA Music Journalism and BA Sports Journalism. Most of these have sat within the School of Film and Media, with journalism courses moving to the Business School for the Creative Industries in 2019. All the media studied in this chapter was produced at UCA's campus at Farnham in Surrey (previously the Surrey Institute for Art and Design University College) though, on occasion, students have attempted to report on news from UCA's other campuses in the south of England.

Academic interest in student journalism in the United States has grown as it is seen as a '*nontraditional data source*' (Seitz et al. 2018) and a more effective way of understanding students' opinions than either official university documentation or external news media. Reimold (2010) argues that the distinctive feature of student journalism in the first decade of this century was the growing number of sex columns and sex magazines and the boldness of their content. In the second decade, students began to realise that employers might be able to look up their student journalism or that opinions expressed while at college could be used against them as they started out in professional media careers (Guardian 2021). As a result, student journalism appears to have become more cautious when addressing sexuality with significant self-censorship or external censorship (Nicolini and Filak 2020).

By contrast, there has been less analysis of student journalism in the UK and, while this chapter can offer no more than an imperfect snapshot of a single university, one of its aims is to find out whether some of the same trends can be detected.

Method

The inspiration for this article was the discovery, in summer 2020, of a pile of old student newspapers and magazines found in a previously underused office when staff returned to UCA's Farnham campus after the first pandemic-induced lockdown. The collection, ranging from 2003 to 2017, is clearly incomplete; it includes, for example, issues one and four of *Canvas*, published in December 2007 and May 2009 respectively, but there is no sign of issues two and three nor five or later. Just three pages of The Tribune (2005) and Blackwater Bulletin (2012) have survived, possibly suggesting they were intended as practice exercises in page layout rather than papers intended for wider distribution.

There were plans for an exhibition of student work in summer 2021 and the organisers kindly accepted the newspapers. The first draft of this article was an attempt to contextualise the collection for visitors to the exhibition which ended up being cancelled due to a lockdown in late Spring. By this time, it appeared that the student journalism warranted more sustained analysis.

The first stage in this research involved collecting all the available student publications from 2003 to 2019. This did not entail finding every piece of student journalism from this period (which would have clearly generated an unmanageable amount of content) but, rather, publications produced by entire cohorts of students and intended for wide distribution among the student body. This included newspapers, magazines, radio and television news programme and websites.

The process itself proved quite interesting. A surprising number of newspapers—traditionally derided as tomorrow's fish and chip wrapping—had survived. A few TV and radio programmes had been stored on DVDs but these were largely unplayable; the television programmes used in this analysis date from 2015 or later and were stored online but, even in recent years, some episodes have been taken down and lost for copyright reasons. Contrary to expectations, online journalism proved the most perishable; generally, websites were set up for specific projects and then not maintained or links lost. There may be more UCA journalism available online but it is not always easy to find. For more reflection on the challenges of maintaining an archive of student work, see Barwell 2015).

Some media was excluded: anything incomplete and work where external influences appeared to dictate the content (for example, a television bulletin made up solely of pictures supplied that day by Reuters).

The next stage involved analysing the covers or lead stories from the various media. From this, a very general narrative emerged which is summarised in part one, below.

Finally, all the stories in the surviving media were analysed and divided into a set of broad categories with a view to finding out how student interests changed between the earlier part of this period (2003–2009) and the later part (2015–18). (There was very little surviving media from 2010–2014.) This is explained in part two.

Findings: Part One—Covers or Lead Stories

In 2003–2005, *The Tab's* covers appeared to be deliberately provocative with eye-catching tabloid-style stories. The newspaper's strapline was '*The Tab—you gotta pick it up*' and the writers appeared to be stretching their creativity to get fellow students to do just that. The December 2004 issue of *The Tab* has three front cover stories. The top half of the cover is promoting the paper's page 3, on which a male and female student pose largely naked except for underwear. Below that, is a dramatic headline '*Terrorists hit London*' with a picture of St Paul's cathedral exploding. T his turns out to be the work of a first-year photography student. '*I want to get a reaction from people who actually see their own town and country getting rampaged*,' says the photographer Sveinung Skaalnes. (This was published eight months before the first major terror attack in London on 7th July 2005.) Finally, the '*lead*' story '*Pavement Porn*' which claims that a stack of pornographic magazines was left, by a distributor on a Farnham street.

The Tab appears to have been heavily influenced by the '*lad culture*' of the late 1990s, typified by the magazine *Loaded*. Although, creditably, it does attempt to aspire to a degree of gender balance such as by including a page 3 girl and boy, a feature on Ann Summers parties and a review of sex toys, the headline '*Hello Boys*' appears more targeted at male readers. There is also little consideration of readers who are not heterosexual. Its one foray into '*political*' opinion is to criticise Surrey Institute for building a lecture hall, taking up part of the carpark: '*outraged students have been left confused over SIAD's £1m extension as they feel the money could have been better spent on refurbishing the car park*' (The Tab, 2004).

Three years later, *The Tab* had been succeeded by a very different publication *Canvas* which published its first edition in December 2007. Staff who were at the university during this period (2007–2009) have revealed that this was a student-led publication. As well as writing the magazine, students paid for printing by selling advertising and through grants from the Student Union although a study of messages exchanged on Facebook suggests there was some organisation and direction from staff. Although the two surviving issues date from 2007 and 2009, as late as February

2011, students were still offering ideas for the paper though it seems unlikely that one was published that year.

The tone of *Canvas* is more overtly political. Its first headline (Canvas 2007) is '*We Want Wireless: Why Keycom isn't working*', referring to a crude early form of wifi which was supplied, in return for a subscription fee, to students living in halls of residence. The front cover of the other surviving issue of *Canvas* (number 4, 2009) shows students carrying placards and wearing bin bags as part of a protest against a round of staff cuts that was taking place at the time. *Canvas* clearly opposes the cuts in the editorial pages of the paper. (The bin bags were being worn because students thought the proposed changes were '*rubbish*'.)

It is tempting to suppose that *Canvas* died due to official pressure from University management. Staff from the time, however, say that the University leadership approved of *Canvas* as its existence provided more evidence that UCA was a true university (it was granted full university status in September 2008). Instead the problem was more that student interest was shifting more towards broadcast and online journalism and away from print. This is borne out by the Facebook messages which show only passing interest in production meetings, and frequent cancellations, throughout 2010–2011.

This may, partially at least, explain why, when the current author arrived at UCA as Course Leader for Journalism, Sports Journalism and Journalism & Creative Writing in 2014, there was no student newspaper. The next to be published was *The Scoop* in 2016. *The Scoop* was in the fortunate position of having a major national news story on its doorstep: junior doctors were out on strike—only the second National Health Service strike in the previous 40 years—in response to new contracts that were being brought in as part of Health Secretary Jeremy Hunt's attempts to create 7-day-a-week provision. Hunt was Farnham's Member of Parliament and, as a result, doctors' leaders and other protestors were regular visitors to the town. Although the strike dominates the front page (Scoop, 2016), it is interesting to note that there is no editorial comment on the dispute anywhere else in the paper.

The Scoop was to be the last newspaper produced by UCA students. Thereafter, this study focuses on a selection of magazines and television news bulletins. While the headline stories on UCA television tend to follow a serious news agenda (stories include the redevelopment of Farnham, the impact of Brexit and ram raids on cash dispensers), the magazines offer more clues to student concerns. Perhaps the most eye-catching cover is for one titled No Idea (2017). It shows a crudely drawn human head and brain. Inside the brain, are words such as Reading, family, LECTURES, STRESS, bills, £££, friends, work, sex, cleaning, drugs? COOKING, EVERYTHING. It is an attempt to depict the inside of a student's mind, one that is cluttered and congested. Several articles in the magazine discuss mental health; not always as a central topic but as something to discuss with interviewees. There was evidence of this in the other magazines and even in the television programmes (for example, a series of '*vox pop*' interviews asking whether human beings will have chips implanted in their brains in the near future).

So, a broad overview of the media produced at UCA suggested that one of the major changes between the early years of the twenty-first century and the late 2010s was an increased sense of stress, anxiety and worry and a move away from the journalism of politics and protest. However, this was not supported by closer study of the media.

The Findings: Part Two—Quantitative Analysis

For quantitative analysis, only complete media products were studied. This excluded the newspapers from which only a few pages have survived. Publications produced on behalf of other organisations (eg Glue, a magazine for the Student Union) were not studied, nor those where the content was heavily influenced by external companies (eg television or radio bulletins made up of material shared by Reuters or Independent Radio News). This left two distinct '*clusters*' of media: four newspapers from 2003–2009 and mixed media (magazines, television bulletins and one newspaper) from 2015–2019.

In the first cluster, 177 separate stories were identified; in the second, 290. These were split into the following categories:

University News;
Local News (Surrey and North-East Hampshire);
National News;
International News;
Local/student arts and entertainment;
National or International arts and entertainment;
Health and Wellbeing;
Sport;
Technology;
Travel and Motoring;
Finance;
Study or career advice;
Cookery.

The categories are inevitably arbitrary. Fashion was included in '*arts and entertainment*', whereas video games were categorized under '*technology*'. There were stories that could have gone under '*career advice*' or '*finance*' and some that could have been classed as '*finance*' or '*cookery*'. For example, a piece from *The Tab* compared the cost of a basket of food at the four main supermarkets which revealed that you could buy a loaf of bread, a Pot Noodle, a block of cheese, a tin of baked beans, a pizza and a bottle of white wine for just £5.59 at Lidl in 2004 (op. cit.).

Four stories from 2003–2009 defied classification: the aforementioned Page Three, a first person piece about visiting a tattoo parlour, advice on how to play air guitar and a comment piece asking whether today's students are more boring than their predecessors. There were three stories that were not classified in the 2015–2019 section: one giving advice on buying Christmas presents, a report on where to find a decent Vegan Christmas dinner in Farnham and a vox pop which asked whether we start celebrating Christmas too soon.

In the 2003–2009 period, the most popular categories were:

1. National or International arts and entertainment (22.6% of stories);
2. University News (12.99%);
3. Sport (12.43%);
4. Local/student arts and entertainment (9.6%)

For the later period, this had changed to:

1. Sport (23.1%);
2. Local News (20.69%—up from 7.34%);
3. National or International arts and entertainment (16.9%);
4. National News (14.14%—up from 5.65%)

University News had fallen to 0.69% while Local/student arts and entertainment fell slightly to 7.59%. (For full results, see Appendix one.)

Some of these changes can be explained by institutional factors. Most obviously, during the later period, UCA was running a Sports Journalism degree which only began life at the tail-end of *Canvas'* existence. The sharp decline in university news may be a reflection of the priorities of the accrediting body, the Broadcast Journalism Training Council, which discouraged students from reporting their own friends' and peers' activities. There is a nearly six-fold drop in the number of travel and motoring stories reflecting the fact that it is hard for broadcast journalists to film abroad—though one pair of students did make inventive use of green screen to film a report about the cost of holidaying by the Mediterranean, the Caribbean or in ski resorts.

In both periods, the classification method, counting *stories,* probably led to an overemphasis on '*National or International arts and entertainment*' because many of these stories were very short. For example, a five line review of a film or album was counted as one story just as a double page spread about changes to student funding also counted as one story. Had another method been deployed, such as column inches, the outcomes would have been very different.

Nonetheless, there are some clear patterns that can be detected. The overall proportion of news, across the four categories listed, has increased by nearly ten per cent from just under 30% to nearly 40%. This may, in part, owe something to the more '*newsy*' nature of television bulletins (though not of magazines) but it hardly suggests that the 2015–2019 students were apathetic and not interested in politics or current affairs. In a similar vein, the idea that these later students were obsessed with deadlines and careers is not born out by the data as the number of stories focussing on study or career advice dropped from 2.26% to just 0.69%.

Perhaps the most surprising finding was that, notwithstanding the arresting cover of *No Idea,* the expected growth in stories dealing anxiety, wellbeing and mental health did not materialise. This category dropped slightly from 7.34% to 4.14%. Although the words *'mental health'* do not appear in any issues of either *The Tab* or *Canvas,* anxieties about money, friends and sex very clearly do. The language may have changed but the issues have not.

Conclusions

The past, even the recent past, has a capacity to surprise us. Current students, when shown the 2004 issue of The Tab with its attention-grabbing headlines, are often surprised that their predecessors adopted such a *'lad-dish'* approach—or that their lecturers would let them. Conversely, the 2004 generation might wonder why the team responsible for No Idea chose such a downbeat cover.

Broadly speaking, Reimold's idea that students were much bolder in their handling of sex matters in the first decade of the twenty-first century is repeated at UCA. As well as the Page Three and sex toys stories already referred to, students produced a bullish advice page (including recommending to one letter writer that she go ahead and have an affair with her step-brother). As well as being a form of lad, or ladette, culture, this is perhaps a reflection of young people's excitement at the freedom that the world wide web, in its early days, appeared to offer.

There is also support for Webster's thesis that British students continued to be engaged with politics and protest throughout the period under discussion; UCA students covered protests against student fee changes and conflict in Syria. However, this research did not find any evidence of political party membership or *'campaigning for NGOs and pressure groups'* among UCA students.

It is notable that there is less journalism in the later period which is critical of UCA, or its management, directly. As journalism lecturers, we often discouraged students from writing about student issues on the basis that we want students to develop the confidence approach external organisations to request interviews but there is a place for bold student journalists who are prepared to investigate their own university, such as those at Penn State who have reported on the impact of a sexual assault on their college (Allen 2021).

One story crops up on three separate occasions, in 2003, 2007 and 2018–2019. In it, students are sent to the charity shops of Farnham to try to find stylish outfits for as little money as possible. This highlights the most striking finding of this research: the extent of continuity across the period studied. While the brash style of *The Tab* may have disappeared, its concerns are very similar to those of modern students. The notion that twenty-first century students are either more apathetic or more '*woke*' than their predecessors is not shown in this collection of journalism.

Appendix: Analysis of UCA Student Journalism by Story Category

Table One: Stories in UCA student newspapers 2003–2009

	2003	2004	2007	2009	TOTAL	%
University news	1	9	6	7	23	12.99
Local news	2	7	3	1	13	7.34
National news	5	1	2	2	10	5.65
International			7		7	3.95
Local or student arts & entz	1	2	9	5	17	9.60
National or international arts & entz (including music & fashion)	10	6	9	15	40	22.60
Health and wellbeing	8	2	1	2	13	7.34
Sport	6	7	4	5	22	12.43
Technology (including games)	2	7		2	11	6.21
Travel and motoring	5	1		1	7	3.95
Finance	3		1		4	2.26
Study or career advice		1	1	2	4	2.26
Cookery		1	1		2	1.13
	43	44	44	42	173	97.74
Unclassified		3	1		4	2.26
Total	43	47	45	42	177	100.00

Table Two: Stories in UCA student journalism (mixed media) 2015–2019

	2015 (TV)	2016 (TV)	2016 (newspaper)	2017 (magazines)	2017 (TV)	2018–2019 (TV)	Total	%
University news	1	1					2	0.69
Local news	18	19	2		8	13	60	20.69
National news	9	17	5		8	2	41	14.14
International	3	1	1		6		11	3.79
Local or student arts & entz	7	4		4	5	2	22	7.59
National or international arts & entz (including music & fashion)	8	10	17	6	8		49	16.90
Health and wellbeing	1		2	5	2	2	12	4.14
Sport	13	25	8	8	7	6	67	23.10
Technology (including games)	1			3	2	4	10	3.45
Travel and motoring					2		2	0.69
Finance		2		3	2		7	2.41
Study or career advice				1	1		2	0.69
Cookery		1	1				2	0.69
	61	80	36	30	51	29	287	98.97
Unclassified	1					2	3	1.03
Total	62	80	36	30	51	31	290	100.00

References

Albertine, V (2014) *Clothes, Music, Boys A Memoir,* London: Faber & Faber

Allen, B (2021) *The 10-year anniversary of the Jerry Sandusky indictments challenged Penn State journalists to dig deep and stand by their work* at https://www.poynter.org/reporting-editing/2021/the-10-year-anniversary-of-the-jerry-sandusky-indictments-challenged-penn-state-journalists-to-dig-deep-and-stand-by-their-work/ Last accessed 10/01/2022.

Barwell, C (2015) *Whose Memory? Reflections on the Construction of an Archive, or Canute Against the Waves of Oblivion* Cahier Louis-Lumière 2015, 9 pp. 11–15

Canvas (2007) *Canvas Issue One 2007* [author's own collection]

Canvas (2009) *Canvas Issue Four 2009* [author's own collection]

Dearing, Sir R (1997) *The Dearing Report: Higher Education in the learning society, Main Report* at http://www.educationengland.org.uk/documents/dearing1997/index.html. Last accessed 10/01/2022.

Department for Education (2021) *Participation measures in higher education* at https://explore-education-statistics.service.gov.uk/find-statistics/participation-measures-in-higher-education/2019-20#releaseHeadlines-charts. Last accessed 10/01/2022.

Freeman, R (2014) *Student Voice: New forms of power and governance in Higher Education in England (2003-2013),* thesis submitted to the University of Birmingham for the degree of Doctor of Philosophy

Guardian (2021) *Outcry after Associated Press journalist fired amid row over pro-Palestinian views* at https://www.theguardian.com/media/2021/may/21/associated-press-emily-wilder-fired-pro-palestinian-views Last accessed 10/01/2022.

Hanna, E. (2008) The English Student Movement: An Evaluation of the Literature, *Sociology Compass,* 2:5. pp. 1539–1552.

Hensby, A (2014): *Exploring participation and non-participation in the 2010/11 student protests against fees and cuts,* thesis submitted for the degree of Doctor of Philosophy at University of Edinburgh

Matheson, Donald (2010) "The Watchdog's New Bark: Changing Forms of Investigative Reporting". In *The Routledge Companion to News and Journalism,* Edited by: Allen, Stuart. 82–92. London: Routledge.

McLoughlin, M. (2019). The textile student needs little Giotto, (or a little will go a long way)' (Pevsner. Nov 1968). The 1970 Coldstream Report in response to the art school unrest of 1968. *Journal of Design History,* 32(2), 170–187. https://doi.org/10.1093/jdh/epy049 Last accessed 10/01/2022.

Nicolini, Kristine M. & Vincent F. Filak (2020) *Overt censorship, self-censorship, and gender bias: an examination of high school journalism students and controversial media topics*, Atlantic Journal of Communication, https://doi.org/10.1080/15456870.2020.1832094

No Idea (2017) *No Idea Term Two 2016–2017* [author's own collection]

Reimold, D (2010) *Sex and the University Celebrity, Controversy, and a Student Journalism Revolution* New Brunswick: Rutgers University Press

The Scoop (2016), *The Scoop April 2016* [author's own collection]

Seitz M, Kabir Z, Greiner BA and Davoren MP (2018) *Student, Faculty, and Staff Approval of University Smoke/Tobacco-Free Policies: An Analysis of Campus Newspaper Articles, Tobacco Use Insights* Volume 11: 1–10

The Tab (2004), *Friday 10th December 2004* [author's own collection]

Webster, S (2015), *Protest Activity in the British Student Movement, 1945 to 2011* A thesis submitted to The University of Manchester for the degree of Doctor of Philosophy in the Faculty of Humanities

11

Hyper-Reality: A Dangerous Modern Phenomenon

David Faulkner

Abstract Hyper-reality is a concept whose coinage can be traced back to the sociologist Baudrillard in his work Simulacra and Simulation (1981). In this philosophical thesis Baudrillard tries to explain shared experience. By Simulacra he means a description of things that either never existed or are copies of those which no longer have an original. Simulation is the imitation of the operation of an existing way of doing things by others. It was substantially further popularised by the literary and philosophical polymath Eco (Travels in Hyper-reality C. Steiner, *Journal of Tourism and Cultural Change* 2010, Taylor and Francis, 1985). In the new digital world of the 2020s however, it is being superseded by the evolution of virtual reality, augmented reality and extended reality (Microsoft 2021) and subsumed into the new Metaverse (Facebook 2021), a strong perceptual competitor amongst the young to the world of traditional reality. The chapter explores hyperreality as a modern phenomenon.

D. Faulkner (✉)
Business School for the Creative Industries, University for the Creative Arts, Farnham, UK
e-mail: Philip.Powell@uca.ac.uk

© The Author(s), under exclusive license to Springer Nature Switzerland AG 2022
P. Powell, B. Shankar Nayak (eds.), *Creative Business Education*,
https://doi.org/10.1007/978-3-031-10928-7_11

185

Introduction

Hyper-reality is a process of distorting reality or realities. This is how it is generally used in modern times, but it should be noted that this form of 'reality' has been in existence as long as homo sapiens has existed, although not with such an evocative title. Animals on cave walls from pre-historic times could credibly make claims to be examples of hyper-reality, as could all attempts to develop 'models' of reality rather than to explicitly describe 'the real thing'.

In Times Past and Present

Within this broad definition hyper-reality may be applied with justification to all fantasies and dreams, to the paintings and other similar artefacts and stories of religious orders from at least mediaeval times and more recently; all paintings that are less accurate in depiction than photographs; even some '*artistic*' photographs can also be thought of as examples of hyper-reality under the above definition.

Moving on in the modern world, movies and videos may come within the definition of hyper-reality, but more pertinently perhaps are the imaginary worlds created by Walt Disney (2001–2066) and in the late twentieth century by J.K.Rowling (1956–)with her fictional tales of witches, spells and wizards at Hogwarts with the friends and enemies of Harry Potter. Even more fantastically are the areas of digital games and of avatars and other fictional beings clothed in human form, but owing their existence to the wonders of artificial intelligence.

Current 'Reality'

Much of what purports to be current affairs or even the writings of eminent historians may be claimed by hyper-reality rather than factual evidence-based reality. Books on the second World War (as well as the first) will tell different stories depending on whether they are written in

Japan, Russia, UK or the USA and this is how it is always been. Some of this is due to writers' bias of historians and others to the accepted myths of totalitarian governments deliberately distorting the recounting of past events in order to brain-wash the minds of their citizens. Note in December 2021 how the Russian establishment is resisting any history which describes the savage events of the Stalin era where it is estimated that 20 million Russians died at the hands of the state. History it is said with some truth is *'the story told by the winners'*.

More intentionally fictional, but still claiming some aspect of reality for the reader, are the writings of historical novelists. Can Hilary Mantel's (2020) recounting of the supposed conversations between Thomas Cromwell and King Henry VIII be regarded as real. I suspect not. They are but the surmising of a historical writer imagining what might have been said given certain *'real'* outcomes. Who is to say, if Ms. Mantel's work survives and that of others does not, whether future generations may come to regard historical fiction as historical fact.

However, the writing of history even by those without any ideological or national bias is likely to depend on which written evidence survives the damages of time. Egyptian stone and parchment information gives us an idea of the past when all are long dead, and from archaeological digs we have to construct the more distant past often with much imagination and guesswork. To many non-scientists the theories of the origins of the universe as a result of Big Bang and the claims of quantum mechanics seem like hyper-reality, even if they are accepted as true by scientists. Of course, we are generally unlikely to accept that the claims of flat-earthers that the world is flat and not spherical is nonsense. There is adequate understandable evidence for the spherical explanation as there is for the contention that the world goes around the sun and not vice-versa. However, Michael Angelo got into some trouble with the church in claiming heliocentricity some centuries ago. So, which of our current scientific certainties may be disproved in subsequent years?

In the field of politics few members of that fraternity can with hand on heart claim veracity in all the speeches they make and writings they publicise. Which of the worlds of Presidents Trump and Biden are the closer to actual reality will be judged differently by their respective supporters.

When we see the Crown on TV in 2021 how much are we to believe? The writers even admit they made up certain characters to improve the story. Was Princess Margaret really like that? How much of the iconography of Princess Diana can we believe?

Even Economics and Management varies according to when you were taught; students from the 1960s will swear by John Maynard Keynes (1883–1946) and his theories of controlling the economy through the manipulation of effective demand. Those between 1970 and the noughties are more likely to look at money supply and the Chicago school. However, by 2020 Keynes was returning as the received doctrine. Where is truth?

In sum, all our narratives and the stories we tell get embellished with retelling. Our inclination as we get older is to replay our life's history in our minds, so that we appear in a good light. We need to do this, if we are to retain our self-respect, and thereby the reality of the past gets insidiously replaced by the hyper-reality of the present.

Does It Matter?

In many situations the encounter with hyper-reality is quite harmless and indeed entertaining. For example Disney, Harry Potter, Philip Pullman's character Lyra, like the Famous Five of Enid Blyton (1942) before them have entertained many millions of people of all ages, and neither lured them into believing in the unbelievable or into anti-social forms of behaviour clearly damaging to society. Rowling's books have not led to the growth of many schools of witchcraft in the UK or elsewhere or to the belief by young people that the spell '*expecto patronus*' if uttered with an appropriate wave of the wand will have dramatic and magical results.

But not so harmless are statements attributed to Donald Trump that '*Bleach may cure COVID*' or the dismissing by leaders like Bolsinaro of Brazil of COVID as an illness of little importance. Many Brazilians have died as a result of such irresponsible statements. Hitler's depiction of the Master race in the 1930s led to the second world war, many millions of dead and a ravaged world economy. The ISIS ideology with its violent distortion of the tenets of the Muslim religion has also led to terrible suffering in the regions where ISIS has gathered support and in an area like

USA which is seen as the Great Satan and has led to the Twin Towers disaster of 2001. S imilarly, the recent overrunning of Afghanistan by the Taliban has led to a whole nation of women in that country losing their chances of having a life appropriate to their talents or even any reasonable life at all beyond that of housewife.

Perhaps less dramatically, but still insidiously, distortions of history in national educational syllabuses and out of date courses has led to poor education of the young. Ian Hislop, a perceptive humourist and commentator, in a series on the BBC in 2021 described the English public school system and by imitation the grammar school one too, as being founded on the need by a smallish middle class elite to govern India in the times of the British Raj with the principal value system being to ' *keep a stiff upper lip*' and demonstrate a calm amateurism rather than exhibit the professionalism of skills such as engineering. Generations have suffered as a result and still do.

Conventional opinions presented as fact are also dangerous to society and may be included broadly in the damaging list of hyper-reality. In England Northerners are sometimes portrayed (especially in the North) as more friendly than Southerners. Similarly, different society damaging conventional opinions are attributed by the English to the Welsh, the Scottish and the Irish. This is of course not limited to the British Isles as any Scandinavian will admit. Insular nationalism exists in their part of the world too and elsewhere.

Much of Social Media, where there is little or no censorship of hate speech, extreme pornography, violent ideology or personal vilification of those of whose opinions the writer disapproves, may be classed as falling within the bounds of hyper-reality that matters to society in a damaging way.

In the work of Matsuda (2016) what is real and what is fiction are blended together so that there is no clear distinction between where one ends and the other begins. Genies is an avatar company that believes everyone will need an avatar to represent themselves one day.

What Is Truth?

Hyper-reality is a simulation that does not in fact depict anything with a real existence at all it is suggested, but which nonetheless comes to constitute reality. Or in a broader definition it represents untrue pictures of the world.

So what is reality to one person may be hyper-reality to others. In 1955 national grieving and the sending of a multitude of wreaths to the BBC and the jamming of the BBC switchboard for 48 hours followed the fictional death of Grace Archer, a much-loved character in the Archers on the BBC Radio soap series of that name.

Against all the evidence, Trump supporters still believe that their champion won the 2020 US presidential election and had it stolen from him. No amount of evidence seems to have had any effect in changing their minds.

What is truth then? We need to consult philosophy in order to make a sensible attempt to answer the question, which is one that has been troubling moral philosophers for millenia. Speaking as no philosopher, but as someone who studied the subject for one year at University, I have concluded the following.

There are four possible basic statements that can be made:

1. Logical or mathematical statements—eg. $2 + 2 = 4$. Such statement are true when you accept the basic axioms of mathematics.
2. Beliefs, especially religious doctrine—These are based on faith and have no need for evidence. They cannot be said to be objectively either true or untrue. Believers accept them and unbelievers do not. That is all there is to it in the end.
3. Facts—Some philosophers say facts cannot ultimately be proved to be true as they all depend on the sense data of the writer or speaker and this may vary from person to person. However in deference to Descartes (1596–1650) whose aphorism *cogito ergo sum*, '*I think therefore I am*', has survived the centuries, we should not totally dismiss this idea. However to deny the truth of known and accepted facts defies common sense and would make lives unliveable. Even sceptical

philosophers get in their cars, turn the key and expect the engine to start, despite their professed scepticism of the external world. It is a fact that London is the capital of the UK and that this is a chapter of a book and I am working on a lap top computer. These are facts.

4. Opinions—What are called opinions are somewhere between facts and hyper-reality, and some are credible but still quite uncertain to many people. For example: the statement '*the UK will benefit from having left the EU*' is a credible opinion, backed by evidence and held by many. However, the statement '*the UK will be irrevocably damaged by leaving the EU*' is also a credible opinion with evidence to support it, and also supported by many. Credible arguments can be advanced for both opinions. Therefore, an opinion is more fact than a belief, but not enough to make it a universally accepted fact.

Problems with Hyper-Reality

Someoftheproblemswithhyper-realityinitsbroaderdefinitionarethefollowing:-

- Pornography; real human beings are sometimes disappointed because their real life partners or possible partners are not as physically perfect as those seen on screen.
- With sex and violence so prevalent in movies, the impressionable may well seek to emulate this behaviour in real life. Knife crime growth may well have been stimulated by this.
- Seduction into believing in an imaginary world may result in taking unwise decisions as a result. Perhaps the growth of drug-taking may be influenced here.
- Stimulated by hyper-reality, distortion of judgement may lead to many of the above movements away from stable reality-based lifestyles.
- Sometimes commitment to extreme cults such as the Amish, Scientology or Plymouth Bretheren and consequent limitations to ones life chances may result.
- Additionally, the damage to the cohesion of society from movements away from reality and toward hyper-reality may lead to cynicism, or

the adoption of these way out cults in order to seek certainty or even to the acceptance of totalitarianism for the same reason.

Where Is Hyper-Reality Most Commonly Found?

The Entertainment Industry

The entertainment industry is where hyper-reality is to be found in abundance from science fiction to avatars or fantastic creatures like Lyra's daemon pantalaimon (Pullman 2012). This is generally harmless as no one reading watching or listening believes what is presented to be factual real life. This is as it claims, entertainment. The exploits of Batman, Wonder Woman and many other fictional characters are enjoyed but not seriously imitated. However, there is a dark side to the entertainment industry seen in excessively violent movies, crude language and hard-core pornography which would be given a poor rating by people concerned with the health of society, and much of this can be classed as hyper-reality.

News and Current Affairs

News and current affairs is an industry where the most all-embracing term used by its detractors as a purveyor of truth is '*Fake news*'. This combination of lies, distortions and deceitful propaganda is said to have originated in Macedonia in 2017, but was popularised energetically by Donald Trump in his campaign for the US presidency and with amazing effect. Huffpost through its contributor Johnson (2017) has identified five types of fake news most prominently but not exclusively found on Social Media.

1. 100% false statements eg. Pope Francis is dead; Sir Paul McCartney is dead.
2. Slanted and biased reporting eg. denying climate change or the efficacy of the covid vaccines.

3. Pure propaganda; an overlap with 2. but often specifically directed towards political objectives and programmes.
4. Misuse of data; statistics can always be used to claim as facts surveys using undisclosed often extreme assumptions.eg *beer is good for your brain* a research project tested on mice not humans.
5. Imprecise statements; eg 1 in 5 CEOs are psychopaths.

The Digital Gaming Industry

This industry is strongly focused on the creating of hyper-reality games and figures, eg Pokemon, generally to attract young participants who then spend an inordinate amount of time on their smart phones rather than interacting with fellow human beings in the real world. The games designers create new and attractive worlds like Fortnite, Minecraft, Pokemon and Roblex to attract the young. Arguably this may stunt the development of their social skills if they spend too much time on their smart phones and tablets.

Education

Perhaps the most important and also the most vulnerable area where hyper-reality has an impact is the education industry. Many untruths and biased statements are smuggled into educational courses and claim the minds and evolving value systems of the young. Hyper-reality blends the fictional and imaginary with the real and true and makes distinction between the two nigh on impossible when the ideas are professed by authority figures. Thus, children taught in China are likely to graduate believing in Communism, and those taught in religious schools are likely to adopt and profess a faith reflecting that of the school. This is not inevitable and many are able to exercise independent judgement, but it would be unwise to underate the impact of specifically directed teaching on human minds if subjects and themes are carefully selected. Here hyper-reality is to be regarded with caution.

In Sum

Hyper-reality in its broad definition above covers a very wide range of activities and statements including pretty well everything that is deliberately and intentionally untrue. This is too wide an area for an apparently technical term to be definitionally useful in language. It needs a narrower definition and therefore a sharper focus.

As described above and used on-line and journalistically, hyper-reality covers four quite distinct and different groups of activities and writings

1. Historical fiction
2. Fake news
3. Imaginary worlds
4. Artificially intelligence (AI) enabled games and allied activities

1. Historical fiction is a popular form of literature, in content half-way between a novel and a history book. We may learn a lot in British history that we never knew or have forgotten from our school days of the lives and times of the Tudors, Stuarts and Plantagenets inter alia; of the wars and their outcomes that shaped out nation and of the supposedly grand figures whose reputations were made or marred by them.

We have many authors of such very readable books at the current time but we can also legitimately go back to Shakespeare or further to find earlier such works. Was Richard III really such a bad man as Shakespeare portrays him? It would be difficult to resurrect his reputation given the play by the bard. And did Henry IV really undergo such a spiritual and character epiphany on achieving kingship as Shakespeare suggests? These writing were and are created to entertain, but they may also distort and perhaps have the last word if other countervailing evidence is no longer available to historians of the future. But tag them with the label of hyper-reality?. Let just call them historical novels.

2. Fake news, Within this category we can include a substantial proportion of the utterances of politicians, the writings of left or right wing political journalists or TV chat show commentators not bound by the requirements to be '*balanced*' in their comments. Without stretching too great a point we can include in this category virtually all advertisements

saying how great the offerings of their company are and how they will satisfy the needs of everyone who buys their products. We can also include much of social media that is for wide consumption and not merely chit-chat between friends. Much of this category is destructive of truth, damaging to society and encouraging of racism, ageism and all the other negative '*isms*' that plague our times. However, let's call the category fake news and not dignify it with the hyper-reality label.

3. Imaginary worlds. This is a category traced back to Walt Disney (1901–1966) who through animation and other then existing technologies starting in the 1920s brought to life Mickey Mouse, Cinderella, Snow White and the Seven Dwarfs and many more entrancing creations that have long outlived him. H e also created amusement parks in California, Florida and Paris that excited young children with their imaginary worlds and did no harm to anyone and certainly made great profits for the Disney Corporation. These imaginary worlds are not however limited to Walt Disney. J.K.Rowling conjured a fascinating fictional world from her imagination building on myths of witchcraft and wizardry, plus Scandinavian folklore tales and the basic structures of the British Public school system exemplified by Hogwarts. This has entranced children and their parents around the world for the past quarter century. Philip Pullman (1946) created another world with his series of books and films entitled His Dark Materials, describing and showing the exploits of Lyra Belacqua and her associates. This also included supernatural happenings and entry to a number of worlds and even universes plus a bedrock of Oxford University, Pullman's alma mater. These three imaginary worlds in particular have attracted audiences way beyond children themselves and can genuinely claim to be life and literature enhancing products of hyper-reality.

4. The world of AI entertainment. Digitally based entertainment is probably the greatest growth area of entertainment and of games in particular in the modern world and is mostly attributable to artificial intelligence. The recent announcement by Facebook (2021) that it would now use Meta as the name for its parent company drew the world's attention to a new and perhaps superseding concept to replace Hyper-reality, namely the Metaverse (Facebook 2021).

Virtual reality has been a minor part of movie experience for half a century or more. Older members of society remember '*going to the pictures*' back in the fifties and sometimes being given a pair of coloured glasses to help them see the screen in 3D. It never really caught on at that time. However virtual reality (VR) is now a major part of the gaming industry and seeks through its real world excluding headset to replace the actual world with a virtual one for the wearer. At the same time augmented reality (AR) another suite of contemporary technologies still lives in the real world but adds digital and virtual content to augment the environment the participant is actually experiencing. It is used in games such as Pokemon but also in industrial uses like construction. AR and VR plus holographic avatars combine their technologies within what Facebook and no doubt others in their futuristic world have dubbed the Metaverse (2021).

Once we delve into AI, we move out of the entertaining world of our teenagers and into the substantial world of AI where such matters are discussed. It poses the question What if AI is able to create a machine many times more intelligent and many times faster in evolutionary terms than humans? (Vinge 1993), This year's (Russell 2021) Reith lectures have focused on this issue. Scientists have grappled with this and allied issues since at least 1993, note the technological Singularity of AI (1993). Most of the points discussed in this chapter relate broadly to moral philosophy and the consideration of how we should behave in the interests of the planet's survival and the spreading of truth rather than fiction, and where it is fiction at least it should be of the harmless and entertaining kind.

The Singularity, possible through technology advance, is a much more serious matter and brings into question the possible either partnership or substitution of man by machines (Vinge 1993). There is a large literature on this subject some of it quite frightening. However AI in the world of the Singularity is quite distinct in terms of purpose to the world of hyper-reality of Baudrillard (1981).

Conclusion

So what are the boundaries to the world of Hyper-reality envisioned in its infancy by Baudrillard in 1981? The term has been expanded so that it has become almost meaningless, if it can be used for any experience which cannot be proved to be factually true. Thus it can be used to include propaganda, fake news, historical fiction and perhaps stories of any kind. There lies the end of a useful definition. This chapter suggests a tighter definition for hyper-reality. It should be applied to situations where an imaginary world is created, whether that be in Disney or Harry Potter mode or in the futuristic world of AR and VR where avatars tussle for space and prominence and mainly US based corporations vie for competitive advantage while the next generation of consumers excitedly embraces the next AI invention in the newly created Metaverse. But Hyper-reality, by this definition stops short of the vast literature on the Singularity.

It will be for social scientists, psychotherapists, PhD researchers and others to assess whether the largely young human psyche will be stable enough to withstand the convincing and sometimes probably overpowering assault on its traditional sense data streams and be strong enough to understand the difference between the worlds of reality and hyper-reality and maintain healthy social contacts and relationships with its real friends and other human contacts. We have all seen otherwise normal couples in restaurants ignoring their partners whilst engrossed digitally and exclusively on their smart phones. It could get worse in the Metaverse. All of this is challenge enough without embarking on exploring and indeed creating the possible future worlds of the Singularity, but who knows what the future might bring?

References

Baudrillard, J (1981) *Simulacra and Simulation*, University of Michigan, Ann Arbor

Blyton, E (1942) *The Famous Five*, Hodder and Stoughton.

Hilary Mantel, H. (2020) Wolf Hall, Fourth Estate, London.

Johnson, J. (2017) *Huffpost*

Matsuda, K. (2016) A Hyper-reality film

Pullman, P. (1946) The Subtle Knife, Scholastic, London

Pullman, P. (2012) *Dark Materials Omnibus: The Golden Compass; The Subtle Knife*; Knopf Books.

Russell S, (2021) Living with AI, Reith lectures BBC

Vinge, V. (1993) "The Coming Technological Singularity: How to Survive in the Post-Human Era" Archived 2018-04-10 at the Wayback Machine, in *Vision-21: Interdisciplinary Science and Engineering in the Era of Cyberspace*, G. A. Landis, ed., NASA Publication CP-10129, pp. 11–22.

12

Creative Tourism and Creative Tourists: A Review

Shawn Li and Gareth Shaw

Abstract Over the last two decades, creative tourism has been used in many countries to create tourism products, enhance the destination image, and develop sustainable tourism. This new type of tourism shifts the experience away from tangible sites towards the intangible heritage of the destination. Visitors develop their creativities through participation and engagement in the learning experience that is characteristic of local destinations. Due to its nature of growing the local economy through local skills and intellectual property relating to creativity and culture, creative tourism is seen as an extension of culture tourism that contributes to the creative economy. The concept and framework of creative tourism brings together an ecosystem that enhances the destination attractiveness and stimulates creative exports (OECD, *Tourism and the Creative Economy,*

S. Li (✉)
Business School for the Creative Industries, University for the Creative Arts, Farnham, UK
e-mail: Philip.Powell@uca.ac.uk

G. Shaw
University of Exeter, Exeter, UK

OECD Studies on Tourism. https://doi.org/10.1787/9789264207875-en, 2014). This paper reviews the birth and growth of creative tourism and the marketing theory underpinning this new type of tourism. A meta-analysis follows this to exhibit the recent output relating to the motivation to take creative tourism.

Introduction

The need for joint development between culture and tourism was first claimed in the 1970s (see for example IUOTO 1974; Patterson 1976). The notion of creative tourism was developed from cultural tourism, one of the major themes in tourism research since the 1970s. MacCannell referred to the term *'Culture Production'* (MacCannell 1976, p. 25), which entailed products that resulted from the process of culture. MacCannell further commented that tourism is the ideal subject in which to research culture production. Following this, Ritchie and Zins identified twelve key cultural elements of a region that attract tourism. Those are Traditions, Gastronomy, History, Architecture, Handicrafts, Leisure Activities, Art/Music, Language, Work, Dress, Education, Religion (Ritchie and Zins 1978). During their holiday, many tourists consume an element of culture, which was conceptualised as Culture Tourism by Smith (Shaw 1992a; Smith 1977).

The World Tourism Organisation brought a very early definition of cultural tourism: *'Culture tourism can also be defined in broad or in narrow terms. In the narrow sense, it includes movements of persons for essentially cultural motivations such as study tours, performing arts and cultural tours, travel to festivals and other cultural events, visits to sites and monuments, travel to study nature, folklore or art, and pilgrimages … In the broadest sense, all movements of persons might be included in the definition because they satisfy the human need for diversity, tending to raise the cultural level of the individual and giving rise to new knowledge, experience, and encounters'* (World Tourism Organization 1985, p. 6). This statement extended the organisation's earlier definition of cultural tourism, which focused only on the tourists' activity of discovering sites and monuments (World Tourism Organization 1985).

An early attempt to understand travellers' motivation to visit Europe highlighted the importance of the cultural aspect. According to a survey carried out by the European Travel Commission, the most prominent segmentation of travellers, accounting for 60 per cent of all travellers from the United States, was attracted by Europe's unique cultural qualities. In the UK, practitioners' attempts had been made as early as 1985 to stimulate the local economic growth through cultural activities. The cultural facilities and economic benefits drove the engagement from locals and tourists (Shaw 1992b). From the 1980s, the Greater London Council pioneered labelling Cultural Industries for cultural activities outside the public funding system (O'Connor 1999). As well as attracting overseas visitors, cultural and historic interest act as a vehicle to drive visitors intention for return visits; the strong interlink between culture and tourism contributed to the growth in many developing and developed economies (British Tourist Authority 1989; Shaw 1992a). At the EU level, the European Heritage Group reported that the visitors' volume at museums, monuments, and archaeological sites has doubled between 1977 and 1997 (European Commission 1998).

However, there were chicken-and-egg debates as to whether the growth in this period was attributed to visitors growing interested in culture or cultural attractions were visited more because there were more visitors in general. In the UK, cultural attractions between 1989 and 1997 saw a slower growth rate (Museums and galleries +14%; Historic properties +9%) compared to +15% growth rate of overall visits (British Tourist Authority 1989–1997) despite an emerging of cultural attractions. Taking museums, for example, the number of museums in the UK increased from 876 in 1963 to 2500 in 1989 (Walsh 2002). Similarly, in Spain, the number of museums doubled in the twenty years from the 1980s (Richards and Raymond 2000). Arguably, some fast-growing attractions (measured by visitor volume) such as Garden and Steam railways have a strong culture affiliate yet are not classified as cultural attractions. Richards (2001) agreed that the disproportional growth might have to do with the definition of culture—some new forms of cultural attractions may not be included in the tourism statistics.

Nevertheless, the supply of cultural attractions grew faster than demand in the 1990s (Richards 2001). General criticism argued that the mass and 'serial reproduction' of culture tourism dilutes the local culture for being commercialising the cultural activities and creating unnecessary cannibalisation (Crandall 1987; Harvey 2002; Shaw 1992a). Scholars and practitioners at that time started to explore more sustainable means of developing cultural tourism.

It is unclear how the term 'creative industry' has derived from the culture industry. One widely accepted explanation lies in the emerging and mass media production in the 1990s, such as software and audio-visual products, which is beyond the convention of the culture industry (Ratzenböck et al. 2004; Richards and Wilson 2007). Richards and Wilson (2007) point out that culture is perceived as static representing the past; creativity is needed to enhance the dynamism. Nevertheless, the establishment of the UK Creative Industries Task Force (CITF) in 1997 is seen as the formal origin of the concept of creative industry (Flew 2002). In its mapping document, the Creative Industries is defined as 'activities which have their origin in individual creativity, skill and talent, and which have a potential for wealth and job creation through the generation and exploitation of intellectual property' (2001, p. 5).

Since the conceptualisation of Creative Industries, there has been rapid growth in the literature surrounding policy, creativity, clusters and region (Flew 2002; Florida 2002; Richards and Wilson 2007; Rogerson 2007). In particular, Florida (2002) brought in a profound creative strategy, which connects creative production and consumption through the development of creative people, seeking to stimulate and capitalise on creative resources. In his book 'The Rise of the Creative Class', Florida suggested that regional economic advantage is shifting from fixed stocks such as natural resources, raw material or production lines to attracting and retaining talented people under low entry barriers and tolerant policies. The creative people collectively make up the Creative Class, so that the economy is shifting from the 'consumption of goods' to 'consumption of experience' (Florida 2002, p. 132). This idea somewhat resonates with Pine and Gilmore's view that the economic progression will evolve the consumption from commodities and goods to services and, eventually, experiences (Pine and Gilmore 1998). Many economics theories, including Pine and Gilmore's experience economy, were grounded through

Adam Smith's work (Smith 1776) on tangible goods, production, and value in exchange of surplus commodities.

Pine and Gilmore argued that during the economic progress, firms will enter a commoditised business unless they shift from selling goods and services which are considered fungible offers to staging memorable experiences through customer participation and connection (Pine and Gilmore 1998). However, Pine and Gilmore (2011) acknowledged the pitfall that when all competitors are offering experience, the movement will eventually commoditise the business. Therefore they suggested that firms customise and personalise the experience. In doing so, a 'Transformation' (p. 244) is offered to customise the experience, and the experience becomes unique to the customer (Pine and Gilmore 2011). In line with Pine and Gilmore's development of their model of economic progression, Boswijk et al. (2007) pointed out the stagging of fun and enjoyment experience in 1990s is the first generation which was primarily found in retailing, events, and group experiences; while the co-creation is manifested as the second generation of experience which focuses on an individual's own unique experiential needs.

This idea was widely used as a theoretical foundation to underpin the creative tourism literature. A common view is that the progression of economic value and its analysis of business (Pine and Gilmore 2011) were primarily based on the tourism and leisure sectors, such as theme parks, hotels, and restaurants from the United Sates, with evidence from a comparison of Experience and Transformation against other sectors' growth rate in terms of their nominal gross domestic product (GDP) between 1959 and 2009.

However, many studies have highlighted no evidence that GDP per capita and tourism competitiveness are correlated (see, for example, Korez-Vide 2013). On the other hand, Pine and Gilmore contended that the development of the economy would result in staged experience and transformation. However, early forms of creative tourism were identified in less developed economies in Asia (for example, Thailand, as discussed below) in the twentieth century. It is possible that the diffusion of creative tourism is not a linear process as per the experience economy states.

The rise of marketing theories shifts the focus from tangible goods production to the exchange of service provision (Lusch et al. 2007;

Terblanche 2014). Customers' participation in enhancing production was initially mentioned by Lovelock and Young (1979) and resonated by scholars in the following two decades, see, for example, Fitzsimmons (1985), Bowers et al. (1990), Firat et al. (1995), Prahalad and Ramaswamy (2000). Since Bowers et al. (1990) unlocked the idea that firms could view customers as employees in value creation, the advantage of customer co-creation has been found in effectively enhancing service quality (Lengnick-Hall 1996), achieving customer satisfaction (Van Raaij and Pruyn 1998) and value creation in innovation diffusion (Alexander et al. 2009). The most prominent work in analysing the changing role of consumers was the introduction of 'service-dominant logic' (S-D logic), as it connects with a wide range of work relating to 'consumption within both marketing itself and in the humanities and social science' (Alexander et al. 2009, p. 534). Vargo and Lusch (2004) argued that marketing inherited value exchange ideas from economics but more customer-centric and service-driven, that a reformulated thought, a service-dominant logic has emerged. This approach promotes the foundational principle (Table 12.1) that knowledge and skills is the fundamental basis of exchange. The idea is that customers are seen as a so-called 'operant resource'—a resource that that is 'capable of

Table 12.1 Foundational principles from S-D logic

Foundational principles	Service-dominant logic
FP1	Service is the fundamental basis of exchange
FP2	Indirect exchange masks the fundamental basis of exchange
FP3	Goods are a distribution mechanism for service provision
FP4	Operant resources are fundamental source of competitive advantage
FP5	All economies are service economies
FP6	The customer is always a co-creator of value
FP7	The enterprise cannot deliver value, but only offer value propositions
FP8	A service-centered view is inherently customer oriented and relational
FP9	All social and economic actors are resource integrators
FP10	Value is always uniquely and phenomenologically determined by the beneficiary

Source: Vargo and Lusch (2008)

acting on other resources' to co-create value (Lusch et al. 2007, p. 6). In this view, customer participation plays the central role of the exchange, with a service-oriented provision instead of goods. During this process, there is no value until an offer is used. Therefore the experience is essential to value determination in such activity (Lusch et al. 2007).

In this sense, the business and customer are no longer on the opposite sides but jointly to produce mutual needs with interactions. Galvagno and Dalli (2014) defined co-creation is *'the joint, collaborative, concurrent, peer-like process of producing new value, both materially and symbolically'* (Galvagno and Dalli 2014, p. 644). The engagement during the co-creation process meaning customers now have greater control. We argue that S-D logic and tourism are closely related despite existing references to the co-creation of tourism experience and creative tourism gave undue emphasis to the experience economy. Pine and Gilmore focused on *'stagging experiences that sell'* (Pine and Gilmore 1998, p.98) with the belief that experience and transformation are the ultimate stages of economic progression. We, however, view creative tourism is not for everyone—as an extension of culture tourism (Richards 2011), and it is unlikely to be fully diffused by all tourists. Therefore, it is critical to recognise customer views from this niche market.

Thanks to technology diffusion, especially web 2.0, customers become significant value producers through their engagement and conversation in the tourists' online communities making the S-D logic a useful framework for gaining the tourists' insights (Shaw et al. 2011). In contrast to the view of the experience economy, where business remains the leading performer of the output, S-D logic implies value is defined by and co-created with the customer, rather than embedded in output (Lusch and Vargo 2014). Therefore, at this front, S-D logic is more of an appropriate framework for the context of creative tourism as its fundamental concern is around knowledge and skills. There is a great deal of focus on building customers roles as co-creator for production.

Conceptualising Creative Tourism

Richard and Raymond initially defined creative tourism as '*Tourism which offers visitors the opportunity to develop their creative potential through active participation in courses and learning experiences which are characteristic of the holiday destination where they are undertaken*' (Richards and Raymond 2000, p. 18).

Before the conceptualisation of Creative Tourism by Richard and Raymond, various basic forms for creative tourism were practised in Thailand (Singsomboon 2014). In the 1950s, visitors and migrants came to the *tambon* of Dan Kwien attracted by the place's over 200 years history of pottery making, and unique metallic lustre moved into the *tambon* and co-developed the production (Cohen 1995). In the early 1990s, many smaller craft-making businesses relocated their workshops to attached to the shops in order to perform the finishing stage of production to tourists (Cohen 1995). This movement would encourage visitors to observe or try out the making of the crafts. The tourism-related craft-production, marketing, and dynamic workshop relocation emerged hybrid communities for craft-making and tourist centres in Thailand (Cohen 1995). At the same period, some other early forms of crafts tourism were identified in Finland, Greece and Portugal (Richards 2005). The notation Creative Tourism was first mentioned by Pearce and Butler (1993) as a potential form of tourism but lacked a clear definition (Richards 2011).

Since its conceptualisation, there have been emerging practices and scholarly attention from both developed and developing economies. Policies relating to creative experience began to be developed (Duxbury and Richards 2019; Richards and Wilson 2007). The United Nations Educational, Scientific and Cultural Organization (UNESCO) refined the definition as a '*travel directed toward an engaged and authentic experience, with participative learning in the arts, heritage, or special character of a place, and it provides a connection with those who reside in this place and create this living culture*' (UNESCO 2006, p. 3). This marks a new phase of creative tourism which reflects a macro perspective in

Tourism style

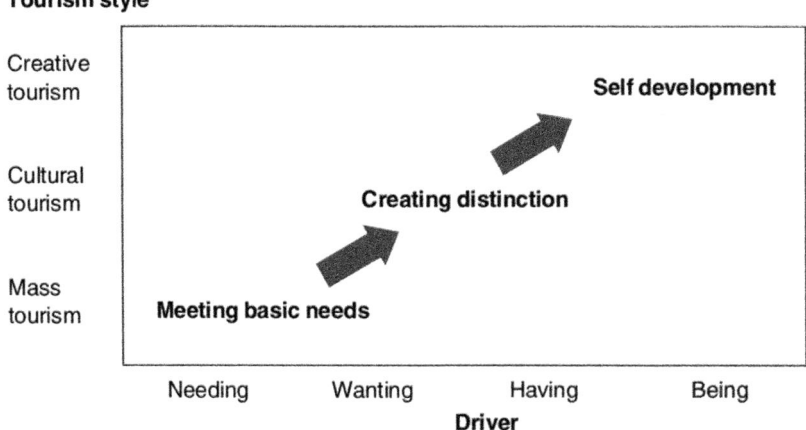

Fig. 12.1 Changes in the drivers of tourism over time. (Source: Richards and Wilson 2007)

using creative activities for destination marketing (Duxbury and Richards 2019).

As an extension of culture tourism (Richards 2011), creative tourism emphasises the shift of tourists' involvement from tangible resources (for example museums, monuments and mountains) to intangible resources (for example lifestyle, atmosphere, and media). In this complex process, the traditional cultural tourism experience derived into a practice of co-creating fashion, design, media, entertainment, cuisine, traditions, folklore, etc. (Richards and Wilson 2007).

Richards and Wilson (2007) highlighted (Fig. 12.1) the movement of tourism consumption from a basic value of '*needing*' in participating in mass tourism towards the value of '*being*' when taking creative tourism. In view of the S-D logic, it is the co-creation of tourists' personal and authentic memory that encourage value and self-actualisation, which is above and beyond the experience-centric view, resonating with Maslow's (1943) Hierarchy of Needs Theory.

Creative Tourists

What drives tourists to take creative activities in distant places or an unusual environment sometimes beyond their comfort zone?

The unique character and its niche market suggest the creative tourism is not for everyone. One common theme modern consumers and tourists asked for is the authentic experience in which they balance the self-expression and the control from the experience stager (Binkhorst and Den Dekker 2009). As S-D logic indicates a customer-view, finding creative tourists and understanding their motivation as co-creators is the primary focus that hosts from the destinations need to draw upon.

In the attempt to identify the heterogeneous groups of creative tourists, some studies were carried out at the regional level, mainly in the Asia Pacific and European countries. Early studies in New Zealand by Raymond identified creative tourism appear to focus around three groups: baby-boomers and newly retired who are actively seek intellectual stimulus and new interests. Students and backpackers under 30s looking for creative experiences after travel adventures, and the general public (New Zealanders) of all ages looking to learn different aspects of the local culture (Raymond 2003). More specifically, Campbell found that creative tourism adopters in the UK are predominantly female, either 45+ or between 22 and 30 years old, with a full-time job and without children. Chang et al. (2014) reported tourists that engage in creative activities in Taiwan largely consist of those who travel with family or friends, whilst individual tourists are less inclined to creative activities. In contrast, Tan et al. (2013) argued that the classification of creative tourists should not focus only on demographic factors and they, therefore, suggested in the context of Taiwan, creative tourists can be broadly classified into five groups: novelty-seekers, knowledge and skills learners, those who are aware of their travel partners' growth, those who are aware of green issues, and the relax and leisure type. In a similar way, Remoaldo et al. investigated the motivation and demographic characters of tourists in continental Portugal and segmented creative participants in three clusters: Novelty-Seekers, Knowledge and Skills Learners, and Leisure Creative-Seekers.

In an attempt to explore the cognitive drivers, we conducted a meta-analysis. Table 12.2 shows a selection of recent publications concerning the antecedents or factors affecting tourists participation in creative activities. Through the 17 publications, it is clear there is an overwhelming use of quantitative methods in understanding the creative tourists. This has possibly resulted in a lack of research on the relative importance of personality traits (such as self-efficacy or perceived innovativeness), and barriers or impediments (such as financial contains, perceived effort, perceived risk, etc.,) to adopt such activity. On the other hand, it is unclear how tourists' demographic factors such as gender and education attainment relate to creative activities' segmentations and how those factors influence or moderate the dependent variable (DV) and independent variable (IV) relationships.

Table 12.2 A meta-analysis of tourists motivation to take creative activities from 2012–2021

	Sample & approach	DV	IV	Notes/contributions	Creative activity/ context	Region
Ihamäki (2012)	Case study + survey n = 52	Share, creative, manage experience	Support Multi-sensory applications User control Creative tools	Design guidance for GPS facilitated creative activities	Geocatcher (GPS-treasure hunt)	Finland
Prebensen et al. (2013)	Survey n = 505	Overall experience value	Service quality Involvement Surrounding nature Other tourists Time spent Resources spent Money spent	Tourist resources, personal service, environment and other visitors, enhance the overall value perception	Nature-based attractions	Norway
Tan et al. (2013)	Grounded theory, interview n = 32	Learning and interacting	Consciousness/ awareness Creativity Needs	Tan et al. did not specify IV and DV but concluded 4 themes in creative tourism, where Learning and interacting was labelled as "outer interaction", Consciousness, Creativity, Needs were labelled as "inner reflections"	Leisure-farm, 'story house', pottery-making museum, and furniture museum	Taiwan

Minkiewicz et al. (2014)	Customer critic approach in two venues n = 27	Co-creation (co-production, engagement, and personalisation)	Previous experience Individual pre-conceptions Perceived Crowding Experience space design	Addressed gap in S-D logic in creative tourism by adding 3 dimensions in co-creation	Museum and Gallery	Australia
Prebensen et al. (2014)	Survey n = 1152	Perceived value	Motivation Involvement Knowledge	Motivation and Knowledge predict perceived value; Knowledge mediates involvement and perceived value	Hybrid nature and cultural attractions: mountain, zoo, aquarium	Norway
Chang et al. (2014)	Survey n = 417	Revisit intention	Motivation Experience Perceived value	Identified that experience has a positive influence on revisit intentions to creative tourism attractions; while motivation and perceived value shows no impact	Pottery, crafts, arts, workshops	Taiwan

(continued)

Table 12.2 (continued)

	Sample & approach	DV	IV	Notes/contributions	Creative activity/ context	Region
Hung et al. (2016)	Survey n = 399	Revisit intention	Creative experience Memorability	Creative experience also found to have strong impact on Sense of achievement, Unique learning, Interaction with instructors Memorability mediate Creative experience and Revisit intention	Pottery making	Taiwan
Ali et al. (2016)	Survey n = 296	Behavioural intention	Creative tourism experience Memories Satisfaction	Creative tourist experience is a second-order construct manifested by Escape and recognition, Peace of mind, Unique involvement, Interactivity, and learning.	Cooking classes, handicraft classes, storytelling sessions of local tales, and "batik painting" in resort hotels	Malaysia
Singh (2019)	Survey n = 388	Creative tourism behaviour Revisit intention	Motivation Experience Perceived value	Motivation, experience and perceived value were treated as reflective measures for behaviour	Various activities including handicraft, dress, and dance in Kashmir	India

Dean and Suhartanto (2019)	Survey n = 369	Behavioural intention	Experience quality Pull motivation Satisfaction	Push motivation and its relationship with behavioural intention was not examined	Gardening, batik painting, and horse riding	Indonesia
Chen and Chou (2019)	Survey n = 281	Perceived "coolness"	Uniqueness Identification Attractiveness	Generation Y sample; Perceived coolness also found has impact on satisfaction and place attachment	Design and contemporary art Centre	Taiwan
Wang et al. (2020)	Survey n = 574	Memorability Authenticity	Creative tourism experience	Creative tourist experience is a second-order construct manifested by Escape and recognition, Peace of mind, Unique involvement, Interactivity, and learning.	Hybrid creative tourism park	China
Suhartanto et al. (2020)	Survey n = 369	Motivation	Experience quality Perceived value Tourist satisfaction	Experience quality is measured by Escape, Peace of mind, Involvement, Recognition, Learning	Coffee making, gardening, painting, and horse riding	Indonesia

(continued)

Table 12.2 (continued)

Xu and Tapachai (2020)	Survey n = 446	Behavioural intention	Attitude Subjective norm Perceived behavioural control	Chinese tourists in Thailand	Learning activities range from carving fruit, painting, dancing, etc.	Thailand
Munawar et al. (2021)	Survey n = 96	Revisit intention	Perceived coolness Destination uniqueness Tourist experience	Tourist experience was measured by joyfulness and attitude, which has no impact on behavioural intention	Gardening tours	Indonesia
Li and Kovacs (2021)	Blog content analysis n = 552	Actively seek out creative activities	Participation Knowledge acquisition experiencing of local life	Revealed connections between creative activities and the three elements: participation, knowledge acquisition, and the experiencing of local life	Crafts and folk arts, design, film, gastronomy, literature, media arts	China

Source: Authors

References

Alexander, A., Nell, D., Bailey, A. R., and Shaw, G. (2009) The Co-Creation of a Retail Innovation: Shoppers and the Early Supermarket in Britain. *Enterprise & Society* 10(3): 529–558.

Ali, F., Ryu, K., and Hussain, K. (2016) Influence of Experiences on Memories, Satisfaction and Behavioral Intentions: A Study of Creative Tourism. *Journal of Travel & Tourism Marketing* 33(1): 85–100.

Binkhorst, E., and Den Dekker, T. (2009) Agenda for Co-Creation Tourism Experience Research. *Journal of Hospitality Marketing & Management* 18(2–3): 311–327.

Boswijk, A., Thijssen, T., and Peelen, E. (2007) *The Experience Economy: A New Perspective*. Pearson Education.

Bowers, M. R., Martin, C. L., and Luker, A. (1990) Trading Places: Employees as Customers, Customers as Employees. *Journal of Professional Services Marketing* 4(2): 55–69.

British Tourist Authority (1989–1997) *UK Tourism Survey*. BTA, London.

British Tourist Authority (1989) *Overseas Visitors' Survey 1988*.

Chang, L.-L., Backman Kenneth, F., and Yu, C. H. (2014) Creative tourism: a preliminary examination of creative tourists' motivation, experience, perceived value and revisit intention. *International Journal of Culture, Tourism and Hospitality Research* 8(4): 401–419.

Chen, C.-F., and Chou, S.-H. (2019) Antecedents and consequences of perceived coolness for Generation Y in the context of creative tourism—A case study of the Pier 2 Art Center in Taiwan. *Tourism Management* 72: 121–129.

Cohen, E. (1995) Touristic craft ribbon development in Thailand. *Tourism Management* 16(3): 225–235.

Crandall, L. (1987) The social impact of tourism on developing regions and its measurement. *The social impact of tourism on developing regions and its measurement.* 373–383.

Dean, D., and Suhartanto, D. (2019) The formation of visitor behavioral intention to creative tourism: the role of push–Pull motivation. *Asia Pacific Journal of Tourism Research* 24(5): 393–403.

Duxbury, N., and Richards, G. (2019) *A Research Agenda for Creative Tourism*. Edward Elgar Publishing.

European Commission (1998) *The Europeans on Holiday*. DGXXIII, Brussels.

Firat, A. F., Dholakia, N., and Venkatesh, A. (1995) Marketing in a postmodern world. *European Journal of Marketing* 29(1): 40–56.

Fitzsimmons, J. A. (1985) Consumer Participation and Productivity in Service Operations. *INFORMS Journal on Applied Analytics* 15(3): 60–67.

Flew, T. (2002) Beyond ad hocery: Defining Creative Industries. In *Cultural Sites, Cultural Theory, Cultural Policy, The Second International Conference on Cultural Policy Research*. Presented at the Cultural Sites, Cultural Theory, Cultural Policy, The Second International Conference on Cultural Policy Research eprints.qut.edu.au.

Florida, R. (2002) *The Rise of the Creative Class*. (Vol. 9). New York: Basic books.

Galvagno, M., and Dalli, D. (2014) Theory of value co-creation: a systematic literature review. *Managing Service Quality* 24(6): 643–683.

Harvey, D. (2002) The Art of Rent: Globalisation, Monopoly and the Commodification of Culture. *Socialist Register* 38.

Hung, W.-L., Lee, Y.-J., and Huang, P.-H. (2016) Creative experiences, memorability and revisit intention in creative tourism. *Current Issues in Tourism* 19(8): 763–770.

Ihamäki, P. (2012) Geocachers: the creative tourism experience. *Journal of Hospitality and Tourism Technology* 3(3): 152–175.

IUOTO (1974) *Charter for Development and Protection of Tourist Resources and Influence of Cultural Traditions on the Formation of Distinctive Supply*. Geneva, Switzerland: International Union of Official Travel Organizations.

Korez-Vide, R. (2013) Promoting sustainability of tourism by creative tourism development: How far is Slovenia? *Innovative Issues and Approaches in Social Sciences* 6(1).

Lengnick-Hall, C. A. (1996) Customer Contributions to Quality: A Different View of the Customer-Oriented Firm. *AMRO* 21(3): 791–824.

Li, P. Q., and Kovacs, J. F. (2021) Creative tourism and creative spaces in China. *Leisure Studies* : 1–18.

Lovelock, C. H., and Young, R. F. (1979) Look to customers to increase productivity. *Harvard Business Review* 57(3): 168–178.

Lusch, R. F., and Vargo, S. L. (2014) *The Service-Dominant Logic of Marketing: Dialog, Debate, and Directions*. Routledge.

Lusch, R. F., Vargo, S. L., and O'Brien, M. (2007) Competing through service: Insights from service-dominant logic. *Journal of Retailing* 83(1): 5–18.

MacCannell, D. (1976) *The tourist: A new theory of the leisure class*. London: Macmillan.

Maslow, A. H. (1943) A theory of human motivation. *Psychological Review* 50(4): 370.

Minkiewicz, J., Evans, J., and Bridson, K. (2014) How do consumers co-create their experiences? An exploration in the heritage sector. *Journal of Marketing Management* 30(1–2): 30–59.

Munawar, F., Munawar, R., and Tarmidi, D. (2021) The Impact of Perceived Coolness, Destination Uniqueness and Tourist Experience on Revisit Intention: A Geographical Study on Cultural Tourism in Indonesia. *Review of International Geographical Education Online* 11(1): 400–411.

O'Connor, J. (1999) *The Definition of "Cultural Industries",* Manchester. Manchester Institute for Popular Culture http://mmu.ac.uk/h-ss/mipc/iciss/home2.htm.

OECD (2014) *Tourism and the Creative Economy, OECD Studies on Tourism.* https://doi.org/10.1787/9789264207875-en.

Patterson, W. D. (1976) Pacifica Nostra. *Tourism International Policy, 3rd*: 2–6.

Pearce, D. G., and Butler, R. W. (1993) *Tourism Research: Critiques and Challenges.* Routledge.

Pine, B. J., and Gilmore, J. H. (1998/1/July) Welcome to the Experience Economy. *Harvard Business Review*: 97–105.

Pine, B. J., and Gilmore, J. H. (2011) *The Experience Economy.* Harvard Business Press.

Prahalad, C. K., Ramaswamy, V., and Others (2000) Co-opting customer competence. *Harvard Business Review* 78(1): 79–90.

Prebensen, N. K., Woo, E., and Uysal, M. S. (2014) Experience value: antecedents and consequences. *Current Issues in Tourism* 17(10): 910–928.

Prebensen, N.K., Vittersø, J. and Dahl, T.I (2013) Value co-creation significance of tourist resources. *Annals Of Tourism Research* 42: 240–261.

Ratzenböck, V., Demel, K., Harauer, R., Landsteiner, G., Falk, R., Hannes, L., and Schwarz, G. (2004) *An analysis of the economic potential of the creative industries in Vienna.* Österreichische Kulturdokumentation, MEDIACULT and Wifo, Vienna.

Raymond, C. (2003) *Cultural renewal + tourism: Case study—Creative tourism.* Creative Tourism New Zealand.

Richards, G. (2001) *Cultural Attractions and European Tourism.* CABI.

Richards, G. (2005) Textile tourists in the European periphery: New markets for disadvantaged areas? *Tourism Review International* 8(4): 323–338.

Richards, G. (2011) Creativity and tourism: The State of the Art. *Annals of Tourism Research* 38(4): 1225–1253.

Richards, G., and Raymond, C. (2000) Creative tourism. *ATLAS News,* (23), 16–20.

Richards, G., and Wilson, J. (2007) *Tourism, Creativity and Development.* Routledge.

Ritchie, J. R. B., and Zins, M. (1978) Culture as determinant of the attractiveness of a tourism region. *Annals of Tourism Research* 5(2): 252–267.

Rogerson, C. (2007) Creative industries and tourism in the developing world: The example of South Africa. In *Tourism, Creativity and Development.* Routledge.

Shaw, G. (1992a) Culture and tourism: The economics of Nostalgia. *World Futures* 33(1–3): 199–212.

Shaw, G. (1992b) Growth and employment in the UK's culture industry. *World Futures* 33(1–3): 165–180.

Shaw, G., Bailey, A., and Williams, A. (2011) Aspects of service-dominant logic and its implications for tourism management: Examples from the hotel industry. *Tourism Management* 32(2): 207–214.

Singh, R. (2019) Investigating the influencing factors of Tourist Behavior towards Creative Tourism and its Relationship with Revisit Intention. 8(1).

Singsomboon, T. (2014) Tourism promotion and the use of local wisdom through creative tourism process. *International Journal of Business Tourism and Applied Sciences* 2(2).

Smith, A. (1776) The wealth of nations. *na* 11937.

Smith, V. L. ed. (1977) *Hosts and Guests: The Anthropology of Tourism.* University of Pennsylvania Press.

Suhartanto, D., Brien, A., Primiana, I., Wibisono, N., and Triyuni, N. N. (2020) Tourist loyalty in creative tourism: the role of experience quality, value, satisfaction, and motivation. *Current Issues in Tourism* 23(7): 867–879.

Tan, S.-K., Kung, S.-F., and Luh, D.-B. (2013) A model of 'creative experience' in creative tourism. *Annals of Tourism Research* 41(C): 153–174.

Terblanche, N. S. (2014) Some theoretical perspectives of co-creation and co-production of value by customers. *Acta commercii* 14(2).

UK Creative Industries Task Force (CITF) (2001) *Creative industries mapping document.* London: Department for Culture, Media and Sport.

UNESCO (2006) *Towards sustainable strategies for creative tourism.* Santa Fe, New Mexico, USA: International Conference on Creative Tourism.

Van Raaij, W. F., and Pruyn, A. T. H. (1998) Customer control and evaluation of service validity and reliability. *Psychology & Marketing* 15(8): 811–832.

Vargo, S. L., and Lusch, R. F. (2004) Evolving to a New Dominant Logic for Marketing. *Journal of Marketing* 68(1): 1–17.

Vargo, S. L., and Lusch, R. F. (2008) Service-dominant logic: continuing the evolution. *Journal of the Academy of Marketing Science* 36(1): 1–10.

Walsh, K. (2002) *The representation of the past: museums and heritage in the post-modern world.* Routledge.

Wang, C., Liu, J., Wei, L., and Zhang, T. (christina) (2020) Impact of tourist experience on memorability and authenticity: a study of creative tourism. *Journal of Travel & Tourism Marketing* 37(1): 48–63.

World Tourism Organization (1985) *The State's Role in Protecting and Promoting Culture as a Factor of Tourism Development and the Proper Use and Exploitation of the National Cultural Heritage of Sites and Monuments for Tourism: Report of the Secretary-General on the General Programme of Work for the Period 1984–1985.* World Tourism Organization.

Xu, R., and Tapachai, N. (2020) Chinese tourists' intention of and preference for attending Thailand's creative tourism activities. *Sustainable tourism: Shaping a Better Future*: 286.

13

Accelerated Times: Post-Capitalism and Music Industry Pedagogy

Gareth Thomas

Abstract This chapter explores the post-Covid adoption of livestreaming as both a pedagogical tool and as a development within the live music industry. This meta-narrative will draw on research around the efficacies of on-line and blended teaching and update that knowledge though an analysis of the current landscape. With a particular reference to music courses, I will interrogate how universities have adapted teaching to the online environment and what part the pandemic has played in this. At the same time, I will use my own students' experience of on-line teaching to understand its benefits and drawbacks. Third, I will compare and contrast those experiences with how music fans have taken to livestreamed gigs and how the industry has embraced the format, or otherwise. In the same way as tutors have had to adapt their teaching to the on-line environment, so acts have adapted their live offering to the on-line world, for example by including interviews and other '*extra content*' to their streams.

G. Thomas (✉)
Business School for the Creative Industries, University for the Creative Arts, Farnham, UK
e-mail: Philip.Powell@uca.ac.uk

© The Author(s), under exclusive license to Springer Nature Switzerland AG 2022
P. Powell, B. Shankar Nayak (eds.), *Creative Business Education*,
https://doi.org/10.1007/978-3-031-10928-7_13

221

The chapter will look at the popularity of livestreaming and the '*long tail*' nature of livestreamed gigs where the shows are recorded and can build up a considerable audience over time, despite potentially having had only a few views for the original live performance. On the other hand, large concerts can pull in thousands of fans from all over the world. I also look at this aspect from the pedagogical perspective by researching whether students watch recorded lectures and, if so, what do they consider to be the pros and cons. As well as this, I draw on current and recent academic research around blended learning and music livestreams. There is no doubt that on-line has established itself as a platform in future for the live music industry and for higher education teaching. This chapter will interrogate just how big a role it is set to play.

Introduction

These are interesting times. Times when razor-sharp critiques of capitalism made just a few years ago now seem outdated. Times when the leftist love of populist masses has turned into an embarrassed revulsion of extreme, polarising populism itself. Teaching in these times has been equally revelatory in terms of what young people are saying, thinking and feeling about the 2020s and the fissures and breaks in society's tectonic plates caused by the pandemic, populism, progression, acceleration and revanchism.

In this chapter I aim to present experiences in higher education and in particular music industry pedagogy within the context of a critique of the current conditions of what is commonly described as late-capitalism with a view to capturing the enigmas of post-capitalism.

Capitalist Realism

Fellow university lecturer and theorist Fisher famously popularised the notion of capitalist realism in his unexpectedly popular book of the same name (Fisher 2009). Fisher posited the notion—something which had been hibernating in leftist circles for decades—that capitalism had crept into every crevice of our existence. This was not a new idea, but it was an explicit, contemporary description of a dialectical movement which had first been expounded by Marx and Engels (1992).

Later, the theory of an ever-encroaching capitalism was picked up by the Frankfurt School thinkers (Horkheimer and Adorno 1982) and Gramsci (1971). Theirs was the realisation that culture was a corollary aspect of the capitalist machine, reflecting, supporting and reifying its exploitative brutality. Later still, French theorists Deleuze and Guatarri allied this critique of capitalism's invasion of our unconscious through invoking Freud and suggesting a return to the pre-oedipal state (2004). Fisher picked up the mantle in the wake of American philosopher Fredric Jameson declaring that '*someone once said that it is easier to imagine the end of the world than to imagine the end of capitalism*' (1994).

Original k-punk and founding member of the Cybernetic Culture Research Unit at the University of Warwick, Fisher was exploring the notions of post-capitalism before he committed suicide in 2017. Since then the cult status he has achieved online is a testament to his place as one of the foremost radical thinkers of recent times. Following Fisher's death, world events have shaken up the situation to such a degree that a re-think is in order.

The rupture across society caused by the Trumpians and Brexiteers dragging time back towards the past while young progressives were modelling a new future has been enormous. These divisions have called everything into question, including the music industry and higher education business pedagogy.

The pandemic only served to heighten these divisions while at the same time illustrating the crucial role the previously marginalised and exploited social support jobs play in society. The Covid pandemic forced upon us the realisation that without healthcare and social care we do not have a society—just a business and political class feverishly trying to make as much money as possible through a systematic depletion of resources, bearing in mind that ecological pressure is what potentially caused the virus outbreak in the first place (Gillespie and Chapman 2006).

In the UK, train companies are slowly becoming nationalised and the privatised energy sector is in turmoil with 29 UK energy companies having collapsed under the pressure of price increases. The energy crisis reveals the dark, unspoken truth that multiple companies trying to sell exactly the same public good for different prices does not make any sense and renders the government's neo-liberal mantra of simply '*switching*' to find a better deal non-sensical. The only reason not to re-nationalise energy is through a blind adherence to the bankrupt ideology of the free market.

So now the so-called Great Resignation reveals that Americans are slowly waking up to the concept of socialism, not as the much-feared evil stepchild of communism, but as a valid political system in its own right which we are, to all intents and purposes, gravitating towards.

The idea of the weekend had been around since the early nineteenth century, yet it's only now, some two hundred years later, that the validity and efficacy of a five-day working week is being properly examined. In the UK, a four-day working week is being piloted by campaign group 4 Day Week Global (4 Day Week, 2022) alongside university academics and is running in parallel with similar programmes in the US, Ireland, Canada, Australia, and New Zealand. The governments of Scotland and Spain have also launched trials of the four-day week.

Ghosts and Barometers of Change

Fisher was a music nut and, as such, could not help but include critiques around music into his theories. Perhaps his dalliance with hauntology, which he resurrected from the writings of post-structuralist Derrida, who declared that '*time is out of joint*' (Derrida 2006), is the most well known iteration of his obsession.

This notion of hauntology in music was perhaps most apparent in the strange vaporwave movement of the early 2010s when artists re-imagined 80s and 90s synthpop. Outside of music, it is—in essence and inevitably reductively—the notion that the past contains echoes of the future and that past '*failures*' could be re-evaluated, repositioned and most importantly, reimagined in the context of a ludic '*what if?*' moment (Fisher 2014).

Meanwhile in 1977, French writer and political figure Attali had declared that music is the barometer of social change and that it reflects and indeed anticipates the way society is headed (Attali 1985). Attali's is an interesting notion. Indeed, music has been the first artistic expression to embrace technology—or perhaps the other way around. Radio and audio-video tapes quickly became the media of music and no sooner had Berners-Lee invented the world wide web than music lovers, with a little help from Napster's Fanning, were using it to swap music files. YouTube announced its entry to the market with the slogan '*Broadcast Yourself*' with the idea that you would film yourself doing everyday things—like going to the zoo in the first ever YouTube video—and post it on the platform. But within weeks artists began uploading their music videos on to the site and it quicky became the go-to place to watch music film, swiftly putting paid to MTV in the process.

Traditionally, of course, it is artists who are hyper-sensitive to the times we are living through and who are naturally equipped with the antennae to express and respond to those changes. From dadaism and surrealism to abstract expressionism and pop art, the visual art avant-gardists were the touchstones of the times and the cultural frontrunners in mapping out the path to advance along towards the future. That was pretty much the case until dada came along and announced the end of art. It was announcement which, of course, was premature, yet prophetic. The end of art as a radical instrument with which to torture capitalism and at the same time triumph over it was finally put paid to by the Situationists, a number of whom were originally artists—including its leading light the filmmaker, Debord.

The proto-Situationists got together in northern Italy in 1957 to renounce art and herald the '*revolution of everyday life*' through the '*creation of situations*' (Debord 2006) as its historically necessary replacement. Sure enough, it was Situationist theories which fuelled the Paris riots of May 1968, manifestations of a radical movement which nearly overturned the government of the day.

Music did not suffer the same fate at the hands of the Situationists as the visual arts. On the contrary, more than anything music took the place of art as the medium through which rebellion was expressed and reflected. T hrough the voices of The Rolling Stones, Bob Dylan, The Who and The MC5—among many others—it became the mouthpiece for reflecting and amplifying young people's dissatisfaction with the old establishment and their dream of a new world.

In the 1970s, popular music slowly became the miserable, phony soundtrack of dropping out and a hippy retreat from society. Mainstream hippies were more concerned with making money than revolution. Branson and his ilk used their alternative *cultural capital* (Bourdieu 1977) to reinvigorate capitalism. And he was lucky too to have signed a failing folk singer, Mike Oldfield, who produced Tubular Bells, the mesmeric, metronomic opus which chimed with the monotonously transcendental times.

But music's inability to *actually* change anything at all came into sharp focus during and after the two-year-long punk explosion which sounded popular music's death knell. vIts radical bankruptcy was finally announced in 1978 by the north-east's answer to Raoul Vaneigem, Situationist brothers David and Stuart Wise (Wise 2014).

Music is representation, not real life and yet the contradiction for the counter-culture lies in the fact that while music may have lost the sense of itself as a force for revolutionary change, people are still drawn to it, a love or talent for music, musicality cannot be denied—just as, ultimately, Debord could not totally renounce his love of film-making.

Never Work

So, the decision to renounce all art and the making of artefacts in the Situationist times was a painful one for many who sacrificed their creative urges and desires at the altar of revolution. For others the determination to '*ne travaillez jamais*' ('*never work*'), an exhortation spray-painted on to the walls of riot-torn Paris in 1968, had equally existential consequences—which does not mean that these idealistic edicts were wrong, just that they were incompatible in terms of operating within a capitalist society.

Darling of the young New Left in the 1960s, Herbert Marcuse had influenced the Situationists in this regard, arguing that human emancipation could only be achieved with the abolition—not the liberation—of labour and with the affirmation of the libido and play in social relations

(Marcuse 1962). His Great Refusal envisioned society's dregs and cast-offs forming a united front against capital in its refusal to work.

And the '*never work*' mantra is getting ever closer in terms of realisation within late/post-capitalism with the realities of artificial intelligence and robotics and the notion of a universal wage. There are more mainstream spin-offs too, including the Financial Independence and Early Retirement movement.

This is part of the experimentation in how to live fulfilled lives when, over the past ten thousand years or so, societies have used people, in the words of computer scientist Russel, as '*performative robots*' (2021).

Singularity

Everything is rapidly moving towards its dissolution. This is in a way pure Hegelian Marxism—the proposition that capitalism's seeds of destruction lie within the system itself. It is, like everything in nature, subject to entropy. It is not a resurrected culture which opposes the decline of the west, but '*the utopia that is silently contained in the image of its decline*' (Horkheimer and Adorno 1982).

Part of this inexorable movement is the mad drive towards subjective desire which has been underway for a long time. From the 1960s onwards, this privileging of the self and the innate power of subjectivity was uppermost in much counter-cultural thought—the realisation of the emotional human being in contrast to the machinic nature of capitalism or, more reductively, the little person against The Man. It was underlined more toxically by advertising which began to place *you* at the centre of everything; *you* deserve this product, why shouldn't *you* have it? because *you're* worth it.

This articulates itself now in the realisation of all your needs and desires—from visiting the coolest places and eating great food to '*living your best life*' and fulfilling and expressing every aspect of yourself ('*your truth*' in today's parlance). If something can be imagined it will, inevitably, at some point be reified. Thus, we've entered unknowingly into a world of mirrors where we are reflected—and it is far more mysterious and unknowable and menacing than anything the Situationists could have dreamed up.

This is indeed the desert of the real (Baudrillard 1994), as referenced by philosopher Žižek (2002) and featured in The Matrix (1999)—a kind of hyperreality within a society of the spectacle—the commutation of relationships through images where the metaverse is the spectacle entering its ultimate form.

This drive towards subjective desire is apparent, as Attali suggested it would be, in music too. When streaming entered the technological landscape, music was the first in line. And livestreaming was accelerated under Covid conditions. Once seen as a complete no-hope platform for live music, it is cementing itself as an alternative way of experiencing live events. It can never replace the sweat, noise, tactility and emotion of being together with others in the same room or field, but it can provide an alternative.

My second-year students had to put on livestreamed gig as part of their Live Music Industry unit. The streams were live gigs, but often with something different—apart from lighting and showtime effects, some featured interviews with the acts in question and fans could react to the show in real time through the chat.

This drive towards realising subjective desires sees music is returning to its roots and the idea that anyone can create music. The gatekeepers have fled and the power of creation is being transferred back into the hands of the people, so that making music, with so-called creator tools, is becoming as easy as filming a TikTok video or recording your own podcast.

The meta-narrative of streaming a live lecture about livestreaming nicely encapsulates where we are now in a time where scientists have posited our universe could be one of many multiverses. We are indeed '*all watched over by machines of loving grace*' (Brautigan 2015). But will this bring us happiness, or is it just something we communally dreamed of forever which, in the end of days, we will finally be able to touch before the ecology collapses. In other words are we seeing that rising tide before the tsunami?

Covid has taught us to realign our priorities and reset out psyche to understand what is important. Now the healthcare worker is as important, if not more so, than the lawyer—even though capital is trenchant in its refusal to acknowledge this is in fair rewards or indeed in any other way. If life can be taken away so easily then our time here becomes more precious, so is it about working mechanically at high speed all your life just to have a comfortable pension when you are too old to enjoy it?

The acceleration of capitalism saw the American model of resizing—reducing departments incrementally to minimum staffing levels—and multi-tasking (both connoted as positive terms by the corporate elites) spread across the globe. Yet, while in the short term these business practices may work, in the long term it has led to burnout and resentment.

Atomisation, Acceleration and Music

In its sociological sense, atomisation—a notion birthed by the Greek philosophers and scientists—sees the individual as the '*atom*' of society and therefore the only true object of concern. Early capitalist thinkers like Locke (1997) and Hobbes (1969) used the atomic idea to lay the basis to their version of self-interested capitalism, which later developed into free market neo-liberalism.

Harking back to Hegel's account of alienation (1807) and later that of Lukács (1990), the Situationists claimed that capitalism would triumph if it managed to successfully atomise everyone, if we were all so consumed in ourselves and our own struggles that we abandoned the collective, which has historically been the real people power. In the wake of a breakdown in cultural and class solidarities, people have been '"atomised" *and forced onto the market against one another, as competitiors*' (Sabbaghzadeh 2020), where '*society was now in an economic Hunger Games, accelerated via digital connectivity*'.

But the collective has also been tainted. Left-wing thinkers now find it harder to champion populism after they've witnessed the Trump era and the Brexit vote (both powered by the '*working class*'). In a similar way to when the Soviet Union invaded Czechoslovakia and even the more hardcore communist sympathisers in the west began to slough off their Bolshevik skins, left-wing thinkers have been forced to reassess their blind, reverential working-class allegiance and address that abstractive othering of the '*people*' as a mythical saviour lying outside of ourselves.

Accelerationism and the idea of '*sustained growth*', a phrase commonly used by the Conservatives in the 2000s and 2010s as a way of détourning the '*sustainability*' agenda of the environmental movement, was reimagined by radical thinkers and expressed as the way that revolution—or at least a more equitable society—could be brought about not by the hindering and slowing down of neo-liberalism and the free market, but by accelerating all its most malignant tendencies to a point where the system implodes or is resolved in a final cataclysm.

The idea of acceleration is typically apparent in the cultural dynamics which take place towards the end of a movement, scene or era—from the orgiastic heights before the fall of the Roman Empire and the excesses of Nick Leeson at the tail-end of Yuppieism to the frenzied phone hacking by the tabloids before the collapse in print journalism.

Just like society, the music industry is atomising and accelerating. Young people are at the forefront of this movement—the students I teach are interested in NFTs, in entrepreneurship, in establishing their own start-ups, in creating experiences, in a return to the physical artefact and in using all the digital tools out there to facilitate exactly what they want to achieve.

Although this has been much slower in this realisation that futurologists were predicting, 3D printing could eventually see everyone have the ability to make their own products at home. Music too moves towards its dénouement. Soon we will all be artists and creators as well as fans.

Now you can have a '*record label in your pocket*', as online music distribution company United Artists' slogan goes. You make a track at home on your computer and you upload it to United Artists, they distribute it for you and you wait for the royalties to roll in—or get snapped up by a major label for big bucks.

If you view the major labels as reflective of corporate greed then this is welcome as a means to their destruction. It is the triumph of the little man, the independent artist who toils away in their garret. And who now does not have to pray that the major labels that they will sign them up, but can do it all themselves and find their audience, distribute their music and then reap the rewards. And there is no reason not to assume that new technologies and trends—such as 5G, social audio and the metaverse—will not pretty quickly embrace music as part of its world. Moving on from social media groups such as WhatsApp, social audio elevates the audio element. Why spend your time typing when you can talk? That already seems like an alien idea when people did the opposite.

As Attali predicted, music is utilising all the digital tools which are coming of age. Music is at the avant-garde again.

A Young Idea

Young poeple are, in a true Situationist sense, realising their own desires. But is it all too late? Is this the final swansong before we call get washed away in the flood, baked dry by the sun, frozen by the blocked gulf stream or swept away by gales and high tides in the terrible feedback loop of terminal climate change. This is also acceleration—like Covid it is the incremental and, more dangerously, exponential growth of the virus of ecological meltdown of mass extinction.

Generation Z's mental health issues are the result of, as Debord described it in his overlooked 1971 post-situ tome, Living On A Sick Planet, the threat of environmental collapse. Even before the idea of the first ever World Environment Day was established, Debord saw the way society was heading. This was ironically also the time when hippy tech geeks were musing on how a digitally connected work could bring about the peace and love they had dreamed of in the 1960s, but which was already being brutally repressed in the 1970s.

It was, lest we forget, young people who determinedly drove home to the mainstream the urgency of the agendas of mental health, LGBT+ rights and racial justice. These are issues which were prominent in the struggles of the 60s and 70s but which, rather unexpectedly, remain unresolved to this day. There is a true heroism in that which young people will probably never be recognised for. But, again, in a world which perhaps even Fisher would not have predicted, the stream is flowing in two opposite directions; one progressive and one deeply conservative. It is change versus stasis writ large.

And that is why the students seemed to open up during my lecture series on cultural theory as applied to music; this is their world and it was the most positive response I have ever had to a unit. Yes, these are difficult questions and theories, but is not that what university is all about—challenging stereotypes, fresh thinking, broadening horizons. My students appeared to finally got to where they thought they'd be heading all along, echoing Derrida and his '*no difference without alterity, no alterity without singularity, no singularity without here-now*' (2006).

So, it is often not so much about the information we can feed our students (they can get that anywhere online), it is more about the context, the societal changes which are taking place, the emerging theories, the way we perceive things. The students' high level of receptivity and aliveness to current popular societal debates is an argument for incorporating more contextual studies and cultural theory into the curricula of business school pedagogy.

Influence, Confluence and Socialism

The students are coming at this from their own desires and perspectives. It is a subjective drive towards realisation of everything. It is what the radicals dreamed about and it is happening but it is taking place in an accelerated frenzy under the cloud of a pandemic and under the spreading shadow of climate change.

Teaching in a time where everything is available online raises fundamental questions about the profession itself and the idea is being challenged of what value a human being can add to the algorithms and search engines, datasets, information highways and rabbit holes of today. We can provide anecdotes and context, a human face and storytelling, be an inspirer and guide. We can, as suggested, expand horizons, discuss theories and explore societal change but, just as holograms and avatars exist in the world of music, we can be replaced by a version of ourselves delivering content.

This accelerationist tendency is apparent in how the mainstream has become the radical stream, in how Daily Mail readers have become Covid-deniers demonstrating on the streets and in the way football fans chant political songs denouncing BJ as a c ***. In how the word '*revolution*' can roll off the tongue of the man in the street.

Ironically, in the spirit of acceleration, one of the things AI could excel at is education, providing the tailored '*individual learning plan*' many universities are striving for. There is a certain amount of trepidation among academics that their lectures, now recorded and with the copyright belonging to the university, can be simply made available to students next year while tutors become, literally, redundant.

Interestingly—and no doubt coincidentally—the software used by a number of universities to record and archive lectures is called Panopto—calling to mind Bentham's prison control system (Bentham 2017) and, more currently, the all-seeing eye of Artificial Intelligence—while one of the most common university financial management systems is called Agresso.

We are in the age of influence. A music business gradate I was talking to recently referred to '*socialism*' during our conversation, but the way he used the word was imbued with the concept of the influencer. Socialism, for him, connoted social media. In other words he viewed the real power in society as having shifted towards those who have, to quote Bourdieu '*social capital*'. Social media kudos and caché are the modern forms of social capital and will, in the student's eyes, foreshadow the path of socialism. In his eyes—and this is a grand re-interpretation of the Marxist strand of thinking—'*social capital*' in this day and age is the ability to change people's ideas, to create a groundswell and shift opinion. Elon Musk has that power, whether that be raising the awareness of autism or inflating the price of cryptocurrencies.

Conclusions

The world of automation is beset by visions of machines taking over, the morbid take on singularity as exacted on humanity by Skynet the Terminator films (the first email service was called Arpanet). But it has an equally bucolic, gentle aspect where creativity is liberated in a golden age of fulfilment of human potential and '*visions of the "epoch of rest" (Morris) can energize and compel us to action*' (Jameson 2004).

In a reification of Situationist theory, it will be the practice of real life which will be the playground and workplace of the future. When real robots finally take over the grunt work of capitalist drudgery, the creation of situations will replace the mechanistic slavery of capitalist production where previously '*machinic desire (…) rips up political cultures, deletes traditions, dissolves subjectivities, and hacks through security apparatuses, tracking a soulless tropism to zero control* (Land 2017).

And this is exactly what is happening with the so-called Great Resignation, with people actively turning their backs on the nine-to-five, clocked-on, psychic servitude of consumer capitalism. This is the world dreamed of by the internet pioneers and radical thinkers, the haunted fragments of utopia hidden in the folds of historical time, the freedom from slave labour and the instinctive, desire for creating community.

References

4 Day Week Global (2022) https://www.4dayweek.com/. Accessed on 18 January 2022.

Attali, J. (1985) *Noise: the political economy of music*. Minneapolis, University of Minnesota Press.

Baudrillard, J. (1994) *Simulacra and Simulation* . Translated by S. Glaser. Ann Arbor: University of Michigan Press.

Bentham, J. (2017) The Correspondence of Jeremy Bentham, Volume 1, 1752 to 1776.

Bourdieu, P. (1977) Cultural Reproduction and Social Reproduction. In J. Karabel and A. H. Halsey (Eds.), *Power and Ideology in Education* (pp. 487–511). New York: Oxford University Press.

Brautigan, R. (2015) All Watched Over by Machines of Loving Grace. *Brautigan. net*. Available at: http://www.brautigan.net/machines.html. Accessed 15 January 2022.

Debord, G. (2006) *"Report on the Construction of Situations"*. Translated by K Knabb. Situationist International Anthology. Bureau of Public Secrets, Berkeley.

Deleuze, G. and Guattari, F. (2004). *A Thousand Plateaus: Capitalism and Schizophrenia*. London: Continuum.

Derrida, J. (2006) *Specters of Marx: The State Of The Debt, The Work Of Mourning And The New International*. London: Routledge.

Fisher, M. (2009) *Capitalist Realism: Is there no alternative?* Winchester: Zero Books

Fisher, M. (2014) *Ghosts of my life: Writings on depression, hauntology and lost futures*. Winchester: Zero Books

Gillespie, T.R. B. and Chapman, C.A. (2006) Prediction of parasite infection dynamics in primate metapopulations based on attributes of forest fragmentation. *Conservation Biology* 20 (2): pp. 441–448.

Gramsci, A, (1971) *Selections from the Prison Notebooks of Antonio Gramsci.* New York: International Publishers.

Hobbes, T. (1969) *Leviathan, 1761.* Menston: Scolar P

Horkheimer, M., & Adorno, T. W. (1982) *Dialectic Of Enlightenment.* New York: Continuum.

Jameson, F. (1994) *The Seeds of Time.* New York: Columbia University Press.

Jameson, F. (2004) *Archaeologies of the Future: The Desire Called Utopia and Other Science Fictions.* New York: Verso.

Land, N. (2017) *Fanged Noumena: Collected Writings 1987–2007.* Falmouth: Urbanomic x Sequence Press.

Locke, J. (1997) *An Essay Concerning Human Understanding (Volume 1).* London: Penguin Classics

Lukács, G. (1990) *History and Class Consciousness: Studies in Marxist Dialectics.* Translated by Livingstone, R. Decatur: The Merlin Press.

Marcuse, H. (1962) *Eros and Civilization: A Philosophical Inquiry into Freud.* New York: Vintage Books.

Marx, K. and Engels, F. (1992) *The Communist Manifesto.* Oxford: Oxford University Press.

Russel, S. (2021) *The Reith Lectures.* Accessed on 22 December 2021 on the BBC iPlayer https://www.bbc.co.uk/programmes/m0012fnc.

Sabbaghzadeh, D. (2020) *On The Atomization Of Human Experience & The Factory Of Privatised Stress In The Individualized Self-Care Economy* Accessed at https://www.aqnb.com/2020/10/06/lookoutfornumberone-on-the-atomization-of-human-experience-the-factory-of-privatized-stress-in-the-individualised-self-care-economy/ on 14 January 2022. AQNB.

Wise, D. (2014) *King Mob: A Critical Hidden History.* Bristol: Bread and Circuses Publishing.

Žižek, S. (2002) *Welcome to the Desert of the Real: Five Essays on September 11 and Related Dates.* New York: Verso.

14

Cultural and Creative Districts: A Literature Review and a Taxonomy

Elisabetta Lazzaro

Abstract Cultural and creative districts have become a popular instrument of socio-economic regeneration and governance in many areas of the world. This chapter is a concise overview of main economic research on cultural and creative districts or cultural and creative clusters, their main features and different types that exist, as well as their theoretical background. It accounts for types of governance and administration models, and discusses various elements of monitoring and indicators that are usually used for the measurement of districts and cluster performance, and relative recent developments. It, finally, offers a taxonomy based on some examples of case studies of successful districts, where they are located, and their characteristics at start, growth and maturity phases of their life.

Introduction

In the last decades, cultural and creative districts or clusters have become popular governance instruments adopted by policy makers for the sake of socio-economic development or revitalisation of territories in many regions

E. Lazzaro (✉)
Business School for the Creative Industries, University for the Creative Arts, Farnham, UK
e-mail: Philip.Powell@uca.ac.uk

© The Author(s), under exclusive license to Springer Nature Switzerland AG 2022
P. Powell, B. Shankar Nayak (eds.), *Creative Business Education*,
https://doi.org/10.1007/978-3-031-10928-7_14

237

worldwide, from industrialised countries to less developed ones. Cultural and creative districts or clusters refer to the role of cultural and creative industries (CCI) in local development and regeneration (Chapain and Sagot-Duvauroux 2018). They encompass at the same time the cultural, economic, social, political, geographical and historical spheres (De Propris and Lazzeretti 2009; Scott 1997), offering an interdisciplinary perspective. The geographical units that are mainly considered are municipalities—even of small size and in rural areas—, cities, metropolitan areas and regions. The economic perspective considers local development, job creation, attraction of investment and tourism and regeneration. The social perspective focuses on local communities, and the level of social cohesion, networking and engagement, and an overall sense of community that characterise them.

Creative districts also relate to urban and regional capital (Brooks and Kushner 2001), as well as to the types of interventions that are needed in order to leverage such capital for the sake of their socio-economic impact (Le Blanc 2010). Urban and regional capital bears at least five dimensions: physical (buildings, infrastructure), natural (ecosystem and landscape), human (residents' skills and capacity), cultural (tangible and intangible cultural goods and their creation) and social (community, identity, engagement and cohesion) (Markusen and Gadwa 2010; Landry and Bianchini 1995). In this context, governance's types of intervention include the creation of new goods and endowment, the management of the existing ones, and their renovation and reuse. Stakeholders that exercise this governance in different ways and at different levels are public (e.g., local governments and administrations) and private (e.g., owners, reals estate investors, citizens, associations, etc.), following different interests and motives, such as efficacy, efficiency, measurement and accountability, as well as sustainability and quality of life (Goldberg-Miller and Heimlich 2017).

Theoretical Background

In the economic literature, former concepts related to cultural and creative districts and clusters are those of *creative cities*, as economic units endowed with individuals' skills that contribute to national wealth (Jacobs 1984), and (European) *cities of culture*, as coined in 1990 and then implemented, by the European Union, in order to promote a common European cultural identity, together with local regeneration and tourism (Myerscough 1992). Tourism attraction as such particularly connotates 'art cities' (Costa 1991), which are characterised by a dense, large, complex and interconnected artistic and cultural capital, which is continuously accumulated and consolidated (Richards 1999).

Remarkably, the notion of creative city (Pratt 2010) implies a wider connotation of culture, namely creativity, better allowing for urban planning strategies and intervention (Landry and Bianchini). The creative city was further associated with the creative class (Florida 2002), which emerged as a new social class, where creativity replaced raw materials, physical work and financial capital flows. Correspondingly, municipalities and their governance aimed to actively promote the growth of the creative class and hence its economic performance. The creative city is based on a social and cultural infrastructure, and its socio-economic functioning is considered in terms of urban dynamism and cultural activities. As such, the creative city is able to attract a high concentration of creative work and financial investment.[1]

The general theoretical reference of 'creative districts' (Gdaniec 2000) and 'cultural districts' (Brooks and Kushner 2001) dates back to Marshall's (1890) industrial districts, characterised by internal and external economies of specialised small enterprises that locally compete and cooperate at different stages of production. About one century later, Porter (1990, 1998), among others, developed the concept of cluster, defined as a local agglomeration of firms that are economically interconnected and interdependent and characterised by cooperation, exploitation of local human and financial resources and sharing of information and social networks. Being part of a cluster confers a competitive advantage in terms of productivity—generated by economies of scale and of scope or variety—and innovation, which are fostered by knowledge and network spillovers. Moreover, clusters lower information asymmetries and uncertainty. First applications of clusters to the cultural and creative sphere include Russo's (2000) study on sustainable tourism,[2] and the study on European cities' growth by Van den Berg et al. (2001).

---

[1] Further to some criticism to Florida's creative city and in particular to the creative class—including a too broad definition of creativity, and the assumption of a strong causality, leading to copy-and-paste recipes—, the concepts of creative class and creative city have been revised by Florida himself.

[2] Though Russo's general theoretical framework is based on innovative clusters of Audretsch and Feldman (1995) and not on Porter.

Governance and Performance

Although in their infancy creative clusters tend to present natural or unplanned forms of governance, Scott highlights how creative clusters are not fully self-organising entities, requiring governance interventions. From a governance perspective, local development designed and implemented through cultural and creative districts and clusters can follow a more traditional culture-centric approach or a rather relatively more recent economic-centric approach, implying different values (diversity, inclusion, etc., for the former, vs. innovation, competition, etc., for the latter) and models of a decentralised governance (civic vs. business and public-private-partnership oriented), whose processes can be more or less collaborative and inclusive (Smith and Warfiled 2008; Andres and Chapain 2013).

For their geographical connotation, creative districts and clusters have been the object of economic-impact assessments. First examples date to the early 2000s in the Unites States (e.g., Greater Philadelphia, 2006; Boston Symphony Orchestra, 2008; New York City Waterfalls, 2008). However, this measurement approach was not without criticism. That also offered the chance to expand a sole economic perspective to include also physical and social perspectives (Evans 2005).

Cultural districts, especially when they geographically correspond to metropolitan or regional areas, have made the object of economic measurement in terms of employment, number of firms, turnover, value added, etc. (see for example, Amez et al. 2017). The purpose of these indicators is to assess the contribution of the cultural and creative industries to the economy of these areas. Noticeably, the application of these rather standard indicators is not obvious in the case of cultural and creative industries (Lazzaro and Lowies 2015).

More recently, creative clusters, together with learning, creative and experimenting labs, hubs, incubators, universities and science parks can embody innovative bottom-up initiatives of cross-sectoral cooperation at local, national and international levels, generating important cluster externalities. Especially in the case of regional development, such contribution of the cultural and creative industries to socio-economic growth is favoured by the support of institutional governance (Gustafsson and

Lazzaro 2021). Creative clusters allow a better flexibility and adaptation can generate key knowledge and innovation spillovers at intra- and inter-sectoral levels, for instance in terms of division of labour, or exchange of input, expertise or information. However, the identification and assessment of these spillovers is not straightforward (Lazzaro 2017, 2021).

While the literature offers some perspectives and definitions of performance of cultural and creative districts and clusters, fewer studies attempt to combine and measure them. Indeed, the assessment of cultural performance in urban planning is relevant to capture and foster cultural activities that contribute to local cultural and socio-economic sustainable development and growth. That is particularly relevant through a benchmarking approach, which allows comparisons. The definition of performance can be articulated into different dimensions that make cultural activities possible, where these dimensions need to be measured through accessible and reliable data, which are synthetised in composite indicators. For instance, Jackson et al. (2006) refer to *'cultural vitality'* or *'vibrancy'*, and empirically define it on the basis of interviews to arts professionals, encompassing existing arts organisations, arts participation in its multiple ways, and support systems for arts participation. In Montalto et al. (2019), cultural vibrancy, as defined by surveyed experts, corresponds to the presence of and participation to cultural venues and facilities, as distinguished from the more functional dimensions of jobs creation and innovation generation, and the conditions that enable them. Similar contributions focus more or less on arts supply, arts participation and their environmental conditions, and especially on a relatively more availably measurable arts supply.

A Taxonomy

Table 14.1 below offers a taxonomy of cultural and creative districts applied to a combination of examples of analysis of case studies of cultural and creative districts and clusters taken from the literature in the last fifteen years of so. References were sampled in order to offer and compare a variety of approaches and case studies. Not surprisingly, given also the considerable support put forward by the European Union in the last

Table 14.1 A taxonomy of cultural and creative clusters based on the literature

Reference	Wording	Main perspective(s)	Governance/ administration models	Start
Andres and Chapain (2013)	Networks, CCI in local development strategies, regeneration, rebranding	Institutional design and governance: Degree of inclusion and collaboration between different mixes of public and private stakeholders	Culture vs economic-centric models, and the alternation of their relative importance in time	Industrial and social crises, followed by local public policies of regeneration, driven by national government with key EU financial support
Catungal et al. (2009)	Placemaking, creative city	Discursive and material strategies, and their impacts	Non-profit development agencies for artists, private actors, especially Local property management firms, culture of networking and collaboration	Attractiveness of size, aesthetics, availability and affordability of abandoned industrial spaces to artists
De Propris and Lazzeretti (2009)	Industrial district, urban creative district, clustering and networking	Firm demography and population ecology, local systems, Cross-fertilisation, life cycle	Institutionalisation through creation of professional associations and professional education	Skilled labour, raw materials availability, technological change, small firms' specialisation, localised trade, thick social environment
Della Lucia and Trunfio (2018)	Creative cities	Heritage and creativity, regeneration, tourism, Experience design, community engagement, representation	Formal governance, role of private actors, co-creation, co-design, bottom-up design, local participation, joint public-community strategy	Heritage preservation/ restauration

Growth	Maturity (and possible threats)	Performance/ monitoring indicators	Case study(ies)
Development of different types of institutional collaborations, especially economic-centric (public-private partnerships)	Drop in EU funds, return to more traditional and local culture centric model, less collaboration and/or inclusion	Number, diversity and lasting of partnerships	Birmingham (UK), Marseille (France)
Rise of dotcom industry, site redevelopment, influx of Creative professionals in new media, advertising, film, television and design, attraction of investors and better access to lifestyle amenities, branding	Gentrification, dominance of economic rationales, lack of diversity and experimentation, inequality, working poverty, racialised exclusion, displacement, sustainability	Rental rates, artists' displacement	Liberty Village, Toronto (Canada)
Industrial revolution External factors: Fashion, Input prices and raw-material availability, technological changes, Skilled labour Transportation infrastructure	World wars, recession From manufacturing to direct retailing: From industrial district to urban creative district	Historical, economic, industrial, demographic and ecologic analysis, firms' birth, survival and death	Jewellery quarter, Birmingham (UK)
Heritage-creativity hybridisation	Community engagement	Social inclusion and sustainability, organisational value	IlCartastorie museum, Naples and the farm Cultural Park, Favara, Sicily (Italy)

(continued)

Table 14.1 (continued)

Reference	Wording	Main perspective(s)	Governance/ administration models	Start
Evans (2005)	Culture-led regeneration	Physical, economic and social regeneration, good and bad practices, impact measurement	Integrated and inclusive cultural planning, community consultation, toolkits	Symptoms of local physical, social and/or economic decline that can be mitigated by regenerative effects driven by culture
Richards (2020)	Creative placemaking and design principles	Cultural and creative tourism, creative development, experience design, value creation process, dynamics, creativity as a strategy	Clear vision, consideration and mobilising of resources, structure, programming, implementation Different programmes and design strategies depending on the scale (small-rural to cities and regions)	Resources, meaning and creativity
Sacco and Blessi (2007)	European capitals of culture; cultural districts, cultural clusters	Long-run impact of systematic cultural policies; culture as engine of self-sustaining local socio-economic development; different forms of capital, exogenous and endogenous tangible and intangible assets; "ephemeral"/ tourism vs. "structural"/ cultural-innovation approaches	Official EU programme selection and funding; City-management boards' and temporary agency's capacity building aimed to increase place attractiveness and social capacity building and competitiveness through investment in the CCI and HR; bottom-up design; simple policy making vs. complex polycentric culture-based development process through strictly hierarchical organisation	Former industrial cities; physical infrastructure, organisation of events; redefinition of city image and massive communication plan at national and international levels; blockbuster exhibitions concentrated in city Centre vs. disseminated multicultural and hybridised events in the metropolitan area

Growth	Maturity (and possible threats)	Performance/ monitoring indicators	Case study(ies)
Culture-led regeneration / cultural regeneration / culture and regeneration	Too much ambition in projections (in terms of audience and income), community ownership not secured	Physical, economic and social regeneration; correspondingly, various tests and measurements of policy imperatives and examples of evidence of impacts	Several, from cited literature
New local meanings to resources, participation, creative expression development of coherent narrative	Gentrification, exclusion and serial reproduction, over-tourism	Tangible and intangible resources, meanings and locally embedded creativities	DASTA (Thailand), Den Bosch (Netherlands), Recife (Brazil), Nordrhein-Westfalen region (Germany)
Creation of a dense local Networking of cultural initiatives and involvement of area residents and associations	Long- vs. short-term cultural impact; attraction of qualified tourists vs. dense local networking of cultural initiatives involving residents	Quality of: Cultural supply, local governance, production of knowledge, local entrepreneurship, local talent; attraction of: External firms, external talent; management of social criticalities; capability building and education of the local community; local community involvement	Genoa (Italy), Lille (France)

(continued)

Table 14.1 (continued)

Reference	Wording	Main perspective(s)	Governance/ administration models	Start
Zukin and Braslow (2011)	Cultural or creative districts; gentrified or hipster districts	Real estate development, geography, relocation	Unplanned and natural at start, lack of explicit public support, regulation of artists' house prices (though not able to compensate for gentrification effects on retaining artists)	Concentration of artists, creative and designers in affordable areas, bohemian lifestyle

decades, examples are concentrated in Europe, although examples from other areas are also present.

The taxonomy includes main terms more specifically used to refer to the general category of cultural and creative districts and clusters, the main perspectives and theoretical background considered, and the underlying governance and administration models of reference. This taxonomy can be applied for sake of analysis, as well as to support design and monitoring of creative clusters through their different life-cycle phases (from Start to Maturity through Growth) and more or less explicit, simple versus complex performance and monitoring indicators.

From the different studies, or real cases, presented in Table 14.1, we can see a plurality of wording used for cultural districts and alike, and of main perspectives and aims underlying their analysis. Governance models range between an economic and a social orientation, between a hierarchical organisation to pure unplanning, through a bottom-up approach. Emphasis is often placed on the variety and number of public and private stakeholders that are involved or mobilised in cultural districts. Notwithstanding the plurality of approaches, the analysis allows to identify evolving and maturity (and even decline) patterns in the life cycle of districts, their causes, and hence the performance of districts, more or less explicitly assessed by different possible indicators.

Growth	Maturity (and possible threats)	Performance/ monitoring indicators	Case study(ies)
Public art on streets, neighbourhood reputation, creative entrepreneurs, rise of a small number of celebrity artists, vibe, media, attraction of non-creative cultural consumers	Higher housing prices, more intensive capital investment, artists' displacement, redevelopment Gentrification	Housing prices, capital investment, presence vs displacement of artists	New York (USA)

Conclusions

This chapter dealt with the growing interest cultural and creative districts and clusters have enjoyed in the economic literature, as well as in the practice of local governance in the last decades. After having contextualised cultural districts and the main drivers of their popularity, the chapter discussed their theoretical background, initially focused on a simple economic paradigm, that has been further developed toward a more social dimension, allowing for a variety of cultural district definitions and features, and, correspondingly, underlying aims and perspectives and corresponding governance models. This increase in multiple diversity has called for the concept and application of a taxonomy, enabling to offer a cross comparison of cultural districts for sake of analysis and policy design and monitoring in different environments and purposes.

References

Amez, L., Lazzaro, E., Mauri, C., Vlegels, J. & Ysebaert, W. 2017. *The Cultural & Creative Sectors in the Brussels-Capital Region.* Brussels: Government of the Brussels-Capital Region.

Andres, L. & Chapain, C. 2013 The integration of cultural and creative industries into local and regional development strategies in Birmingham and

Marseille: Towards an inclusive and collaborative governance? *Regional Studies*, 47(2): 161–182.

Audretsch, D.B. & Feldman, M.P. 1995. Innovative Clusters and the Industry Life Cycle. *CEPR Discussion Paper Series*, n. 1161, London.

Brooks, A. C. & Kushner, R. J. 2001. Cultural districts and urban development. *International Journal of Arts Management* 3: 4–14.

Catungal, J. P., Leslie, D. & Lii, Y. 2009. Geographies of displacement in the creative city: the case of Liberty Village, Toronto. *Urban Studies*, 46, 1095–1114.

Chapain, C. & D. Sagot-Duvauroux. 2018. Cultural and creative clusters—a systematic literature review and a renewed research agenda. *Urban Research & Practice*, 1–30.

Costa, P. 1991. Managing tourism carrying capacity of art cities. *The Tourist Review*. 46 (4): 8.

De Propris, L. & Lazzeretti, L. 2009. Measuring the Decline of a Marshallian Industrial District: The Birmingham Jewellery Quarter. *Regional Studies*, 43:9, 1135–1154.

Evans, G. 2005. Measure for Measure: Evaluating the Evidence of Culture's Contribution to Regeneration. *Urban Studies*, 42(5/6), 959–983.

Della Lucia, M. & Trunfio, M. 2018. The role of the private actor in cultural regeneration: Hybridizing cultural heritage with creativity in the city. *Cities*, 82, 35–44.

Florida, R. 2002. *The Rise of the Creative Class: And How It's Transforming Work, Leisure, Community and Everyday Life*. New York: Basic Books.

Gdaniec, C. 2000. Cultural industries, information technology and the regeneration of post-industrial urban landscapes. Poblenou in Barcelona—a virtual city? *Geojournal*, 50(4), 379–388.

Goldberg-Miller, S. B. & Heimlich, J. E. 2017. "Creatives' Expectations: The Role of Super Creatives in Cultural District Development." *Cities*, 62:120–30

Gustafsson, G. & Lazzaro, E. 2021. The Innovative Response of Cultural and Creative Industries to Major European Societal Challenges: Toward a Knowledge and Competence Base. *Sustainability*, 13(23), 13267.

Jacobs, J. 1984. *Cities and the Wealth of Nations: Principles of Economic Life*, New York: Random House.

Jackson, M. R., Kabwasa-Green, F. & Herranz, J. 2006. *Cultural vitality in communities: Interpretation and indicators. Culture, Creativity and Communities Program*. Washington, DC: The Urban Institute.

Landry, C. & Bianchini, F. 1995. *The creative city*. Demos, London.

Lazzaro, E., 2017. Cultural and creative entrepreneurs. In Doyle J.E. & Mickov B. (eds.), *Culture, Innovation and the Economy*, pp. 33-37. London: Routledge.

Lazzaro, E. 2021. Linking the creative economy with universities' entrepreneurship in a urban context: A spillover approach. *Sustainability*, 13(3), 1078.

Lazzaro, E. & Lowies, J.G. 2015. *Le poids économique des industries culturelles et créatives en Wallonie et à Bruxelles*. Namur: Institut wallon de l'évaluation, de la prospective et de la statistique (IWEPS).

Le Blanc, A. 2010. Cultural Districts, a new strategy for regional development? The South-East Cultural District in Sicily. *Regional Studies*, 44, 905–17.

Markusen, A. & Gadwa, A. 2010. *Creative placemaking*. Washington, DC: National Endowment for the Arts.

Marshall, A. 1890. *Principles of Economics*. London and New York: Macmillan & Co.

Montalto, V., Moura, C.J.T., Langedijk, S. & Saisana, M. 2019. Culture counts: An empirical approach to measure the cultural and creative vitality of European cities. *Cities*, 89, 167–185.

Myerscough, J. 1992. Measuring the impact of the arts: the Glasgow 1990 experience. *Journal of the Market Research Society*, 31, pp. 323–335.

Porter, M. 1990. *The Competitive Advantage of Nations*. New York: The Free Press.

Porter, M. 1998. Clusters and the new economics of competition. *Harvard Business Review*, 11 (November–December), 77–90.

Pratt, A.C., 2010. Creative cities: Tensions within and between social, cultural and economic development: A critical reading of the UK experience. *City, Culture and Society*, 1(1), pp. 13–20.

Richards, G. 1999. European Cultural Tourism: Patterns and Prospects. In Dodd, D. & van Hemel, A-M. (eds), *Planning cultural tourism in Europe. A presentation of theories and cases*. Amsterdam: Boekman Foundation.

Richards, G. 2020. Designing creative places: The role of creative tourism. *Annals of Tourism Research*, 85, 102922.

Russo, A.P. 2000. *The sustainable cultural cluster. Notes on agglomeration, tourism policy and information technologies in tourist cities*. Paper presented at the 40th Congress of the European Regional Science Association, Barcelona.

Sacco, P.L. & Blessi, G.T. 2007. European culture capitals and local development strategies: Comparing the Genoa 2004 and Lille 2004 cases. *Homo oeconomicus*, 24(1), 111–143.

Scott A. 1997. The cultural economy of cities. *International Journal of Urban and Regional Research* 2, 323–339.

Smith R. & Warfiled K. 2008. The creative city: a matter of values. In Cooke, P. & Lazzaretti, L. (Eds), *Creative Cities, Cultural Clusters and Local Economic Development*, pp. 287–312. Edward Elgar, Cheltenham.

Van den Berg, L., Braun, E. & van Winden, W. 2001. Growth Clusters in European Cities: An Integral Approach. *Urban Studies*, 38(1), 186–206.

Zukin, S. & Braslow, L. 2011. The life cycle of New York's creative districts: Reflections on the unanticipated consequences of unplanned cultural zones. *City, Culture and Society*, 2(1), 131–140.

15

Innovation Through Engaged Learning: Working with Mode 2 Knowledge and Intrapreneurship

Anita Walsh and Philip Powell

Abstract The dominance of a market discourse in higher education emphasises private benefit—either through individual human capital for students or through intellectual property for innovation through research. This approach coexists with a debate concerning the importance of students' engagement with learning and the need for universities to be more responsive to the society of which they are a part. There is an emphasis on world-class research but, it is claimed, a neglect of the more '*local*' research which would be valued by communities. The role of pedagogies which support both engagement and practice relevant research is overlooked. A pedagogic approach which recognises the importance of practice knowledge and which supports working students as practitioner researchers in

A. Walsh (✉)
Department of Management, Birkbeck, University of London, London, UK
e-mail: Philip.Powell@uca.ac.uk

P. Powell
Business School for the Creative Industries, University for the Creative Arts, Farnham, UK
e-mail: Philip.Powell@uca.ac.uk

© The Author(s), under exclusive license to Springer Nature Switzerland AG 2022   **251**
P. Powell, B. Shankar Nayak (eds.), *Creative Business Education*,
https://doi.org/10.1007/978-3-031-10928-7_15

their own organisations offers a means of drawing together engagement and knowledge creation. Using an epistemology of practice and drawing on the concept of Gibbons et al.'s Mode 2 knowledge (transdisciplinary knowledge produced in the context of application) a pedagogy can be used to support practitioner research, enabling work-based learning students to be supported in undertaking applied contextual research. The development and application of research skills creates a high level of engagement for students from private, public and third sector organisations. Negotiating the context for their research helps move them from an '*employee*' mindset to an '*intrapreneurial*' mindset, whereby they question, enquire and innovate. Such research is small scale and context specific, yet it can introduce immediate innovation and benefit to organisations which have been difficult to reach through more conventional approaches.

Introduction

The economic environment in which higher education operates, and the increased scale of student participation, have meant that the funding and the purpose of a university education have come under scrutiny. Within UK higher education the dominance of market discourse, and the imposition of policies which are predicated on the assumption that the market model is most appropriate, have shifted perceptions of higher education from a public good to a private benefit. As Neary (2016) points out, the UK Consumer Rights Act (2015) and the UK Higher Education Research Bill (2016) have '*consolidated this rhetoric [of students as consumers] as an objective legal fact*', confirming the university as '*a trader and supplier of educational services to the student in what amounts to a direct, individual contractual relationship*'. Tomlinson (2017) argues that students are encouraged to view the value of their higher education experience as a form of individual human capital creation. With this model of higher education as a consumable good there is little to indicate the desirability of the mutual exchange which has often been seen to be at the heart of the higher education experience. Molesworth et al. (2009) claim that:

With the degree of marketization seen in many HEIs, students and the institutions they attend look only to satisfy a consumer culture which negates even the possibility that higher education changes the individual's outlook. Instead many HEIs prepare the student for a life of consumption by obtaining a well-paid job: a mission of confirmation rather than transformation.

The emphasis on individual investment and return, together with the considerable increases in graduates entering the labour market, has resulted. The focus on the cost of studying for a degree, together with considerations of '*value for money*' has resulted in an increasing emphasis on the need for a degree to deliver individually measurable benefits. Yet, such discussions are taking place in a context in which many students need to work during their studies, and when awards such as, in the UK, the Degree Apprenticeship and a lifelong learning entitlement are prominent in national policy.

HE Research and Pedagogy

There are a number of pressures on UK higher education which call for universities to demonstrate the contribution they make on a range of fronts. Yet, in the UK, the Research Excellence Framework (REF) and the recent Knowledge Exchange Framework (KEF) set the parameters of HEIs' impact quite narrowly, drawing on the established model of higher education as a creator of knowledge.

Despite the expressed concern to ensure the academy makes an active contribution to society, it has been claimed that current metrics reinforce the divide between the two. Alvesson et al. (2017) point to the extent that REF metrics, which emphasise '*quantifiable outputs and publications in the right journals*', have influenced academic practice. Since these directly influence both institutional and individual status, the argument is made that government policies have promoted the employment of '*career academics*' with little or no experience of organisations other than the university (Kumari 2017). It has been claimed that, particularly in business schools, academics who wanted respect from other academic disciplines needed to produce research that could be published in respected journals.

Therefore, many business school academics develop theoretical models which will appeal to an academic audience (Thomas et al. 2013). The result is that '*much business academic research remains founded on issues of experimental design derived from the hard sciences, which becomes the driving force in selecting research questions rather than the needs of the practitioners*' (Syed et al. 2009). The research debate is frequently couched in terms of achieving either rigour, through the use of established disciplinary methodologies, or relevance, through the attempt to address issues which occur in practice—with the implication that the two may be mutually exclusive.

A strong critique of the current approach adopted is put forward by Alvesson et al. (2017) who argue that, '*The demand for rigour—or rather a particular version of rigour—is one that accounts for the continuing preponderance of papers based on quantitative methodologies, no matter how trivial their conclusions*', leading to a failure to engage with the major social challenges society is currently facing.

The emphasis on quantifiable approaches is likely to have arisen because the model of impact assessment often used is based on one which works well for subjects which are hard sciences, but which is difficult to use effectively in the social sciences. The impact of academic social science research outside the academy is therefore extremely hard to evidence. However, the impact of research inside the academy, via research-informed teaching, is often assumed. The benefits of students learning from active researchers who teach on their specialist topic are consistently referred to. Weertz and Sandmann (2010) point out that research intensive universities have '*cosmopolitan faculty who have developed national and international relationships based on their success in advancing traditional forms of scholarship*'. General claims are made that '*top level research is one of the best quality assurance mechanisms for classroom teaching*' (Steffens and Grote 2016). Yet, Grand et al. (2015) found that the most common terms provided by academics relating to public engagement with their research involved '*dissemination*', '*communication*' or '*presentation*' of research. This may be why Alvesson et al. (2017) report that, when considering activities of academic staff, research orientation and student orientation are often negatively correlated. Moreover, Brown (2013) states that, '*I have lost count of the number of times I have heard representatives of the sector, and especially Vice Chancellors, make assertions about the necessary inter-relationship between research and teaching which lack any serious evidential basis'.* Despite this, relatively little attention has been paid to the student engagement and knowledge co-creation achieved through teaching research skills to students, and supporting them in applying such skills in contexts outside the academy.

Practice Knowledge

Business and management schools in universities are mainly structured along disciplinary lines, and, as Schoenberger (2001)points out, '*Disciplines are bound up with epistemological commitments .. we have to internalize a set of practices and understandings about how valid knowledge is created'.* Inside the academy there is a preference for formal theoretical models which are refined over time through peer critique and a belief that separation from society ensures detachment. Hager and Halliday (2009) argue that the approach taken by the academy assumes that there are general solutions to particular problems which can be development outside of the practical situations i.e. that decontextualised models can be developed in the university and applied elsewhere. The primacy given by the academy to theoretical formal knowledge has the effect that more tacit and informal aspect of professional are overlooked or devalued (Boud and Hager 2012). The result being that many models of knowledge exchange between universities and other organisations conceptualise knowledge as the '*professionally packaged outputs of research'* (Ward, Smith et al., Ward et al. 2012). The case has been made that organisations need to meet the challenge of gaining '*a better understanding of the applicability of academic knowledge'* (Rosli et al. 2018). Yet the pace of academic knowledge production and refinement is slow, and the nature of the knowledge is different to the knowledge which serves organizational interests (Avis 2003).

When considering different types of knowledge, Boud (2015) points out that learning about practice is not the same as practising, in that knowledge use is involved in the latter. Susskind and Susskind (2017) distinguish between people who are experts and people who are knowledgeable—expert practice involves having a successful track record of using one's expertise. Adopting a perspective of knowledge in use involves a shift in focus from one on knowledge to one on knowing, and entails a shift from an epistemology of possession to an epistemology of practice (Webster Wright 2010). As Boud (2015) points out, a practice-oriented approach would see practice knowledge to be as valuable as scientific or technical knowledge. This involves not displacing formal knowledge, but recognising that more than one type of knowledge is necessary for effective professional performance, and that each type of knowledge fulfils a specific role. Such a recognition is present in Eraut's (2000) claim that '*to focus only on the explicit learning of formally presented knowledge is to fail to recognise the complexity of learning*', as well as in the discussion relating to the importance of supporting students in the development of 'soft skills'.

Eraut (2004) argues that '*professional, managerial and technical performances are normally complex and typically involve the simultaneous use of several types of knowledge and skills*'. However, codified formal knowledge is explicit and has a particular epistemological status, whereas personal practice knowledge tends to be informal and can be explicit or tacit (Eraut 2000). The result is that it is easier to discuss and identify formal codified knowledge, while overlooking tacit aspects of personal professional knowledge (Eraut 2004). Yet, the performative aspect of practice knowledge production and application is fundamental to the solution of the immediate problems which arise in practice (Avis 2003). In addition, theoretical knowledge must be adapted to suit the demands of a given situation—it has to be interpreted in order to be used (Eraut 1998).

The recognition of the importance of practice knowledge allows a different perspective to be taken on the value of knowledge gained outside the academy and facilitates a different approach to student research which is applied and context specific.

Practitioner Research

Many higher education institutions will have students who are in work during their studies. At postgraduate level, the proportion of students who study part-time is high as people often take postgraduate programmes to enhance their existing careers, and many undergraduate students will work as they study due to financial constraints. Paid employment, either full-time or part-time, provides a contrast to the conventional work placements and internships undertaken by young, full-time students. In paid employment students primarily self-identify as employees, whereas during work placements and internships they retain their primary identity as student. The opportunity to integrate curriculum content from their work into their programme of study through undertaking an applied research project instead of a text-based dissertation is attractive to working students. Such students to not intend to become academic researchers—they are not intending to add to the sum of disciplinary knowledge, but appreciate the opportunity for their research to demonstrate the relevance of their studies. They acquire research skills to investigate specific aspects of their professional practice and/or context, thus adopting the perspective of the practitioner-researcher.

As Jarvis (1999) points out, the role of the practitioner-researcher provides a clear contrast to the image of researchers as academics who enter the work context as '*outsiders, usually university-based, coming into the world of practice, seeking to understand it*' (Jarvis 1999). Academic researchers attempt to theorise practice from the perspective of a given academic discipline and the audience for their findings is other academic researchers. In contrast, practitioner research is '*about seeking, in a most rigorous manner, to understand and create efficient working practice*' (op cit). Practitioner researchers take an interventionist stance to the area under study. Because they are employees they are already socialised into the organizational culture of the context in which they will be researching—they are established members of communities of practice and are familiar with both formal and informal aspects of organisational functioning. They have access to the '*cultural knowledge that has not been codified [but that] plays a key role in most work-based practices and activities'* (Eraut 2004). The research undertaken by practitioner researchers is directly informed by their professional practice and therefore addresses '*real*' issues. Direct workplace experience provides knowledge of where to look for information, and also knowledge of what to look for and why such knowledge is useful (Paloniemi 2006).

Recognising what they term the '*wider social production of knowledge*' Gibbons et al. (2000) distinguish between knowledge produced inside the academy and knowledge produced in other contexts; they define the former as Mode 1 knowledge and the latter as Mode 2 knowledge (knowledge produced in the context of its application). Discussing the different modes of knowledge production, Syed et al. (2009) claim that Mode 1 knowledge is the traditional, discipline-based, largely theoretical work aimed at understanding how the world works, while Mode 2 knowledge is transdisciplinary and tries to get things to work in practice.

The explicit recognition of potentially valuable knowledge in workplace practice supports a different relationship between academic and student when undertaking work-based research projects. As Boud and Costley (2007) point out, the power of the discipline and the requirement for students to research within specific disciplinary parameters has meant that historically the control of the research project has been with the tutor. However, as Helyer (2011) states, work-based learning students have their own professional expertise '*which, if of a specialist nature, sometimes exceeds that of the lecturers they encounter*'. Acknowledging such expertise requires a different role from the academic involved. Boud and Costley (2007) argue for a change in terminology to reflect the need for a different academic practice—they advocate use of the term '*adviser*' rather than '*supervisor*'. Moving away from a single focus on disciplinary expertise, advisers become experts in the epistemology of practice and levels of achievement. They support students in shaping the knowledge they produce to meet academic standards and to address professional requirements.

This research approach allows for the co-production of knowledge between the academic adviser and the student. The student has inside knowledge of the work context and can identify issues which are relevant to the organisation. In this way the setting influences the shape of the project, with the practice focus driving the use of theory rather than the requirements of an academic discipline—it is transdisciplinary. Such an approach is taken in recognition that specific methodologies that have developed in the context of and for the purposes of particular academic disciplines are unlikely to offer effective and appropriate approaches to support and codify a practice-oriented production of knowledge (Garnett 2016). There is, therefore, no attempt to confine students to the boundaries of a specific discipline. This leads to project outcomes which are a mix of the pragmatic/organizational and the academic, and are applied in or recommended for real settings (Boud and Costley 2007). They reflect the characteristics of Mode 2 knowledge production, in that as Gibbons et al. (2000) point out, they represent knowledge produced in the context of its application. In such a context it is not possible to distinguish between '*pure*' and '*applied*' knowledge, the process becomes '*a mixture of theory and practice, abstraction and aggregation, ideas and data. The bounds of the intellectual and its environment have become blurred*' (Gibbons et al. 2000).

A transdisciplinary approach to knowledge affects the perspective taken on research methods, Kincheloe (2005) refers to a '*methodological bricolage*' which draws on a combination of an understanding of the research context, together with previous experience of research methods. This combination is provided through the combined contributions of the student for the context and the adviser for the research methods.

A research methods module introduces students to a range of research approaches, together with the epistemological assumptions which are embedded in them. In considering the different research perspectives students learn that the knowledge produced depends on the research approach taken, which depends on assumptions made about the nature of the research focus.

As Kincheloe (2001) points out, '*It is not difficult to understand the epistemological contention that the types of logic, criteria for validity, and methods of enquiry used in clinical medicine as opposed to teacher effectiveness in teaching critical thinking will differ*'. Engagement with this perspective supports students in selecting the most appropriate theoretical framing for their work, and their approach to research methods is active rather than passive—selecting a method from those to hand, rather than accepting a method defined by a particular academic discipline.

The shift to academic adviser from supervision within a discipline gives students more of a role in the structuring of their project. As practitioner/researchers students take responsibility for the focus and structure of their research, with the research questions set reflecting the interests of the student and their organisation. For those students researching their own professional context, it is necessary to gain organisational consent for access to resources—either data which is collected by the organisation, or access to respondents for interviews or questionnaires. They, therefore, enter into a different relationship with their employing organisation through their research activities.

The secondary research undertaken to inform students' thinking on their project is focused on topics which are relevant to the main area of research, to alert students to issues which have previously been identified in the literature. This engagement with theory on topics which are directly relevant to workplace problems provides a new way of framing the students' perception—it supports them in '*problematising*' a work situation with which they may be quite familiar. Theory can be used as a lens through which to interrogate practice.

Creating a distinction between the student as '*worker*' and the student as '*researcher*' is a fundamentally important aspect of a successful project, and students are introduced to the requirement for all research—whether academic or professional—to be evidence-based. This distinction is emphasised drawing on Oakeshott's (1985) concept of '*ways of seeing*'— that an item can be seen differently according to the world of ideas into which it fits. An example given by Oakeshott is that of a Minoan pot, which he points out was created for purely practical purposes yet, as a survival, is seen as evidence for a particular way of life by the historian. This helps students to appreciate that something which they judge according to its practical usefulness as a worker can also be seen as evidence from a researcher's perspective, and that researchers need evidence to support any case put forward. The emphasis on the fundamental importance of a valid method of data collection to underpin conclusions and recommendations and build confidence in them helps distance students from the workplace in which they are embedded. As Siebert and Mills (2006) explain, the adoption of a '*robust methodology and a meticulous audit trail will ensure that interpretations are justified … and that the voice of the researcher will dominate over the voice of the worker*'.

It is through the undertaking of embedded research in a workplace context that the student develops relevant research skills and an intrapreneurial mindset.

Mode 2 Knowledge, Transdisciplinarity and Intrapreneurship

The parameters of innovation are set relatively narrowly in terms of the research and knowledge exchange activities envisaged in the REF and the KEF—the assumption appears to be that academic knowledge produced in the conventional disciplinary manner will be able to support effective innovation outside the academy. This may be the case where medical or highly technical areas are involved, but it is difficult to see how direct translation of research can take place in a social or business context. In terms of entrepreneurship, often workshops offered in higher education focus on developing a particular concept ab initio, and high-profile entrepreneurs offered as potential role models are individuals who have built large business interests from small beginnings. Such approaches would be suitable only for a small minority of students—with the majority wanting formal employment at the end of their studies or working to enhance their prospects in their current career or wishing to change career direction. It could be argued that the concept of the intrapreneur—someone who innovates on behalf of an existing organisation, rather than on their own behalf—although less discussed and smaller in scale, is of greater relevance to most students.

The parameters of intrapreneurship are set more widely than those for entrepreneurship. As Carrier (1997) points out, innovation through intrapreneurship can be commercial, organizational, institutional, procedural or social in nature, which means that such activity can be of collective as well as individual benefit. In addition, intrapreneurial activity can take place at any level of an organisation, with the innovation involved being incremental or radical (Seshadri and Tripathy 2006). These characteristics mean that students could achieve intrapreneurial activity in a wide range of spheres. It is recognised that the established context and usual job conditions will structure the type of innovation which is proposed (Carrier 1997). There are, however, fundamental characteristics without which intrapreneurship cannot be effective. One is that the intrapreneur must have a measure of autonomy, and that their role in an organisation must allow for an innovation to be introduced (Antoncic and Hisrich 2003). The other characteristic is attitudinal. Seshadri and Tripathy (2006) claim that intrapreneurs operate with an entrepreneurial mindset, and that, to achieve such a mindset, individuals need to experience a shift away from an employee attitude. There needs to be a transformation of perspective to an attitude which is more engaged and which demonstrates psychological ownership of their project and the activities associated with it. This is a key part of building the credibility that is needed when introducing a change into a context where both processes/products and individuals are familiar (Seshadri and Tripathy 2006).

The case is made here that students who undertake work-based projects are supported in shifting their perspective from purely that of an employee. They are required to demonstrate independence of thought both in the choice of the project, and in the manner in which they choose to undertake it. Through their introduction to research methods and the requirement to consider the workplace as a provider of evidence, students build their competence and their confidence, increasing their autonomy. Siebert and Mills (2006) point out that having to see the workplace from the perspective of the academy means that students are better able to gain an autonomous understanding of the world of work of which they are a part. The framework set by secondary research, with theory being used as a lens through which to consider workplace practice, leads to the '*recognition of cross-situational significance, particularly the notions of transferability and applicability, which set higher level forms of learning apart*' (Cope 2003). Here, Cope is referring to the mindset of the entrepreneur, but the experience of intellectual challenge and perspective change achieved through applied practitioner research achieves this shift to intrapreneurial activity in students who are practitioner researchers.

As stated, the requirement to agree a research focus with their employer and to negotiate access to relevant organisational resources requires a different relationship than that of employee. The structuring of an appropriate research method and the '*ownership*' of the relevant research activities places a clear responsibility on the student to complete the project they have proposed. The change of perspective outlined above means that new organisational insights can be offered, or new and creative solutions can be proposed to existing challenges confronting the organisation. There is, therefore, a clear and direct benefit to organisations from the findings of research undertaken by practitioner researchers, which is supervised by the academy, but which adopts a transdisciplinary perspective.

In addition, the benefit to the individual can be considerable. As Seshadri and Tripathy (2006) state, an intrapreneurial approach is not chosen by most employees in any profession because the demands involved are much more than those which apply to operating with an 'employee mindset'. Yet, those individuals who do undertake intrapreneurship find it challenging, fulfilling, and personally and professionally rewarding.

Discussion and Conclusions

In a social and economic context of turbulent markets and technological complexity, the pace of change is such that, as Marques (2015) points out, '*The concept of stability has changed from remaining the same for a long time into flexibly and undauntedly riding the tides of today's corporate sea*'. It is in this context that there has been an emphasis on the need for intrapreneurship in small and medium sizes businesses (Carrier 1997). Increasingly it is also the case that public and third sector organisations need to be able to draw on innovative practice in order to help them maximise the use of resources which are constrained.

Hager and Halliday (2009) argue that the approach to knowledge production and innovation taken by the academy assumes that there are general solutions to practical problems, and that such solutions can be developed outside the practical situations in which they are to be used. The relevance of context is completely overlooked from this perspective.

The slow pace of academic knowledge production and refinement requires the relatively static formalisation of long-term agreements, often including the presence of an academic researcher as a boundary spanner between the two organisations. This entails an increasing emphasis on working through formal contractual relationships and operates to disadvantage the smaller, less well-organised and resourced groups, who rely more on informal structures and communication (Benneworth and Osborne 2013). Such an approach means that partnerships are available mainly to large organisations, and tends to exclude major sectors of the economy and society, many of whom could benefit from the input of a different perspective on their practices or their problems.

In addition, the difficulty of effectively applying much of the theoretical knowledge produced by the academy means that, despite considerable efforts over time, the track record of success is relatively limited. It is also the case that the purpose of academic knowledge is disputed—many in the academy would argue that the creation of knowledge should be the main focus of the academy, not the development of knowledge for direct application and use in problem solving (Steffens and Grote 2016). Susskind and Susskind (2017) distinguish between those who are knowledgeable and those who are expert. The knowledgeable often possess wide ranging knowledge about something yet this does not by definition equip them to be effective practitioners. In contrast, those who are expert have a track record of successfully using the knowledge they possess. This emphasis on the importance of knowledge for professional use highlights the perceived limitations of a purely academic approach. When discussing the relationship between academic knowledge and practice, Boud (2015) points out that, if what academics do exists only in educational institutions and cannot translate to other contexts, then the knowledge gained from them will have limited value.

Through practitioner research and work-based projects students can make a discernible different to the workplace practices of themselves and their colleagues (Helyer 2011), and practitioner research can take place in organisations of any size. The practitioner researcher needs formal consent to be able to access relevant resources, but the timing of any project will fit with the requirements of the programme involved and of the organisation. Small scale contextual projects can be completed in a relatively short timescale, leading to visible outputs which are directly focused on the organisation concerned. From the perspective of the academy the integration of real-life, real-time projects as part of the curriculum moves pedagogy away from the dominant transmission model towards co-creation of knowledge with students. Since the project is based on actual practice it provides an authentic assessment experience which is meaningful for the student both at the time of undertaking it, and for the future in terms of the skills developed (Murphy et al. 2017). The full integration of the student as '*worker*' helps build organizational confidence in their activities and enables them to operate as an effective boundary spanner between the university and the wider community (Weertz and Sandmann 2010).

The flexibility offered by the transdisciplinary approach adopted in the pedagogy means that, rather than engaging only with decontextualised theoretical models, students get a more rounded perspective from being able to learn from real world experience, while at the same time benefitting their employers (Harris et al. 2013). Some lack of confidence in such an approach comes from the established link between the academic disciplines and quality assurance of knowledge production. However, as Gibbons et al. (2000) state, disciplinary boundaries matter far more inside the university than outside it, and their distinction between Mode 1 and Mode 2 knowledge indicates that transdisciplinary knowledge is different but not by definition inferior. It could be argued that, in having to engage with the different epistemological assumptions which underpin research approaches in order to appreciate transdisciplinary research, students get a broader picture of how knowledge production works within the academy. This supports them in gaining a more critically evaluative perspective on knowledge claims more generally—an important skill in today's information rich environment. Moreover, it is recognised that the pace of change of social and technical knowledge is such that future career success will '*depend less on having great swathes of technical knowledge than on having creativity and strong interpersonal skills*' (Susskind and Susskind 2017). This greater flexibility which will be required in approach to employment may be one of the reasons that the Institute for the Future (2011), when listing future work skills includes: transdisciplinarity, social intelligence and adaptive thinking. Such generic capabilities will be necessary to support graduates in the future '*need for self-management, reinvention, and knowing how to manage life transitions*' (Hopson 2009). Shulman (2005) points out that '*professional education is not education for understanding alone, it is preparation for accomplished and responsive practice*', and that a crucial aspect of professionalism is the ability to make judgements in a context of uncertainty. Negotiating the parameters of their project and access to the required resources offers students the opportunity to practice such judgements.

Serrat (2017) claims that the ability to convert intellectual and social capital into novel and appropriate things is now the '*critical organisational requirement of the age*' and it is recognised that flexibility and creativity will be required to negotiate a future which is unclear. The wide literature on innovation and entrepreneurship, supplemented by that on intrapreneurship, indicates the extent to which new ways of approaching things are seen to be fundamentally important. Both entrepreneurship and intrapreneurship are individual enterprises and rely on the commitment and engagement of those concerned. Amabile and Pratt (2016) point out that people are most creative when they are primarily intrinsically motivated. Students who undertake work-based projects have committed themselves to higher level study, and are enthused by gaining the insights provided through a direct relationship between theory and practice—they have the kind of psychological ownership of their project which is a necessary aspect of intrapreneurship. Seshadri and Tripathy (2006) argue that supporting and encouraging intrapreneurship plays a key role in keeping employees motivated and open new avenues for creative innovation which benefits the organisation. It could therefore be claimed that work-based project based on Mode 2 knowledge and transdisciplinarity offer a direct and responsive contribution to organisational innovation.

It is recognised that widescale adoption of the approach outlined above may not be feasible or desirable. However, the case is made here that this mode of knowledge production offers a valuable complement to the more established disciplinary approaches. Knowledge use in practice is fundamentally affected by the context in which it is applied, and transdisciplinary knowledge production leads to results which are both transient and highly contextualised (Gibbons et al. 2000). The results do not directly contribute to building disciplinary knowledge and research. It could be argued that Mode 2 knowledge is therefore more appropriate for practice because whereas '*science assumes a world of stable, unchanging, quantitative fact … practice assumes a world of mutable, transient fact*' (Oakeshott 1985). Moreover, as Derrick (2020) points out, the requirement in practice is for inherently provisional knowledge, i.e. for knowledge which is sufficient for present practical purposes.

Using a pedagogy for research methods which is based on transdisciplinarity and Mode 2 knowledge introduces students to a range of perspectives which enables them to consider their workplace context in new ways, leading to innovative proposals for change. Such changes are small-scale and their impact is contextualised in the organisation of which the student is part, yet the changes are immediate and of direct benefit to those outside the academy. The recognition of such research as part of the academy's research and public engagement activities could help offset the critique that the current emphasis on international research excellence as evidenced through the usual academic indicators—for example, journal citations, patent registrations etc.—leads to a neglect of social and economic issues which are more relevant to local communities. It could also stimulate a discussion which recognises the specificity of institution-based knowledge, while opening up a dialogue between academic knowledge and other forms of knowledge across a range of constituencies, including that of work-based practice in context (Avis 2003).

However, current approaches to identifying and measuring knowledge creation and innovation within the academy cannot accommodate the kind of activity which is dispersed and relatively fluid. The result is that small scale '*local*' research in context which supports innovation and which has an impact which is immediate and of direct benefit outside the academy is currently overlooked.

References

Alvesson, M. Gabriel, Y., and Paulsen, R. (2017) *Return to Meaning: a social science with something to say* Oxford University Press, Oxford

Amabile, T.M. and Pratt, M.G. (2016) 'The dynamic model of creativity and innovation in organisations: Making progress, making meaning' *Research in Organizational Behaviour* Volume 36 pp. 157–183

Antoncic, B. and Hisrich, R.D. (2003) 'Clarifying the intrapreneurship concept' *Journal of Small Business and Entrepreneur Development* Volume 10:1 pp. 7–24

Avis, J. (2003) 'Work-based knowledge, evidence informed practice and education' *British Journal of Educational Studies* Volume 51:4 pp. 369–389

Benneworth, P. and Osborne, M. (2013) 'Knowledge exchange and Higher Education in Europe' in Escriges, C., Granados Sanchez, J., Hall, B. and Tandon, R. *Knowledge, Engagement and Higher Education: Contributing to social change* Global University Network for Innovation (GUNI) Series on the Social Commitment of Universities Palgrave Macmillan

Boud, D. (2015) 'Taking professional practice seriously: implications for deliberate course design' in Trede, F. and McEwan, C. (Eds) *Educating the Deliberate Professional: Preparing practitioners for emergent futures* Springer, Dordrecht

Boud, D. and Costley, C. (2007) 'From project supervision to advising: new conceptions of the practice' *Innovations in Education and Teaching International* Volume 44:2 pp. 119–130

Boud, D. and Hager, P. (2012) 'Rethinking continued professional development through changing metaphors and location in professional practice' *Studies in Continuing Education* Volume 34:1 pp. 17–30

Brown, R. (2013) 'Mutuality meets the market: Analysing changes in the quality assurance in United Kingdom Higher Education 1992–2012' *Higher Education Quarterly* Volume 67:4 pp. 420–437

Carrier, C. (1997) 'Intrapreneurship in small businesses: An exploratory study' *Entrepreneurship in theory and practice* Volume 21:1 pp. 5–20

Cope, J. (2003) 'Entrepreneurial learning and critical reflection—discontinuous events as triggers for 'higher level' learning' *Management Learning* Volume 34:4 pp. 429–450

Derrick, J. (2020) ''Tacit pedagogy' and 'entanglement': practice-based learning and innovation' *Journal of Workplace Learning* Volume 32:4 pp. 273–284

Eraut, M. (1998) 'Concepts of competence' *Journal of Interprofessional Care* Volume 12:2 pp. 127–139

Eraut, M. (2000) 'Non formal learning and tacit knowledge in professional work' *British Journal of Education Psychology* Volume 70 pp. 113–116

Eraut, M. (2004) 'Informal learning in the workplace' *Studies in Continuing Education* Volume 26:2 pp. 247–274

Garnett, J. (2016) 'Work-based learning: A critical challenge to the subject discipline structures and practices of higher education' Higher Education, Skills and Work-Based Learning Volume 6:3 pp. 305–314

Gibbons, M., Limoges, C., Nowotny, H., Schwartzman, S., Scott, P., and Trow, M. (2000*) The New Production of Knowledge: The dynamics of science and research in contemporary societies* Sage, London

Grand, A., Davies, G., Hollman, R., and Adams, A. (2015) 'Mapping public engagement with research in a UK university' PLoSONE Volume 10:4 e0121874

Hager, P. and Halliday, J. (2009) *Recovering Informal Learning: Wisdom, Judgement and Community* Springer, Dordrecht

Harris, M., Chisholm, C. and Burns, G. (2013) 'Using the knowledge transfer partnership in undergraduate education and practice-based training to encourage employer engagement' *Education and Training* Volume 55:2 pp. 174–190

Helyer, R. (2011) 'Aligning higher education with the world of work' *Higher Education, Skills and Work-Based Learning* Volume 1:2 pp. 95–105

Hopson, B. (2009) From Vocational Guidance to Portfolio Careers: A critical reflection 12th Annual Lecture, International Centre for Guidance Studies, University of Derby 10 December

Jarvis, P. (1999) *The Practitioner-Researcher: Developing theory from practice* Jossey-Bass, San Francisco

Kincheloe, J. (2001) 'Describing the bricolage: Conceptualizing a new rigor in qualitative research' *Qualitative Inquiry* Volume 7:6 pp. 679–692

Kincheloe, J. (2005) 'On to the next level: Continuing the conceptualization of the bricolage' *Qualitative Inquiry* Volume 11:3 pp. 323–350

Kumari, P. (2017) *One Size won't fit all: The challenges facing the Office for Students* Higher Education Commission, London

Marques, J. (2015) 'The changed leadership landscape: what matters today' *Journal of Management Development* Volume 34:10 pp. 1310–1322

Molesworth, M., Nixon, E., and Scullion, R. (2009) 'Having, being and higher education: the Marketization of the university and the transformation of the student into consumer' *Teaching in Higher Education* Volume 14(3) pp. 277–287

Murphy, V., Fox, J., Freeman, S., and Hughes, N. (2017) "Keeping it real': A review of the benefits, challenges and steps towards implementing authentic assessment' *All Ireland Journal of Teaching and Learning in HE* Volume 9:3 pp. 3231–32313

Neary, M. (2016) 'Teaching excellence framework: A critical response and an alternative future' *Journal of Contemporary European Research* Volume 12:3 pp. 690–695

Oakeshott, M. (1985) *Experience and Its Modes* Cambridge University Press, Cambridge

Paloniemi, S. (2006) 'Experience, competence and workplace learning' *Journal of Workplace Learning* Volume 18: 7/8 pp. 439–450

Rosli, A., De Silva, M., Rossi, F., and Yip, N. (2018) 'The long term impact of engaged scholarship: how do SMEs capitalize on their engagement with academics to explore new opportunities?' *International Small Business Journal* https://doi.org/10.1177/0266242617749885

Schoenberger, E. (2001) 'Interdisciplinarity and social power' *Progress in Human Geography* Volume 25:3 pp. 365–382

Serrat, O. (2017) *Knowledge Solutions: Tools, methods and approaches to drive organizational performance* Springer, Dordrecht

Seshadri, D.V.R. and Tripathy, A. (2006) 'Innovation through intrapreneurship: the road less travelled' *Vikalpa* Volume 31:3 pp. 17–29

Shulman, L. (2005) 'Signature pedagogies in the professions' *Daedalus* Volume 134:3 pp. 52–59

Siebert, S. and Mills, V. (2006) 'The quest for autonomy: Power and objectivity in work-based research' in *Work-Based Projects: The Worker as Researcher*, proceedings of Universities' Association for Lifelong Learning Work-Based Learning Annual Conference pp 117–123

Steffens, U. and Grote, M. (2016) 'Does academic research have to have impact?' *EFMD Global Focus* Volume 10(3)

Susskind, R. and Susskind, D. (2017) *The future of the professions: How technology will transform the work of human experts* Oxford University Press, Oxford

Syed, J., Mingers, J. and Murray, P.A. (2009) 'Beyond rigour and relevance: A critical realist approach to business education' *Management Learning* Volume 41:1 pp. 71–85

Thomas, H., Lorange, P. and Sheth, J. (2013) *The business school in the twenty first century* Cambridge University Press, Cambridge

Tomlinson, M. (2017) 'Conceptions of the value of higher education in a measured market' *Higher Education* pp 1–17

Ward, V., Smith, S., House, A., and Hamer, S. (2012) 'Exploring knowledge exchange: A useful framework for practice and policy' *Social Science and Medicine* Volume 74 pp. 297–304

Webster Wright, A. (2010) *Authentic professional learning: Making a difference through learning at work* Springer, Dordrecht

Weertz, D.J. and Sandmann, R. (2010) 'Community engagement and boundary spanning roles at research universities' *The Journal of Higher Education* Volume 81:6 pp. 632–647.

16

Professionalisation and Identification in UK Higher Arts Education

Sarah Scarsbrook

Abstract This chapter frames the relationship between UK Higher Arts Education (HAE), government policy, and the emergence and maintenance of professional pedagogies in creative education. Its focus is on art schools and artists' experiences and views of their fine art education and professional curricula. This has been developed from my 2021 study Artists and The Art School which investigated a 30-year period between 1986–2016 in London art schooling. In section one, I discuss the socio-political history of UK art schools, focussing on significant cultural and higher educational policy that shaped the adoption of professionalisation in creative pedagogical activity alongside the institutionalisation of art schooling. In section two, I define the parameters of the arts as professions and artists as professionals, situating the role of professionalisation in UK HAE today. Finally, section three details

S. Scarsbrook (✉)
Business School for the Creative Industries, University for the Creative Arts, Farnham, UK
e-mail: Philip.Powell@uca.ac.uk

© The Author(s), under exclusive license to Springer Nature Switzerland AG 2022
P. Powell, B. Shankar Nayak (eds.), *Creative Business Education*,
https://doi.org/10.1007/978-3-031-10928-7_16

artists' experiences and views of skilling and professional development, as well as considering how artists' form professional identities through/ against this.

Introduction to Professionalisation: Policy and Pedagogy

According to Houghton (2016) six distinct art and design pedagogical models have existed across Europe, including in the UK. They are; the *Apprentice* (circa European Middle Ages), the *Academic* (circa Italian Renaissance), the *Formalist* (circa 1900/60s), the *Expressive* (circa 1950/60s), the *Conceptual* (circa 1970s onwards) and finally, the *Professional Curriculum* (circa 1990s onwards) (ibid.). Some models have left indelible marks on today's fine art teaching in the UK, including; from the *Apprentice Curriculum*, the masterclass (Newall 2019); from the *Academic Curriculum*, the traditional life drawing room and the notion that being an artist '*is not fundamentally about practical skills, but something of higher value, status and even calling*' (Houghton 2016: 110); from the *Expressive Curriculum*, leaving students '*to express themselves and develop their talent*' (ibid.: 113); and from the *Conceptual Curriculum*, the emphasis on process and critical theory (ibid.: 114–115). Some of these claims can be critiqued, such as access to formal and technical skilling, and that the notion of talent is contingent on varying degrees of capital that students have at their disposal affecting development (Bourdieu 1986; Banks 2017). Nonetheless, the present *Professional Curriculum* is understood to embody many of these elements, as well as being deeply interconnected with government agendas. Below, I outline this history of UK art schools and the policies that have formed them, discussing influential political ideologies and the interrelation of changing pedagogical paradigms that have together shaped the *Professional Curriculum*.

Art Schools 1760–1960

UK Art schools have endured strong ties with political agendas since their inception. The primary aim of the first government schools, those of Edinburgh's *School of Art and Design* in 1760, London's *Royal Academy* in 1768, and later, in 1837, the *Government School of Design*, today known as the *Royal College of Art* (RCA), was to plug a deficit in skilled British designers to compete in these industries with Europe (see Strand 1987). These schools fulfilled a role by inscribing standardised styles, producing generically skilled useful graduates to compete in the design and manufacturing economy. While perhaps a seemingly bygone purpose, it is not too different from today's creative education and its' instrumental position provisioning access to the cultural and creative industries (CCIs) (McRobbie 2011; Banks and Oakley 2016). Nor, when contemplating the art school's role as an organisation of the institutions of both education and art, the latter described as the '*art machine*' that includes, '*arts schools, galleries and dealers, art critics, auction houses, fairs and art events, (private and public) collectors, and museums*', which act as an '*interlocking framework of legitimation*' (Rodner and Thompson 2013: 16).

Until the mid-twentieth century, the cornerstone of the UK's original art schools were the exacting standards required of students in drawing the '*"accurate" representation of the visible world' through compulsory classes in 'figure drawing, modelling, still life and pictorial composition*' (Lord c.2008). Elsewhere, vast pedagogical changes were occurring in creative education in Europe and North America.[1] In particular, the influence of the Bauhaus movement, which began in Germany in 1919, was transforming the entire pedagogical/conceptual framework and outputs of art education with its Modern formalist approach that instilled '*abstraction, performance and material experimentation*' (Thorne 2019) over standardised representational techniques. The Bauhaus closed down in 1933, curtailed by Nazi demands (ibid.), and some say under '*the pressure of its own contradictions*' (De Duve 1994: 23), perhaps alluding to its desire to

---

[1] The USA's Black Mountain College (1933–1957) was an influential art school with an avant-garde approach, which rejected 'rote learning' and embraced minimal structure, influenced by the Bauhaus (see Newall 2019: 91).

free art education from the rigidity of the academy yet simultaneously instilling rigorous rules that governed formal art making (Newall 2019: p. 75). Nevertheless, its influence persisted through Bauhaus artists working in exile from Nazi Germany elsewhere (Malherek 2018), and it rippled throughout HAE in the UK. It was seen as the only coherent rival to the '*old academic model*' (De Duve 1994, p. 23), and though its lasting effects are contested for having only a '*residual influence that it once had*' (Llewellyn 2015, p. 17), many accept it still influences creative pedagogies today (Orr and Shreeve 2018; Newall 2019).

It's ripples certainly encouraged the policy reforms implemented through the *First* (and *Second*) *Coldstream Reports* of 1960 (and 1970 respectively), which transformed UK HAE. The two reports were devised by artist and educator Sir William Coldstream, who was both chair of the National Advisory Council on Art Education (NACAE) and Principal of Fine Art at *The Slade School of Art*, one of the UK's oldest art schools, established in 1871, and notably existing within the university framework as a collegiate of *University College London*. Independence and institutionalisation are prominently debated contexts of art schools underscoring discussion on professional pedagogies, which I situate further shortly. The reports profound shift for HAE emphasised giving '*a good deal of freedom to art schools within the limits of a single framework*' (Coldstream, cited in Strand 1987, p. 213). While liberating art schools to devise their own pedagogies was a main aim, the new HAE policies also academicised the schools who sought more intellectual students for the new fine art courses they established. This was achieved through implementing tougher entry requirements, including needing five 'O' Levels,[2] plus the establishment of an extra tier of study in the Foundation Course[3] (or Diploma in Art and Design/Dip.AD), which had to be passed to attend. As well, compulsory History of Art and Complementary Studies were introduced, equating to 15% of student marks achieved through the introduction of written papers and specific classes conducted

---

[2] The GCE 'O' Levels, or General Certificate of Education 'Ordinary level' was the secondary school qualification for compulsory education in the UK, the GCSE (General Certificate of Secondary Education) replaced this in 1988, and is still used today.

[3] The Foundation Course is a one-year Diploma course required for entry onto most art and design undergraduate degrees in the UK.

by accredited teachers (Banks and Oakley 2016), changing the landscape not only for students but for teachers too. These new systems sought to bring arts courses in line with other disciplines in universities (Strand 1987), understood to have been influenced by Coldstream's position as professor at an art school that already existed within a university (Massouras 2012). Raising visual art's academic credentials met the goal of disassociating it from its historical alignment with the trades. The lasting influence of the *Coldstream Reports* is widely considered to have brought the most substantial change to HAE of any reform before or since (Beck and Cornford 2012; Massouras 2012; Banks and Oakley 2016; Willer 2018). It also had an accumulative institutionalising effect on art schools, which I discuss next alongside professionalisation, and influential political ideologies and policies administered since.

Political Ideologies and Professionalising Policies

The *Coldstream Reports* of 1960 and 1970 have been considered main progenitors of professionalised pedagogies in UK art schools (see Massouras 2012). The liberalising and academicising effects these policies had on the new courses are certainly part of the historical professionalising of art and design pedagogies. However, to fully understand art school's *Professional Curriculum* (Houghton 2016) of today, recognising the influence of political contexts and policy objectives of the latter half of the twentieth century is also necessary. Many overlapping factors have contributed to the professionalisation, and interconnected *institutionalisation*, of art schooling. The most predominant is the overarching and successively maintained neoliberal political ideology of UK (and many international) governments since the 1970s. In the UK, this was initially fostered through an allegiance between the then US President Ronald Reagan and UK Prime Minister Margaret Thatcher, who together instigated the 'privatisation, deregulation, financialisation and globalisation' (Radice 2013) of the public sector, and according private ones (i.e. banking and finance), that became the central tenets of neoliberalism. Later, during the 1980s and 1990s, under successive Conservative (1979–1997) and New Labour (1997–2010) governments, even while some dispute the latter's policies as distinctly neoliberal (see Hill et al. 2013; Hesmondhalgh et al. 2015), the dominant ideology was continued through the initiation and embedding of *New Public Managerialism* (NPM). The mission behind NPM was to impose the '*values, structures and processes of private sector management … upon the public sector*' (Radice 2013: 408), some say enforcing '*brutalistic, finance-driven, authoritarian forms of management*' (Hill et al. 2013: 60) on public services. This included higher education, shaping its steady privatisation, embedding an '*audit-culture*' (Radice 2013: 413) through '*increased forms of surveillance and control*' (Hill et al. 2013). In addition, in 1999, the Bologna Declaration (EHEA 1999) standardised EU member's higher education policies and practices into a three-cycle system of BA, MA, and Doctorate programs. Signatories, including the UK, agreed to adopt a system of comparable degrees. This is considered part of 'a coordinated strategy to place higher education in the service of economic growth and global competitiveness', in line with neoliberal expectations. These key situations have all influenced the centralisation of art education's management and its institutionalisation.

For art schools, though alignment with fulfilling government needs began much earlier, the slippage towards institutionalisation, as discussed, had begun in the 1960s with Coldstream's academicising reforms that aligned art and design education with other disciplines of the university. Then, in 1965 another significant transformation occurred with the dawn of the *Polytechnic Era* (Llewellyn 2015). This saw the extensive restructuring of UK higher education with the establishment of seven new universities and thirty polytechnic colleges between 1968 and 1973 (Pratt 1997). The polytechnics were formed by merging local technical colleges, existing art schools, and other colleges together. The impact on independent art schools[4] was significant, reducing their numbers by absorbing them into umbrella institutions. This move essentially cut ties (and funding) with local authorities and moved towards a centrally funded (and

---

[4] Until that time art schools had remained relatively independent as local authority funded colleges, but with significant autonomy from central government's HE policies (Beck and Cornford 2012).

governed) set up that imitated universities (Pratt 1997: 303). Amid these changes came resistance however. In 1968 a rebellion broke out in the UK art schools[5] against these and previous art educational restructures. A wave of art school protests and '*sit-ins*' (ibid.) emerged, beginning at London's Hornsey School of Art. The students were frustrated by a perceived '*lack of relevance to contemporary society, limited or even inadequate facilities, and distant, inaccessible management and decision-making processes*', and opposed '*new course structures and requirements*' (Lyon, c.2008), particularly the entrance qualifications implemented through the *Coldstream Reports*. Their central aim was '*to set the terms of their own education*'. However, in 1992, more changes came which would challenge this, as the *Further and Higher Education Act* (Great Britain, DfE 1992) was implemented. This initiated the *University Era* (Llewellyn 2015), which swiftly condensed polytechnics into universities, diminishing the number of independent art schools further as they became colleges or departments of universities, advancing their entrenchment within the institution of education as a result (Harvey 2012). The substantial, and probably irrevocable, changes of this period for UK art schooling are striking when considering that in 1959 there were 180 independent art schools, and by 2012 this had depleted to around a dozen (Beck and Cornford 2012), the rest had been culled, absorbed, or institutionalised through the *University Era*.

In combination these policies institutionalised UK HAE. The subsumption of art schools into universities meant the structures and policies of the university would permeate art schools as part of legitimisation processes of institutionalisation (Lammers and Garcia 2017: 199–200). The universities' '*social processes, obligations, or actualities [could] take on a rule-like status in social thought and action*' in the art schools, '*driven as much by external forces as functional requirements*' (ibid.). It raised deep concerns that HAE would become '*subject to the same kind of generalising academic and professional pressures that have always been applied in the governance of university subjects*' (Thomson, 2005, cited in Beck and

---

[5] This occurred among wider socio-political unrest in 1968, most notably in Paris, where protesters challenged the 'conservative establishment', opposed 'the negative impact of industrialised work processes', and demanded 'more effective participatory democracy' (Lyon, c.2008).

Cornford 2012: 63). Indeed, a new set of policies (and pressures) were applied to universities throughout the late 1990s and 2000s, felt in the art schools that were now faculties and departments in these institutions. These included New Labour's introduction of tuition fees in 1998 of £1000 per year. Subsequent rises have continued, increasing to £3000 per year in 2003 (New Labour), £9000 per year in 2012 (Conservative-Liberal Democrat Coalition), and to £9250 per year in 2017[6] (Conservative). The discrepancies paid by artists I have studied (see Scarsbrook 2021), range from those who attended art school in 1989 and paid nothing (plus received material stipends from local authorities), to some who, by 2016, paid £27,000 for their fine art education. This highlights the sharp increase in the cost of higher education, resonating with injustices linked to decreased attendance of working class or disadvantaged students, particularly in creative subjects (see Banks and Oakley 2016; Banks 2017).[7] Also notable is the shift towards the individual student paying for their education, rather than this being supported through taxation.

Further pressures on universities, and institutionalised art schools, came in 1999/2002 with government employability agendas (Great Britain, DWP 2002). These have defined the vocationalisation of higher education, based on the reasoning that, '*given the substantial public investment in university students, it is particularly important that they are employable upon graduation*' (Rt. Hon. Gordon Brown, Chancellor of Exchequer, 1999, in Smith et al. 2000: 382). The development and delivery of '*the*

---

[6] Tuition fees continue to be reviewed. In May 2019 the Augar Report recommended decreasing tuition fees to £7500 per annum, reintroducing maintenance grants for disadvantaged students, and increasing repayment plans to 40 years (ibid.), meaning, in real terms, more interest would be paid. It received criticism for being most damaging for arts courses (see Wright 2019), for not considering student housing costs (see Kingham 2019), and for not offering robustly supported/financed delivery of lifelong learning (see Callender 2020). In 2022, The Lords Committee recommended it be reviewed, stating it 'did not take a holistic approach to the funding of universities and made no attempt to assess the potential impact of its recommended changes on the funding of research in universities' (UK Parliament 2022).

[7] Of artists I have studied, those identifying as working class doubted their financial capacity to attend art school now (Artists P3, P10, and P9 cited in Scarsbrook 2021). They felt students are consumers/customers of education today (Artists P3 and P5 cited in Scarsbrook 2021), contradicting government predictions upon introducing fees that stated, 'we do not believe that students will in the future see themselves simply as customers of higher education but rather as members of a learning community' (Dearing 1997: 64).

individual's employability skills and attributes' (McQuaid and Lindsay 2005) became paramount as work-ready graduates were (and still are) anticipated to slot into the according industries that (notionally) await them. Employability and enterprise policies have been exposed as an unscrupulous and transparent mechanism to '*ensure that [governments] and the banks are repaid [the student debts]*' that are a '*financial condition for entrance into higher education*' (Federici 2017). They are linked to disproportionate marketisation and unsustainable expectations of higher education in provisioning the work force, seen as especially unfeasible for creative subjects (Smith et al. 2000; Mason et al. 2006; Wheelahan 2010; Belfiore and Upchurch 2013). There are considerable difficulties for subjects like fine art in preparing/skilling individuals ready for artistic '*employment*', as well as somehow measuring that, when employment itself is indeterminate for many art school graduates.

Measuring taught and applied employability skills have become demands placed on art schools within universities, since a series of performance assessments were launched following the employability agendas. In line with NPM's instilling of competition through the generation of comparable datasets, the aim has been to evaluate the effectiveness of institutions and specific courses, and then pit them against one another. This is achieved through synchronising data from the National Student Survey (NSS[8]), the Research Excellence Framework (REF[9]), and the Teaching Excellence Framework (TEF[10]), introduced in 2005, 2014, and 2017 respectively. The metrics from these are compared against data gathered on graduate employment. Furthermore, since 2017 institutions can raise tuition fees in line with inflation (Universities UK 2022) according to the

---

[8] NSS gathers 'feedback from final-year undergraduate students about the quality of their course experience'. While 'helping applicants to make informed choices of subject, program and institution' and contributing 'to public accountability for teaching', it is criticised for producing generic results attributable to its inability to account for institutional differences (ibid.: 50). It has been boycotted by students for its role in tuition fee increases.

[9] REF assesses 'the quality of research in UK higher education institutions' (REF 2021). However, in valorising only a 'narrow model of research' it is condemned as a 'an instrument of neoliberal governmentality … designed to force institutions to compete for finite amounts of public money'.

[10] TEF consists of three measures: 'teaching quality, including student satisfaction; the institutional environment in which students learn; and student outcomes, including the performance of underrepresented groups' (Gunn 2018).

results of these market driven audits. Under the alias of providing students with '*choice*' (Great Britain, DfE 2017) by supposedly '*placing students at the centre*' (Gourlay and Stevenson 2017: 391), there are deep concerns these methods could '*fundamentally alter the market viability of certain university courses*' (Morris 2017, cited in Kenning 2018: 3). Fine art courses are particularly vulnerable, because employment outcomes are exceptionally difficult to trace when artists' working lives are known to be complex, often precarious, and insecure (Gill and Pratt 2008; Hill et al. 2013; McRobbie 2016). That artists' employment patterns cannot be sufficiently measured means the data is unreliable and works against HAE in an audit-driven educational climate. Moreover, since the advent of tuition fees, the creation of student-customers/consumers has been widely criticised as damaging and unfair (Bishop 2012; Tomlinson 2014; Bunce et al. 2017), whereby situating artist-students[11] in a '*student-as-rational-investor model*' becomes a "*seriously 'bad bet*" (Kenning 2018: 2). This has placed unrealistic expectations and transactional values on arts education, students, and teachers. However, it is easy to see how the *Professional Curriculum* is prevailing, and those planning HAE courses have found it increasingly necessary to instil professional practice as core curricula activity, certainly since the educational reforms and political ideologies of the 1960s and 1970s, and absolutely against the backdrop of the past thirty years. The timeline below (Fig. 16.1) presents an overview of the events and policies discussed above.

Current Perspectives, Acceptances, and Alternatives

In contrast to HAE's challenges I present above, more optimistic outlooks on the allegiance of art schools and universities also exist. Banks and Oakley (2016: 2) see that '*many precarious institutions appear to have had their lives extended by becoming absorbed into singular or federal partnerships within the*

---

[11] I borrow the term 'artist-student' from Buckley and Conomos (2009: 6), who use this when referring to 'artist-teachers' and 'artist-students' in highlighting that those in art schools, whether educators or students, are/see themselves as artists.

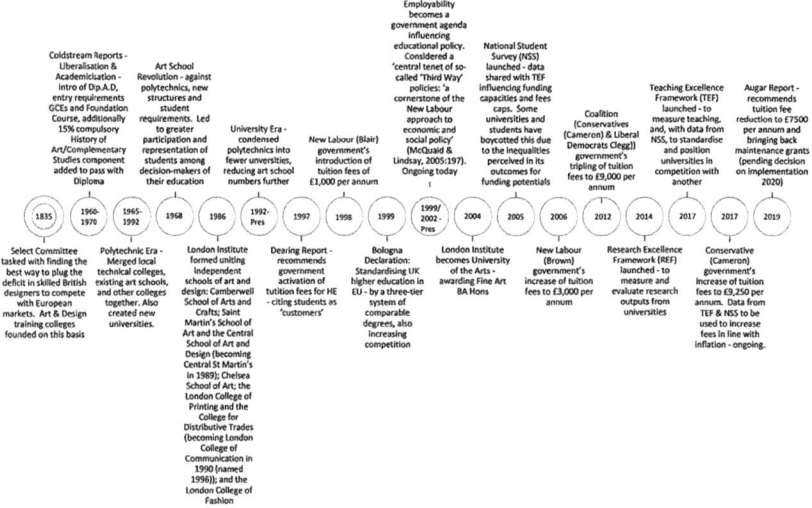

Fig. 16.1 Timeline of influential policies on UK Art Schooling

university system'. Others suggest, that though it is thought art schools have compromised to fit into the academic confines of the university, the university is also learning about and accepting new forms of practice-based knowledge from art schools that *'helps stretch university ideas about what counts as knowledge'* and *'has relevance across the disciplines'* (Orr and Shreeve 2018, p. 157). With practice-based research having been recognised by REF (ibid.), a cynical perspective might conclude it resembles another co-option of knowledge to be measured, benchmarked, and marketised under neoliberal ideologies. Nevertheless, other benefits are suggested, such as that *'art school staff have had to articulate to others, which has helped them understand the nature of their pedagogy and practices'*, leading to *'more literature about creative, studio-based pedagogy that can be shared more widely'* (ibid., p. 156), and that the justification of these practices has meant they *'have become more rigorous'* (ibid.).

It could appear from this that art schools have accepted their fate under the *University Era* (Llewellyn 2015), that some operating within the institution (teachers, students, curriculum developers, critics) have stopped challenging the systematic marketisation of art education, and the concomitant entrepreneurialisation of art practice. Indeed, in 2009, some arts educators were still demonstrably torn, asking, '*should the art school turn itself into a monastery that protects students from the evil forces outside or should it invite the market in and become a kind of lively bazaar?*' (Birnbaum 2009: 238). In contrast, more recently, other arts educators seem more convinced, instead asking, '*how can we capitalise on the opportunities that a more entrepreneurial approach to HE provides for students, staff, academic institutions, communities and the wider cultural and creative industries sector?*' (TCCE 2019). These differing positions demonstrate wider acceptance and absorption of employability and enterprise as deliverable outcomes of HAE. Some art school's complicity in this can be seen in their coordinating and hosting conferences that directly aim to embed employability and enterprise agendas[12] (see CHEAD 2015, and TCCE 2019). In leading the discussion on this, these art schools interlock this agenda into their pedagogies, embedding an entrepreneurial ideology into their brand identities, and the identities of their students. Indeed, the '*entrepreneurial ethos*' entrenched through employability policy and professional curricula, '*offers more than career and professional sustainability advice: it targets student subjectivity itself*', influencing 'attitudes and forms of behaviour thought likely to advantage the individual within established, competitive market conditions' (Kenning 2018, p. 4), a notion I return to later through discussion around skilling.

The picture described above characterises art schools as functional and compliant organisations, that have experienced much adversity in their incorporation into universities in the neoliberal era. There are studies, however, that emphasise art schools within universities can take ownership of pedagogical design despite the regulations imposed by policy (Crippa 2014). Other ways of dealing with the hyper-marketisation and audit-driven culture of HE can be seen in the current bloom of alternative art schools that are non-accredited and independent from the demands faced by HAE (for example: Open School East (2020), The Other MA (2020),

---

[12] The 2015 conference *What is the Point of Employability in Art and Design?* (CHEAD 2015) was hosted by Chelsea College of Arts for art and design educators/curriculum developers to discuss how to embed enterprise and employability at the core of creative education (ibid.). In 2019, the *Culture Capital Exchange Creative Entrepreneurship Forum* was co-organised by UAL colleges Camberwell, Chelsea, and Wimbledon Colleges of Arts (CCW), to discuss 'the coming together of academic life, enterprise and entrepreneurship' (TCCE 2019).

School of the Damned (2020), Islington Mill Academy (2020), Fairfield International (2020), and AltMFA (2020)). Alternative models embed '*pedagogical practices as art practice or artist-driven education*' (Kalin 2012: 43), or '*art-as-pedagogy*' (Bishop 2012). However, mostly, what remains is arts' and art education's entanglement with institutionalisation, professionalisation and entrepreneurialisation, which I consider next as I outline the arts' and artists' relationships with professions and professionalism.

Visual Arts as Professions and Artists as Professionals

It could be that the arts (and artists) have been institutionalised since becoming a profession, and not necessarily vice versa as positioned above. Indeed, theorists of New Institutionalism[13] suggest that 'professions are institutionalized occupations' (Abbott 1988, in Lammers and Garcia 2017: 197). In this section, I consider this as I outline a historical context of the professions, the arts as a profession, and artists as professionals. After, I define the current situation of visual artists' professional and professionalised identities in relation to HAE and the neoliberal backdrop, and outline a working definition of artists' professional identities that are shaped by professional pedagogies.

The Arts and the Professions: Parameters and Participation

The professionalisation of visual arts practice in UK art schools is considered '*an increasingly significant component of higher education study in the UK*' (Kenning 2018: 1). It is also considered the '*enemy of the arts*' (Saltz, 2003, cited in Daichendt 2012, p. 25), because the newly '*professionalized*

---

[13] *New Institutionalism* is defined by 'the symbolic role of formal structure (rather than on the informal organization)' (Lammers and Garcia 2017: 199) in which the organisation is 'constituted by the environment in which it was embedded'. It is distinct from *Old Institutionalism*, which 'focuses more on specific organizations than on environments' (ibid.: 198).

discipline … values the intellectual and the philosophical over the craft and technical origins of art education' (Daichendt 2012, p. 25). This rhetoric implies the recent professionalisation of the arts and artists. However, within this, the meaning of *'professional'* needs defining (or redefining), because the arts have been recognised as a profession and artists as professionals in a European context, according to Durkheim (1957), since medieval and pre-historic times. Ancient craft guilds of Rome (around 600 BC), initiated under King Numa (715–673 BC) and later in the time of Cicero (106 BC), thrived as training and organising bodies of professional arts (ibid.: 17). One British guild, *The Worshipful Company of Goldsmiths* founded in twelfth century London, formed Goldsmiths Technical and Recreative Institute in 1891, becoming Goldsmiths College in 1904 under University of London, and establishing Goldsmiths School of Art that still exists today. The arts have seemingly sustained their position as a profession since the guilds (Freidson 1986: 54), barring fluctuations in historical documentation between the 1300s and 1700s (Prest 1987), during which most professions were *'somewhat overlooked'* because they *'largely served and were recruited from the gentry and nobility'* (ibid., p. 8). I continue to discuss access to professional participation shortly, however, the arts resurface again as professions in the 1800s through the Arts & Crafts guilds.[14] But, by the end of that century, debate was emerging over whether Architecture, the founding discipline of *The Art Worker's Guild*, a major professional organisation for artists and craftspeople, was a 'Profession or an Art' (Stamp, c.1975). This question has continued to be asked of the arts in varying degrees since.

During the First Industrial Revolution (c.1760–1840),[15] the *'professional classes were coming of age'* (Donkin 2001: 106). The status of professionals (skilled labour) was being pit against the industrialists (unskilled

---

[14] These guilds originated through the UK Arts & Crafts movement (c.1860s–1920s), led by artists John Ruskin and William Morris. In reaction to 'the damaging effects of industrialisation' and 'the relatively low status of the decorative arts', they reformed 'the design and manufacture of everything from buildings to jewellery'.

[15] In the UK, the First industrial Revolution (c.1760–1840), moved from agrarian and crafts-based economies to coal and steam powered manufacturing and industry (White 2009). The Second Industrial Revolution, (or Technological Revolution) (c.1860–1940), was epitomised by chemical synthesis of materials and mass-manufacture technologies enabled by the factory. The Third Industrial Revolution (c.1960–2000) is categorised by IT and electronics, nuclear power, and robotics (Schwab 2018). Today, the Fourth Industrial Revolution encompasses digital, the Internet and Smart technologies (ibid.).

labour) who were usually uneducated, whereas professionals had '*the benefit of classical education*' (Donkin 2001: 105). At this point, being educated became a prominent defining factor of the professions, separating professionals and amateurs. Another crucial change for professional parameters and participation was significant democratisation after England's 1832 electoral reforms that opened up professional careers to the middle classes (Larson 2013 [1977]). Along with education this positioned '*merit against birth and patronage*', initiating '*a novel possibility of gaining status through work*' (ibid., p. 5 original emphasis). Considered a 'great transformation' (Polanyi, 1944, cited in Larson 2013 [1977]: xvi), another came at the turn of the twentieth century, which shifted the entire socio-politico-economic landscape towards a market economy that was '*dominated by the reorganisation of economy and society around the market*' (Larson, 2013 [1977], p. xvi), which '*the professions could hardly escape the effects of*' (ibid., p. 9). These changes significantly impacted who could become a professional. Similarly, today's political ideology of neoliberalism continues to influence access to the professions, especially through constricting access to higher education (Burke et al. 2015), that is a common route into creative careers.

Education and access are still markers and hurdles separating professionals and amateurs. Pay is also a factor. Today's professionalism, for artists and more widely, is tightly interwoven with the neoliberalised ability to centralise remuneration, coupled with the ability to brand and market oneself to meet the dominant (free market) economy demands. A far cry from the vulgar and '*grubby*' notion of '*commercial transactions*' and '*receiving money directly from clients*' (Donkin 2001: 105) that professional classes of the nineteenth century would stoop to. Mostly, professionals, including barristers, lawyers, or the clergy, did not '*extend their hands for payment*' (ibid.). Artists were also exempt from this, being supported by patrons of the church or monarchy. I note the historical existence of professionals' condescension of the vulgar business-end, and artists' patronage, because of its relevance to artists who have experienced and attempt to reject these kinds of professionalising effects of art schooling (Scarsbrook 2021). The vulgarity of the business-end attested to by artists (ibid.) may well signify a traditional professional stance of not wanting to be involved in those dealings, as well imbricating historical and somewhat mythologised ideals of patronised and supported artists, notions which can disrupt professional pedagogies. Next, I situate changes in professionalism and the dynamics that have shaped it.

Professions and Professional(ised) Identities

While the arts have been considered professions for centuries, what constitutes a profession, and a professional individual or artist, has significantly altered, shifting with changing social and political paradigms. In sociological (Macdonald 1995) and cultural policy (Paquette 2012) accounts of the professions, different schools of thought have attempted to define what a profession, being a professional, or having a professional identity means. Modern sociological mapping begins with the functionalist's (Parsons 1939, 1964; Durkheim 1957; Wilensky 1964) definitions of the early to mid-twentieth century, who claimed the professions had a rigid set of traits, and compiled lists of qualities for the 'ideal-typical profession' (Macdonald 1995: 3). However, these parameters are now considered narrow and restrictive, such as distinguishing professions by formal '*technical knowledge*', '*professional norms*', regulatory '*associations*', and '*monopoly of the practice*' (Paquette 2012, p. 4). Professional identities were related to a '*function of prestige*' (ibid., p. 5), which though might be still inherent, is not all they are. Later, the interactionists (Becker 1963; Freidson 1986), from the 1960s onwards, repositioned the professions within a broader '*cultural dimension*' as '*ritualised social behaviour*' or '*stabilized social practices consistent with the pressures of a given social world*' (Paquette 2012, p. 5). They centralised the '*inner life*' (ibid.) of professionals, engendering the notion that individuals were capable of professionalising themselves; the term professional became an act. Professional identity was foregrounded and became connected to '*the individual's negotiation between social contingencies of the social world of work he or she evolves in*' (ibid., p. 6).

During the 1970s and after, understanding professions incorporated understanding power dynamics between institutions. These were recognised as shaping the professions and individuals, who were acknowledged as being able to negotiate their professional identities. Larson's (2013

[1977]) theory, the *Professional Project*, encapsulated this combination of social power and collective action as 'the quest for professional status and the strategies that mobilized to gain this status' (Evetts, 1999, cited in Paquette 2012: 7). By that time, art schools were firmly embedded within higher educational institutions through the *Polytechnic* and *University Eras* (Llewellyn 2015), meaning they became more influential as institutions that could shape the profession of visual artists, and significantly, artist-students could individually and collectively negotiate professional artistic identities through art schooling. More recently, identities (professional and otherwise) are thought to '*represent patterns of negotiation between an individual's social aspirations, desires, expectations, and the different forms of socialization one encounters*' (Dubar, 2000, in Paquette 2012, p. 10). This shift has meant that professional identities can be '*inherited, learned, attributed and sometimes rejected by the individuals who enter a professional world*' (ibid.), being that they consist '*of both identifying with and establishing a distinction from certain values and norms*' (ibid.). As well, identities are also considered manifold, in that, '*rather than having one fixed version of who we are, we all move between multiple identities*' (Silverman, 2007, cited in Butler-Kisber 2018, p. 12). Professions and professional identities are consistently in flux due to the changing nature of the complex dynamics that shape their existences. The political ideologies, changing social and institutional powers, and the individual and collective negotiations of identities that create professionals and professions I discuss here underlie this.

Situating Professional(ised) Artists'

In terms of what this means for artists, and in defining parameters of what an art schooled professional(ised) artist entails, is that there are many negotiations to consider. Such as, first and foremost gaining access to the institution/art school; not a simple feat when met with homophilic recruitment processes granting entry only to similar others (Banks 2017). Further, when access has been granted, navigating professionalising pedagogies that embed entrepreneurialism, as noted before, as a '*potent form of self-identification*', entrenching a '*state of mind*' that 'merges with an artistic persona' (Kenning 2018: 9), and operates on the same level as self-employment as a thinly veiled fallacy for autonomy (see Ryan 1992, and Banks 2010); it is an understandably challenging arena to navigate. However, art schools are considered key sites of professional identity work (Orr and Shreeve 2018: 81), and given HE (and HAE) responsibilities in delivering employability agendas for specific industries, industry-related professional identity work could also take place. Though, the notion of an industry in which artist-graduates might '*evaluate their own work and behaviour in the context of a work-place environment*' (Paquette et al. 2016, cited in Orr and Shreeve 2018: 130), as other professionals are considered able to do, seems antithetical and is contested (Bain 2005). Rather, for artist-students it is anticipated there are a '*range of practices into which they will establish their own version of art practice or practices*' (Orr and Shreeve 2018, p. 130) awaiting them for further negotiation post art school.

Ascertaining the outcomes of these negotiations, that might situate what an art schooled professional artist is, is a challenge that becomes deeply complex. Efforts to delineate the parameters of artists' professional status have been attempted. Some, from a cultural economics standpoint (Frey and Pommerehne 1989, in Zanti 2015: 45) suggest eight criteria can be considered. These include, '*time spent*' on and '*income derived*' from artistic work, an artists' '*reputation*' and '*recognition*' among '*the general public*' and '*other artists*', the '*quality of artistic work*', '*membership*' of professional bodies, '*professional qualifications (graduation from art schools)*', and the '*subjective self-evaluation of being an artist*' (ibid.). Though these are not unproblematic and difficult to ascertain/evaluate, they are broad in range, and crucially, the last measure is asserted by and discussed as key to artists I have studied (Scarsbrook 2021). Elsewhere, other criteria lists have been developed. For example, Artists' Union England (AUE), an organisation which supports artists' rights concerning their artistic work and remuneration, has established professional status benchmarks that it uses to determine membership eligibility. This includes '*regularly making and exhibiting*' and receiving '*professional grants*', to being '*featured in an art publication*', '*represented by a gallery*' or having '*a degree in visual or applied arts at undergraduate, post-graduate,*

BTEC or Diploma level' (AUE 2019). However, while many of these might be relevant to artists' working lives, they are object/attainment centred. Critically, they do not incorporate the understanding of more nuanced attempts, such as Frey and Pommerehne (1989), that professional identification is also defined as '*one's professional self-concept based on attributes, beliefs, values, motives, and experiences*' (Ibarra, 1999, in Slay and Smith 2011, p. 85), rather than having been commissioned by a public institution (another of AUE's criteria). I believe it remains that, as Bain (2005, p. 34) suggests, '*there are no official prerequisites or credentials to distinguish artists from non-artists, professionals from amateurs*', and with no '*clear definitional parameters*' (ibid., p. 26) to distinguish them, it is difficult to fully accept criteria lists as defining artistic professionalism when melded with the complexities of identification. I propose an understanding that artists' professional identities are flexible, ambiguous, and contextual negotiations, certainly influenced by art schooling and professional pedagogies, as well as being blended through past, present, and future identifications (Oyserman et al. 2017). Next, I discuss some of the skilling artist-students experience during art schooling through which they negotiate these professional identities.

Skilling

Skills, Talent, and Pedagogy

The concept of skilling artists is a relatively recent phenomenon (De Duve 1994). Art and skills were not always equated with each other, rather, art was usually perceived through the lens of talent (ibid.) and underscored by artistic myth which decrees artists' special creative talents are preordained, God-given, or mystically ascribed innate traits (Kris and Kurz 1979 [1934]; Soussloff 1997; Røyseng et al. 2007). Today, skilling is expressed in binary debates which have divided skills into hard vs soft, practical vs conceptual (Willer 2018), and, art *can* vs art *cannot* be taught (Newall 2019). The latter is usually associated with the argument that creativity is a fundamental human urge. Accordingly, many advocacy reports deem various practical skills necessary from professional art school pedagogies (Slater et al. 2013; Allen and Rowles 2016; Rowles 2016), including networking, preparing CVs, pricing work, and how to fill out HMRC self-assessment forms,[16] the latter being related to assumptions that artists will necessarily become self-employed. This label, seen as '*a category of the tax office, a state-imposed identification*' (Kenning 2018: 6), is discerned as distinct from becoming an entrepreneur (ibid.). However, both are entangled with artists' identities. Being self-employed is considered '*something artists can maintain as separate from their artistic identity*', and being an entrepreneur, as noted previously, is thought to be '*embodied in a set of behaviours*' which merge with identities at '*the most intimate, subjective level*' (Kenning 2018: 6). Artists' identities are at stake in these debates, given that, art schools also provision a '*rich source of resources*' for '*identity work*' (Taylor and Littleton 2012: 135), and that skilling is entangled with this and the anticipation of accepted art-schooled artist identities by different '*art machine*' (Rodner and Thompson 2013) stakeholders (curators, gallerists, the art world etc.).

Alternative fine art skills, and ways to teach them, have recently surfaced in pedagogical theory stemming from art schools/university art departments. Suggestions of more equitable pedagogies which encourage students to design/regulate personal curricula (Orr and Shreeve 2018), or propose students and educators become closer equivalents (Baldacchino 2015), appear to take identity work into account. Pedagogical imperatives centralise embodied knowledge and the development of '*prosthetic pedagogies*' (Garoian 2015) as ways of knowing and being in and through the body, and there is acknowledgement of the need to adopt new onto-epistemological (Barad, 2007, cited in Jagodzinski 2018: 83) modes of enquiry, and pleas for the '*reawakening of curiosity and wisdom*' (Jagodzinski 2018, p. 90), felt to have been lost in professional pedagogies. This is considered key if artist-students are to '*fabulate*' in '*an incompossible New Earth*'[17] (ibid.), enabling art schools to orientate artist-students

---

[16] HMRC (Her Majesty's Revenue & Customs) Self-Assessment is the UK system for collecting Income Tax and National Insurance from self-employed persons who are legally required to complete this annually to pay their tax contributions.

[17] Incompossible refers to that which seems 'paradoxical but mutually existent' (Jagodzinski 2018: 85).

in the age of the post-human, post-anthropogenic, post-ontological Chthulucene (Haraway 2015, cited in Jagodzinski 2018: 83). Though a distinctly different approach to considering HMRC form filling, there is still some concession to these ideas. Jagodzinski (2018, p. 90) admits, whether new modes of enquiry are adopted or not, art educators (and I would add, artists) necessarily continue to '*toil within global capitalism's accounting system*'. A notable consideration among others which surface when artists discuss their views on professional development, as outlined next.

Perceptions of Professional Development

An extensive discourse exists on professional development in UK HAE, centring on both its delivery through embedded or distinct curricula (Rowles 2016), and whether professional skillsets for artists exist (Ferguson 2009), and can be agreed upon (Birnbaum 2009; Bauer 2009). Others question whether artists should be '*professionally*' developed at all, seeing '*art as a de-alienating endeavour that should not be subject to the division of labour and professional specialisation*' (Bishop 2012 p. 3). Such views may stem from desires to protect art's specialness, that is considered to hold symbolic market value, or to avoid the further collapse of art and artists into commodified products of neoliberalised capitalism attributed to professionalisation. It is possibly neither and both, but representative of a field in a state of '*incomplete professionalization*' (Teather, 1990, cited in Paquette 2012: 11), encountering '*contradictory pressures, some pushing toward professionalization, others preventing it*' (ibid.). Whether '*complete*' professionalisation is attainable (or desirable) is disputable, however, other arguments suggest it is '*essential to provide a codified professional development program as part of a wholesome curriculum*'. It is '*codified*' to avoid instrumentalisation through ideas that, '*"the market" is the dominant way for artists to make a living*', considered, '*misleading at best and completely irresponsible at worst*' and 'based on a flawed perception of what it takes to sustain a creative life'.[18] What is clear, across the debates, is an evident distrust of the market, and continuing anxiety over the slippage of art education into becoming an incubator for creative industry workers, whose focus is on the production of a commodified art object that professional development programmes are feared to exacerbate.

Artists I have studied consistently align professional development with unattractive commodification and business practices they preferred not to identify with (Scarsbrook 2021). This is echoed in other studies that indicate '*artists do not see themselves as entrepreneurs and regard associated business practices as unbecoming*', that they, '*demand recognition through the works of art, but regard sales generated as a result of entrepreneurial behaviour as not providing artistic reputation or high-valued standing among their peers*' (Wesner 2018, p. 36). Other accounts show artists deliberately distinguish '"*commercia*"' from "*personal*" work' (Taylor and Littleton 2012, p. 26) as ways of maintaining reputations and protecting their artist identities. These concepts are significant when positioning experiences of professional development alongside the navigations of artistic identities that occur through art schooling. It also helps to understand why artists often do not recognise skills they take from art school as professional development, but instead offer them as resistance to acknowledging being explicitly professionally developed (Scarsbrook 2021).

The pattern of business alignment is apparent when artists define professional skills they took from art school as making websites, contract writing, and writing a proposal or CV (ibid.). Professional development itself is heavily disparaged, and as noted earlier, it was seen as '*vulgar, to talk about the business end*' that, '*it was supposed to be … known, magically. But not actually taught*' (Artist P6, cited in Scarsbrook 2021). This artist, who graduated in the 1990s also perceived differences between themselves and more recent graduates, claiming art schools '*now … make much more of an effort to teach professional development … we weren't as professionalised … it's probably gone a little too far into the direction of professionalising art students*' (ibid.). They also described having minimal

---

[18] Louden's comments come in reaction to the inaugural *MFA Fair* in NYC, calling itself the 'link between academia and industry' its purpose is to 'introduce [the] graduating class to the market' (The MFA Fair 2019) by selling stand space to art schools who in turn sell this to their students.

classes in professional development, recalling '*only … one session, for a couple of hours*' (ibid.). Its nascence in 1990s art schooling perhaps explains this, however, this perception prevailed across artists from different graduate groups in the 1990s, 2000s, and 2010s. A recent graduate disputed its existence entirely, not remembering '*any real discussion about it*' (Artist P12: ibid.). Others said, '*it was not explicit*' recalling '*there may have been one lecture on the business of art in the third year*' (Artist P2: ibid.), and another stated '*there was never talk about what happens next*' (Artist P4: ibid.). Vague recollections of CV support (Artist P1: ibid.) and receiving the advice, '*as long as you're always thinking about your art, you're still an artist*' (ibid.) were remembered by others. Another noted a '*bunch of workshops*' conducted in '*some sort of half-ironic way*' (Artist P7: ibid.) which was (ironically) considered unprofessional. They added they were not interested in how to '*advertise for myself, or making PR for myself*' (ibid.), rejecting business-like practices. These comments made by artist-graduates from London art schools indicate professional development was either forgotten, went unnoticed or unattended if delivered through specific classes, or was deliberately disavowed and disparaged.

These assertions indicate selective self-regulation over professional identities, commensurate with other studies that show, '*knowledge, attributes and beliefs*' at art school are '*taken up or rejected or modified to suit previously held positions … in pursuit of the student's individual version of a professional identity*' (Orr and Shreeve 2018, p. 81). To protect these identities from being perceived as something considered unbecomingly business-like, commodified, and vulgar, artists denied having been affected by professional development. Artists situate their preferred image of an artist based on imagined possible selves (Markus and Nurius 1986), which appears to be one that eschews formal professionalisation. Studying under professional pedagogies and undertaking professional development, or being perceived to have, is entangled with artists' professional identities, and a particular form of self-identification.

Conclusions

This chapter has outlined key historical moments in the formation of professional pedagogies in UK HAE, defining the influential people, governments, and their policies that have shaped this. This is acknowledged as occurring most significantly since educational reforms in the 1960s, and with increasing force under neoliberal agendas during the past thirty years. Political ideologies and policies that have affected this are highlighted as aligning HAE with government aims, provisioning industry with trained individuals; whether plugging deficits in numbers of designers in the 1800s through the establishment of the first art schools, or meeting employability and enterprise agendas for the creative industries today.

The lineage of professionalisation in UK art schools is defined, demonstrating how they became institutionalised into universities, and how the arts as a profession, as well as professional identification, relates to professional(ised) artists today. In recognising the interconnected relationship between professions and institutions, I highlight that the arts and artists have historically been considered professions and professionals. Additionally, the understanding that professional identities are mutable is notable, and a definition for artists' professional identities is distinguished around this. This encompasses not only social prestige and education, but a persons' sense of professional self-concept, based in past, present, and future possible (and impossible) selves (Oyserman et al. 2017) that are negotiated through institutions as well as aspirations and expectations (Dubar, 2000, in Paquette 2012, p. 10).

Professional development is shown to be a cautiously navigated aspect of an artists' creative education. It is often rejected, in part owing to its consistent connection with markets and business practices, but also as part of assertions of a professional identity which eschews having been professionally developed. These negotiations within creative education, as well as alignment with business, employability and enterprise are currently a mainstay in UK HAE, and appear set to continue under the prevailing (and increasingly) *Professional Curriculum* era.

References

Allen J., and Rowles, S., (eds.), 2016. *Professional Practice: 20 Questions*. London: Q-Art.

Artists' Union England, 2019. *Artists' Union England (AUE)*. Online. Available at: https://www.artistsunionengland.org.uk [accessed 28.03.22].

Bain, A., 2005. Constructing an Artistic Identity. *Work Employment Society*, Vol. 19: 25. https://doi.org/10.1177/0950017005051280

Baldacchino, J., 2015. Art ± Education: The Paradox of the Ventriloquist's Soliloquy. *Journal of Education* volume 3, issue 1, 2015, pp. 62–79. Online. Available at: https://www.academia.edu/19394715/Art_Education_The_Paradox_of_the_Ventriloquist_s_Soliloquy [accessed 11.03.22].

Banks, M., 2017. *Creative Justice: Cultural Industries, Work and Inequality*. London: Rowman & Littlefield.

Banks, M., and Oakley, K., 2016. The dance goes on forever? Art schools, class and UK higher education. *International Journal of Cultural Policy*, Vol. 22, Issue 1: Beyond the Campus: Higher Education, Cultural Policy and the Creative Economy. https://doi.org/10.1080/10286632.2015.1101082

Bauer, U. M., 2009, 'Under Pressure', in S. Madoff (ed.) *Art School (Propositions for the 21st Century)*, The MIT Press, London, pp. 220–226.

Beck J., and Cornford M., 2012. The Art School in Ruins. *Journal of Visual Culture*, 11(1), 58–83. https://doi.org/10.1177/1470412911430467

Becker, H. S., 1963. *Outsiders: Studies in Sociology of Deviance*. New York: The Free Press.

Belfiore, E., and Upchurch, A., 2013, *Humanities in the Twenty-First Century: Beyond Utility and Markets*. Basingstoke: Palgrave Macmillan.

Birnbaum, D. 2009, 'Teaching Art: Adorno and the Devil', in Madoff, S. (ed.) *Art School (Propositions for the 21st Century)*, The MIT Press, London, pp. 232–246.

Bishop, C., 2012. *Artificial Hells: Participatory Art and the Politics of Spectatorship*. London: Verso.

Bourdieu, P., 1986. The Forms of Capital. In J. G. Richardson (ed.) *Handbook of Theory and Research for the Sociology of Education*, pp. 241–258. New York: Greenwood Press.

Buckley, B., and Conomos, J., (eds.) 2009. *Rethinking the Contemporary Art School: The Artist, the PhD and the Academy*. The Press of Nova Scotia College: Canada.

Bunce, L., Baird, A., and Jones, S. E., 2017, The student-as-consumer approach in higher education and its effects on academic performance, *Studies in Higher Education*, 42:11, 1958–1978, https://doi.org/10.1080/0307507 9.2015.1127908

Burke, P. J., Stevenson, J., and Whelan, P., 2015. Teaching 'Excellence' and pedagogic stratification in higher education. *International Studies in Widening Participation*, 2 (2), 29–43. Online. Available at: http://shura.shu.ac.uk/11087/ [accessed 05.04.22].

Butler-Kisber, L., 2018. *Qualitative Inquiry: Thematic, Narrative and Arts-Based Perspectives*. 2nd ed. London: Sage.

Callender, C., 2020. Will the Augar Report's recommendations stem the decline in part-time study? Higher Education Policy Institute (HEPI). Online. Available at: https://www.hepi.ac.uk/2020/02/28/will-the-augar-reports-recommendations-stem-the-decline-in-part-time-study/ [accessed on 11.03.22].

Crippa, E., 2014. *When Art Schools Went Conceptual: The Development of Discursive Pedagogies and Practices in British Art Higher Education in the 1960s*. PhD Thesis. London Consortium. Birkbeck College, University of London.

CHEAD, 2015. *What is the Point of Employability in Art and Design?* Conference at Chelsea College of Arts.

Daichendt, G., 2012. *Artist-Scholar: Reflections on Writing and Research*. Bristol: Intellect Ltd.

Dearing, R. 1997. *Higher Education in the Learning Society: Report of the National Committee of Inquiry into Higher Education*. London: Her Majesty's Stationary Office. Online. Available at: http://www.educationengland.org.uk/documents/dearing1997/dearing1997.html [accessed 11.03.22].

De Duve, T., 1994. "When Form Has Become Attitude—And Beyond". In Stephen Foster and Nicholas deVille eds. *The Artists and The Academy: Issues in Fine Art Education and the Wider Cultural Context*. Southampton, UK: John Hansard Gallery, 20–33.

Donkin, R. 2001, *Blood, Sweat and Tears; The Evolution of Work*, Texere, London.

Durkheim, E., 1957. *Professional Ethics and Civic Morals*. New York, Routledge.

EHEA, 1999. The Bologna Declaration of 19 June 1999. The European Higher Education Area. Online. Available at: http://www.ehea.info/page-ministerial-conference-bologna-1999 [accessed 11.03.22].

Federici, S., 2017. Training for Exploitation? Politicising Employability and Reclaiming Education. Precarious Workers' Brigade. *Journal of Aesthetics & Protest Press*, London. Online. Available at: http://joaap.org/press/pwb/PWB_TrainingForExploitation_smaller.pdf [accessed 11.03.22].

Ferguson, B. 2009, 'Art Education', in Allen, F. (ed.), 2011, *Education*, Whitechapel Gallery, London, pp. 175–176.

Freidson, E., 1986. *Professional Powers: A Study of the Institutionalization of Formal Knowledge.* Chicago: University of Chicago Press.

Frey, B., and Pommerehne, W., 1989. *Muses and Markets: Explorations in the Economics of the Arts*, Oxford: Basil Blackwell.

Garoian, C. R., 2015. Performing the Refrain of Art's Prosthetic Pedagogy https://doi.org/10.1177/1077800415581883

Gill, R., and Pratt, A., 2008. Precarity and Cultural Work in the Social Factory? Immaterial Labour, Precariousness and Cultural Work. ON-Curating, Issue # 16/13, pp. 26–40. Online. Available at: http://www.on-curating.org/files/oc/dateiverwaltung/old%20Issues/ONCURATING_Issue16.pdf [accessed 11.03.22].

Gourlay, L., & Stevenson, J., 2017. Teaching excellence in higher education: critical perspectives. *Teaching in Higher Education*, 22:4, 391–395, https://doi.org/10.1080/13562517.2017.1304632

Great Britain, Department for Education, 1992. *Further and Higher Education Act.* Online. Available at: http://www.legislation.gov.uk/ukpga/1992/13/contents [accessed on: 02.04.22].

Great Britain, Department for Education, 2017. Teaching Excellence and Student Outcomes Framework Specification. Online. Available at: https://assets.publishing.service.gov.uk/government/uploads/system/uploads/attachment_data/file/658490/Teaching_Excellence_and_Student_Outcomes_Framework_Specification.pdf [accessed 02.04.22].

Great Britain, Department for Work and Pensions, 2002. Employment Action Plan. Online. Available at: https://dera.ioe.ac.uk/10292/1/DWP_-_Employment_Action_Plan.pdf [accessed 05.04.22].

Gunn A. (2018) The UK Teaching Excellence Framework (TEF): The Development of a New Transparency Tool. In: Curaj A., Deca L., Pricopie R. (Eds.) *European Higher Education Area: The Impact of Past and Future Policies.* Springer, Cham. https://doi.org/10.1007/978-3-319-77407-7_31

Harvey, L., 2012. Institutionalisation. Social Research Glossary, Quality Research International. Online. Available at: https://www.qualityresearchinternational.com/socialresearch/institutionalisation.htm [accessed 02.04.22].

Haraway, D., 2015. Anthropocene, Capitalocene, Plantationocene, Chthulucene: Making Kin. *Environmental Humanities*, vol. 6, 2015, pp. 159–165. Online. Available at: http://environmentalhumanities.org/arch/vol6/6.7.pdf [accessed 22.03.22].

Hesmondhalgh, D., Nisbett, M., Kate Oakley K., and Lee, D., 2015, Were New Labour's cultural policies neo-liberal?, *International Journal of Cultural Policy*, 21:1, 97–114, https://doi.org/10.1080/10286632.2013.879126

Hill, D., Lewis, C., Maisuria, A., and Yarker, P., 2013. Neoliberalism in England. In Hill, D., Ed. *Immiseration Capitalism and Education: Austerity, Resistance and Revolt*. Brighton: The Institute for Education Policy Studies.

Houghton, N., 2016. Six into One: The Contradictory Art School Curriculum and how it Came About. *The International Journal of Art & Design Education*. https://doi.org/10.1111/jade.12039

Jagodzinski, J. 2018. From the artist to the cosmic artisan: The educational task for art in anthropogenic times. https://doi.org/10.4324/9781315143880-9

Kalin, N., 2012. (de)Fending Art Education Through the Pedagogical Turn. The Journal of Social Theory in Art Education (32) (K. Staikidis, Ed.). 42–55. Online. Available at: https://core.ac.uk/download/pdf/51288646.pdf [accessed 11.03.22].

Kenning, D. 2018. Art world strategies: neoliberalism and the politics of professional practice in fine art education, *Journal of Visual Art Practice*, https://doi.org/10.1080/14702029.2018.1500112

Kingham, R., 2019. The Augar Review and Higher Education estates. Online, Available at: https://www.jll.co.uk/en/views/the-augar-review-and-higher-education-estates. [accessed on 01.04.22].

Kris, E., and Kurz, O., 1979. *Legend, Myth, and Magic in the Image of the Artist. A Historical Experiment (1934)*. New Haven: Yale University Press.

Lammers, J. C., and Garcia, M. A., 2017. Institutional Theory Approaches. *The International Encyclopedia of Organizational Communication*. https://doi.org/10.1002/9781118955567.wbieoc113

Larson, M. S. 1977, The Rise of Professionalism: A Sociological Framework, in, Larson, M. S. 2013, *The Rise of Professionalism: Monopolies of Competence and Sheltered Markets*, Transaction Publishers, New Brunswick.

Llewellyn, N., (Ed.) 2015. *The London Art Schools: Reforming the Art World, 1960 to Now*. London: Tate Publishing.

Lord, J. V., c.2008. *Post-war curriculum and assessment development: Post-war curriculum and assessment: Coldstream, Summerson, art history and complementary studies*. Online. Available at: http://arts.brighton.ac.uk/arts/alumni-and-associates/the-history-of-arts-education-in-brighton/post-war-curriculum-and-assessment-coldstream,-summerson,-art-history-and-complementary-studies [accessed 02.04.22].

Lyon, P., c.2008. *1968: the student revolution*. University of Brighton. Online. Available at: http://arts.brighton.ac.uk/arts/alumni-and-associates/the-history-of-arts-education-in-brighton/1968-the-student-revolution [accessed 02.04.22].

Macdonald, K. M. 1995, *The Sociology of the Professions*, Sage, London.

Malherek, J., 2018. The Industrialist and the Artist: László Moholy-Nagy, Walter Paepcke, and the New Bauhaus in Chicago, 1918–46. *Journal of Austrian-American History* , Vol. 2, No. 1 (2018), pp. 51–76. Penn State University Press. Online. Available at: https://www.jstor.org/stable/pdf/10.5325/jaustamerhist.2.1.0051.pdf?refreqid=excelsior%3A8a2fd1b48512d6e4315042c7f673761f [accessed 02.04.22].

Markus, H. R., & Nurius, P., 1986. Possible selves. *American Psychologist*, 41, 954–969. Online. Available at: http://cmapspublic2.ihmc.us/rid=1LQJK1Z9J-16LFNTG-39MK/Possible%20Selves%20ARTICLE.pdf [accessed 02.04.22].

Mason, G., Williams, G., and Cranmer, S., 2006. Employability Skills Initiatives in Higher Education: What Effects Do They Have On Graduate Labour Market Outcomes? *Education Economics* 17(1):1–30. https://doi.org/10.1080/09645290802028315

Massouras, A., 2012. *Patronage, Professionalism and Youth: The Emerging Artist and London's Art Institutions 1949–1988*, PhD thesis. London Consortium, Birkbeck, University of London.

McQuaid R. W., and Lindsay, C., 2005. The Concept of Employability. *Urban Studies*, Vol. 42, No. 2, 197–219. https://doi.org/10.1080/0042098042000316100

McRobbie, A., 2011. *Key Concepts for Urban Creative Industry in the UK*. Online. Available at: https://research.gold.ac.uk/6052/1/october%25202011%2520Wd0000023%5B1%5D.pdf [accessed 02.04.22].

McRobbie, A., 2016. *Be Creative: Making a Living in the New Culture Industries*. Cambridge: Polity Press.

Newall, M., 2019. *A Philosophy of the Art School*. Abingdon: Routledge.

Orr, S., and Shreeve, A., Eds., 2018. *Art and Design Pedagogy in Higher Education: Knowledge, Values and Ambiguity in the Creative Curriculum*. Abingdon: Routledge.

Oyserman, D., Lewis Jr, N. A., Yan, V. X., Fisher, O., O'Donnell, C. S., & Eric Horowitz, E., 2017. An Identity-Based Motivation Framework for Self-Regulation. *Psychological Inquiry*, 28:2–3, 139–147, https://doi.org/10.1080/1047840X.2017.1337406

Parsons, T., 1939. The professions and social structure. *Social Forces*, 17(4), 457–467. https://doi.org/10.2307/2570695

Parsons, T., 1964. Social change and medical organisations in the United States: a sociological perspective. *Annals of the American Academy of Political and Social Sciences*, 346, 21–33. https://doi.org/10.1177/000271626334600103

Paquette, J. 2012, *Cultural Policy, Work and Identity*, Ashgate, Surrey.

Pratt, J., 1997. *The Polytechnic Experiment: 1965–1992. Society for Research into Higher Education*. Online. Available at: https://eric.ed.gov/?id=ED415724 [accessed on 02.04.22].

Prest, W. (ed.), 1987, *The Professions in Early Modern England*, Croom Helm, London.

Radice, H., 2013. "How We Got Here: UK Higher Education under Neoliberalism". *ACME: An International Journal for Critical Geographies* 12 (2), 407–18. Online. Available at: https://acme-journal.org/index.php/acme/article/view/969 [accessed on 02.04.22].

REF 2021, 2019. *What is the REF?* Online. Available at: https://www.ref.ac.uk/about/what-is-the-ref/ [accessed on 02.04.22].

Rodner, V. L., and Thompson, E., 2013. The art machine: dynamics of a value generating mechanism for contemporary art. *Arts Marketing: An International Journal*, Vol. 3 Issue: 1. Online. https://doi.org/10.1108/20442081311327165

Rowles, S., 2016. *Professional practice in art schools: preparing students for life after graduation. a-n The Artists Information Company*. Online. Available at: https://static.a-n.co.uk/wp-content/uploads/2016/12/Professional-practice-in-art-schools.pdf [accessed on 02.04.22].

Røyseng, S., Mangset, P., and Borgen, J. S., 2007. Young Artists and the Charismatic Myth, *International Journal of Cultural Policy*, 13:1, 1–16, https://doi.org/10.1080/10286630600613366

Ryan, B., 1992. *Making Capital from Culture: The Corporate Form of Capitalist Cultural Production*, Walter de Gruyter, Berlin.

Scarsbrook, S. 2021. *Artists and the Art School: Experiences and Perspectives of Fine Art Education and Professional Pedagogies in London Art Schools, 1986–2016*. PhD thesis, Birkbeck, University of London.

Schwab, K. R., 2018. *The Fourth Industrial Revolution. Encyclopedia Britannica*. Online. Available at: https://www.britannica.com/topic/The-Fourth-Industrial-Revolution-2119734 [accessed 02.04.22].

Slater, A., Ravetz, A. and Kwong, L., 2013. *Analysing Artists' Continual Professional Development (CPD) in Greater Manchester: towards an integrated approach for talent development*. Online. Available at: http://www.miriad.

mmu.ac.uk/art/analysing-artists-cpd/MIRIAD_Analysing_Artists_CPD.pdf [accessed 27.03.22].

Slay H., and Smith, D., 2011. Professional identity construction: Using narrative to understand the negotiation of professional and stigmatized cultural identities. https://doi.org/10.1177/0018726710384290

Smith, J., McKnight, A., and Naylor, R, 2000. Graduate Employability: Policy and Performance in Higher Education in the UK. *The Economic Journal*, Vol. 110, No. 464, Features. (Jun., 2000), pp. F382–F411. Online. Available at: http://links.jstor.org/sici?sici=0013-0133%28200006%29110%3A464%3CF382%3AGEPAPI%3E2.0.CO%3B2-F [accessed on 23.03.22].

Soussloff, C., 1997. *The Absolute Artist: The Historiography of a Concept*. London: University of Minnesota Press.

Stamp, G., c.1975. *A Hundred Years of The Art Workers Guild*. Online. Available at: http://www.artworkersguild.org/media/2148/awg-history-by-gavin-stamp.pdf [accessed on 23.02.22].

Strand, R., 1987. *A Good Deal of Freedom: Art and Design in the Public Sector of Higher Education, 1960–1982*. CNAA.

Taylor, S. and Littleton, K., 2012. *Contemporary Identities of Creativity and Creative Work*. London and New York: Routledge.

TCCE, 2019, *TCCE Creative Entrepreneurship Forum—Ideas and Best Practice Exchange*. Online. Available at: https://www.theculturecapitalexchange.co.uk/2019/01/10/tcce-creative-entrepreneurship-forum-ideas-and-best-practice-exchange/ [accessed 30.01.22].

Thorne, S., 2019. *Eight art schools that changed the world*. Royal Academy. Online, Available at: https://www.royalacademy.org.uk/article/eight-art-schools-that-changed-the-world-bauhaus-anniversary [accessed 26.02.22].

Tomlinson, M., 2014, *Exploring the impact of policy changes on students' attitudes and approaches to learning in higher education*. The Higher Education Academy. Online. Available at: https://www.heacademy.ac.uk/sites/default/files/resources/Exploring_the_impact_of_policy_changes_student_experience.pdf [accessed on 29.01.22].

UK Parliament, 2022. *Severe financial consequences for universities if Augar Review recommendations about tuition fees are implemented, Lords Committee warns*. Online. Available at: https://www.parliament.uk/business/lords/media-centre/house-of-lords-media-notices/2019/august-2019/severe-financial-consequences-for-universities-if-augar-review-recommendations-about-tuition-fees-are-implemented-lords-committee-warns/ [accessed 05.04.22].

Universities UK, 2022. *The Future of the TEF: Report to the Independent Reviewer.* Online. Available at: https://www.officeforstudents.org.uk/advice-and-guidance/promoting-equal-opportunities/access-and-participation-plans/fee-limits/ [accessed 02.04.22].

Wheelahan, L., 2010, *Why Knowledge Matters in Curriculum: A Social Realist Argument.* London and New York: Routledge.

Wesner, S., 2018. *Artists Voices in Cultural Policy.* London: Palgrave Macmillan.

White, M., 2009. *The Industrial Revolution.* Georgian Britain. British Library. Online. Available at: https://www.bl.uk/georgian-britain/articles/the-industrial-revolution [accessed on 11.03.22].

Wilensky, H. L., 1964. The Professionalization of Everyone? *American Journal of Sociology*, 70: 137–58. Online. Available at: https://www.jstor.org/stable/2775206 [accessed on 23.02.22].

Willer, J., 2018. *What Happened to the Art Schools?* Politeia. Online. Available at: http://www.politeia.co.uk/wp-content/Politeia%20Documents/2018/Willer/Willer%20text%2019.10.18.pdf [accessed on 04.03.22].

Wright, R., 2019. UK Universities Fear Augar Review Could Starve Funding for Arts. *Financial Times.* Online. Available at: https://www.ft.com/content/79208aae-28b0-11e9-88a4-c32129756dd8 [accessed on 05.02.22].

Zanti, N., 2015. *Artists' identities: a study of the living and working conditions of visual artists in Cyprus.* PhD thesis, Birkbeck, University of London.

17

Interdisciplinary Limits of Creative Business Education

Bhabani Shankar Nayak

Abstract This chapter investigates the disciplinary denials of subjectivities and pluriversal nature of creative business education, examining the interdisciplinary limits of its curriculum produced in response to neoliberal crises in business education. While creative business education is depicted as an alternative way out to regain the legitimacy of mainstream business school education and its dynamism, the programmes often recycle a stance that upholds market values of compliant culture that destroys creativity of labour and the criticality of educational process. The chapter highlights the continuity and growth of alienation within the interdisciplinary praxis of creative business education. It argues against the use of language, methods and conceptual narratives of traditional business education within creative business education for a radical transformation of business praxis that values people, planet and society.

B. Shankar Nayak (✉)
Business School for the Creative Industries, University for the Creative Arts, Farnham, UK
e-mail: bhabani.nayak@uca.ac.uk

305

Introduction

The business schools are transforming their curriculum to stay relevant by responding to the pedagogic and essentialist crisis faced by the compliant culture within business school educational programmes. The failure to understand, explain and offer alternatives to the real-world crisis faced by the planet and people has forced the stakeholders of higher education to change its direction. Therefore, business education is witnessing an emerging area called 'creative business education'. In recent years, interest in 'creative business education' is growing within business schools, though the pedagogic interventions and radical transformation remain tentative and superficial. There are different calls to decolonise, decarbonise and humanise the curriculums for a sustainable and pluriversal knowledge tradition based on reason, science and secularism. The word 'creativity' is used without giving due recognition to the historical origin of 'creative' within 'labour'. It is the workers who are depositories of creativity but do not get the fruits of their 'creative' power. The 'creative business education' is misappropriating the term within its promise of 'interdisciplinarity' by borrowing its language, methods, theories and concepts from different disciplines. Such an essentialist approach reduces the emancipatory abilities of 'creative business education' and its praxis as a growing knowledge tradition. It also follows Eurocentric traditions of 'interdisciplinarity' by bring together narrow silos of different disciplines to stay relevant and pretend to be different, new and unique.

It is central to reject the performative, Eurocentric and essentialist approach to revive 'the social' aspects of 'creative business education' curriculum where labour gets its due within its pedagogic praxis. The 'creative business education' curriculum needs to develop its own methods, language and theories to be independent from the failed promises of the traditional business education and its compliant knowledge traditions. It needs to address the issues and predicaments faced by people and the planet to stay relevant as an interdisciplinary project. This chapter engages with debates around 'interdisciplinarity' within the context of the relationship between 'capital, labour and creativity'. It argues that creative business education and its curriculum needs to get away from the cultures around 'efficiency, productivity and profit' to a culture of socially meaningful business where peace, prosperity and sustainability can flourish, and risk can be minimised for people and the planet.

Historically, 'interdisciplinarity' emerged during 1930s (Abbott 2001: 131–32) to overcome barriers between different subject-based departmentalisations in terms of their languages and methods of seeking new knowledge and understanding the world. Philosophically, interdisciplinarity is not "a shibboleth or a sign of one's advanced thinking. Neither is it an incantation that will magically solve our problems. Interdisciplinary is simply a means. … interdisciplinarity constitutes an implicit philosophy of knowledge—not an 'epistemology,' but rather a general reflection on whether and to what degree knowledge can help us achieve the perennial goal of living the good life. It is the newest expression of a very old question" (Frodeman et al. 2010: xxxii–xxxiii). In this way, interdisciplinarity helps to overcome narrow barriers between different knowledge traditions. Transcending disciplinary boundaries and converging different disciplines, their languages and methods are twin objectives of interdisciplinary research.

Debates Around Interdisciplinarity

Interdisciplinary, transdisciplinary, multidisciplinary and cross disciplinary approaches to research emerged to address complex issues and growing challenges in the society as traditional disciplines failed to understand, analyse and offer alternatives. Interdisciplinary studies and methods emerged in response to the disenchantment of researchers with narrow silos of compartmentalisation and fragmentation of knowledge and departmentalisation terms of subjects and topics. Interdisciplinarity is considered as an integrated approach, which can save research, teaching and learning both in institutional and non-institutional settings.

Interdisciplinarity has emerged as a way out for researchers, teachers and curriculum developers as the narrow silo of disciplinarity and departmentalization of knowledge tradition has failed to understand, analyze and reflect on everyday realities and crisis around the world. The distinctive worldview of disciplines in terms of their language, methods and theories of disciplinary singularity have failed to understand and failed to offer alternatives to recover from different forms of crisis. Such a situation led to the rise of interdisciplinary research. Medical Anthropology, Development Studies, Public Policy, Business Studies, Security Studies and Neuroeconomics are some of the classic examples of interdisciplinary research. The idea of interdisciplinarity is considered as a 'counterculture' by Trow (1984). The debates around interdisciplinary continues to echo in higher education institutions around the world.

From fashion business to music business, human resource management and organisational studies are some of the topics that emerges out of interdisciplinary research and teaching addressing specific issues and areas. The disciplines which failed to develop interdisciplinary research or failed to independently update their own disciplinary language, methods and theories, these disciplines are slowly varnishing from the curriculum i.e., History and Political Science. The agencies, structures, actors and market forces are also forcing some process driven subjects and topics to grow i.e., Business and Management Studies. However, interdisciplinarity as a form of shared dialogical approach requires historical, cultural and political skills to understand different issues, challenges and crisis faced by the people and the planet. In this context, there are both objective and subjective challenges to interdisciplinarity. Scholar like (Jacobs 2013; Jacobs and Frickel 2009) fear that interdisciplinarity can challenge the disciplinary way of seeking knowledge. Therefore, Graff (2015) argues that interdisciplinarity is a process of undisciplining knowledge.

This rise of interdisciplinary, multidisciplinary and cross disciplinary research is a response to canonization of scientific revolution and its Taylorism for the growth of industrial capitalism, which has established positivist knowledge traditions. It has created a pattern of inquiry with set of tools, models and graphs within a specific laboratory like conditions that limit the scope of researcher within its number crunching empiricist knowledge tradition. Fuller (2003) has argued that disciplinarity limits the production of knowledge within a social space free from boundaries of any specific discipline. The interdisciplinary research "also convey a pervasive sense of newness and hint at tensions between applied research and fundamental problems of knowledge or theory, as well as between existing disciplines and emerging ones" (Graff 2016: 776). These tensions and contradictions can be found in the works of both advocates and opponents of interdisciplinarity (Graff 2015; Jacobs 2013). The essentialist and emancipatory knowledge traditions can overcome such contradictions within interdisciplinary praxis by developing language, tools and methods to reflect on everyday realities of people and planet.

Interdisciplinarity is a process of bringing together different disciplinary perspectives, languages and methods to analyse, explain and development an argument which is not possible within a single discipline (Boix-Mansilla et al. 2000). In theoretical terms, interdisciplinarity needs to move beyond its scope of critiquing the narrow silo of disciplines, subjects and topics. It needs to engage to expand both didactic and pedagogical boundaries for a radical transformation of curriculum that reflects material and non-material realities of people by making 'labour' central in understanding 'capital' and 'creativity'. It is labour that contains creativity that produces value for capital.

'Creativity', 'Labour' and 'Capital' in Creative Business Education Curriculum

The idea of 'creativity' is a form of sovereign self-expression (Abercrombie et al. 1986) in different forms of work and material revelation of inner abilities in the form of literature, mythology, music, art, cinema and science. There are attempts by intellectuals to conceptualize creativity as exceptional abilities and skills of few gifted individuals (Henry 2001) in terms of their productivity and achievements. Such half-baked conceptualisations help in creating differences between manual and mental labour. It also contributes to separate 'creativity' from labour. It ignores the social, political, cultural, historical conditions that shape 'creativity' of labour. Such processes of separation has not only created different forms of alienation but also sustained wage inequalities around the world. This creates conditions for capital to control and domesticate 'creative power of labour to expand its empires of profit and alienation of labour. In this way, creativity is a leitmotif of capitalism to normalise alienation and naturalise different forms of inequalities and marginalisation.

The linages of marginalisation of the creative power of labour under contemporary capitalism goes back to industrial revolution, which has not only produced commodities but also started the processes of commodification of labour in a large scale. In the process, the workers have become alienated from their own products, from themselves, from their fellow beings, and from the society as well. The capitalist co-option of labour and its creativity is historically shaped and continues to be relevant in contemporary history (Reckwitz 2017) in the process of accumulation. There is no limit to capitalist accumulation and creative business is a new frontier, where art is separated from artists, musicians are separated from their music, singers are separated from their songs, actors are separated from their films in the same way that manual labourers are separated from their own labour. The workers in creative industries are alienated under the capitalist co-option of creative power of labour. Bourdieu (1971), DiMaggio (1977) and Becker (1982) have argued that there is nothing new in this process of co-option of creativity power of labour within capitalism. The artists and workers of creative industries have always engaged with dealers, agents and brokers to sell their work. However, the contemporary capitalism has created platforms like Google, Amazons, Netflix and many other platforms that controls creative power of labour in an international scale. The contractual contract between capital and labour within creative industries manufacture the crisis of alienation as the legal regimes are created and sustained by capitalism as a system. In this way, the creative workers are complicit agents and victims of capitalist conditions of work (Huws 2006).

Even the creative business and management educational curriculum further narrows down the concept of 'creativity' as problem solving, productivity and efficiency of labour under capitalism. Scholars like Guildford (1967), Rawlinson (1981), and Robinson (2001) have looked at 'creativity' in functionalist and essentialist terms. Cropley (2001) looks at 'creativity' in terms of unique qualities to innovate new technology or new ideas which gives rise to a 'creative class of people' (Florida 2003). These scholars have reduced 'creativity' and its scope to unique ideas, intelligence and imagination to solve problems of business. Such conceptualisation is not only reductionist in its scope and outlook but also denies labour as depository of creativity. Work is creativity and every worker is a creative worker. The universal presence of creativity and its uniqueness is ignored in mainstream creative business and management education. These challenges and limitations can be managed by creative interdisciplinary collaborations (Moirano et al. 2020).

Interdisciplinary Limits of Creative Business Education

Interdisciplinarity in terms of its approach, language, methods and philosophical praxis are important to develop collective foundations of creativity Parjanen and Hyypiä (2019). Interdisciplinarity is used as a "popular strategy for innovation" (Edmondson and Harvey 2018: 347). But there is a gap between promise and practice of interdisciplinarity when it comes to the implementation of interdisciplinary research (Timmis and Williams (2017). Interdisciplinary collaboration is central strategy to overcome the challenges of implementation. However, the interdisciplinary collaborations need to engage with both the ontological and epistemological foundations of business education for a radical transformation of its curriculum. It is possible by engaging with labour within creative industry and ensure that labour remains as central unit of analysis to understand the alienation of artists, musicians, singers, actors, photographers, dancers and many other forms of work in creative industry. Any analysis devoid of issues of labour alienation put further limitations on the interdisciplinary approach to creative business education as a project.

Methodological nonconformity is important for the growth of interdisciplinary research culture. In reality, interdisciplinarity brings together established research methods to study different issues and challenges that follow methodological conformity in an indirect way. This puts a serious challenge to the growth of interdisciplinarity in creative business education.

The philosophical praxis of creative business education is yet to be free from the positivist knowledge traditions. It lacks critical reflection on social, religious, cultural, political and economic conditions that shape both creativity and business. The positivist knowledge tradition and its practice within mainstream business education continues to influence creative business education without understanding conditions and contexts shaped by history of the past and present. The interdisciplinarity as an approach needs to engage within these philosophical gaps within business education curriculum and liberate itself from the promiscuous neoliberal knowledge traditions within mainstream business schools and its curriculums.

Conclusion

In the field of creative business and management education curriculum, the idea of interdisciplinarity is yet to take a great leap forward due to various factors. Firstly, creative business management is yet to be a discipline. It continues to be a subject that borrows language from all traditional disciplines without developing it's a coherent and critical language and methods to reflect on everyday realities of life. Secondly, the creative business management education continues to be driven by an ideologically bias knowledge foundation that serve the market forces. It talks about skills and processes without any intellectual foundations to develop critical and theoretical edge over other disciplines in terms of its knowledge traditions. Thirdly, the creative business education does not engage with labour theory of creativity and failed to offer alternatives to the crisis created by alienation among the creative masses within the market led capitalist society. Finally, creative business and management education lacks universal appeal due to its Eurocentric outlook. It lacks flexibility to incorporate non-European and pluriversal knowledge traditions that exist across the world.

The interdisciplinary limits of creative business and management education can overcome these crises by opening its scope to the wider world of critical pedagogies in different disciplines. It is important to bring back issues of labour and its alienation to the field of creative business in sports, art, cinema, music, fashion, advertisement and branding etc. where labour power is commodified to seek profit. The creative business education needs to develop its mission and vision clearly and coherently without any form of servitude to capitalism and its agencies. In the world of capitalism, the creative business education and business of creativity and its flexibility in terms of working conditions and ownership over work pose a quite challenge where work histories are individualised and disconnected within an erratic work environment. Such a work environment create challenges for creative people who glorify their work in a tinsel town of creativity uncoupled from the masses. Interdisciplinary research can't be designed by focusing on a class of people who tend to work as if they are in a leisurely profession. Therefore, all these issues are central to shape interdisciplinarity as a collective and collaborative project within creative business education curriculum.

References

Abercrombie, N., Hill, S. & Turner, B.S. (1986). *Sovereign individuals of capitalism*. Crows Nest: Allen and Unwin.

Abbott, Andrew (2001), *Chaos of Disciplines*. Chicago: University of Chicago Press.

Becker, H. (1982). *Art worlds*. Berkeley, Los Angeles, London: University of California Press.

Bourdieu, P. (1971). Intellectual field and creative project, in M.F.D. Young (ed.), *Knowledge and control: new directions far the sociology of education*, London: Collier-Macmillan.

Boix-Mansilla, Veronica; Miller, William C.; Gardner, Howard. 2000. On Disciplinary Lenses and Interdisciplinary Work. In: Wineburg, Sam; Grossman, Pam, eds. *Interdisciplinary Curriculum—Challenges to Implementation*. New York, pp. 17–38.

Cropley, A (2001) *Creativity in Education and Learning*, London: Kogan Page.

DiMaggio, P. (1977). Market structure, the creative process, and popular culture: toward an organizational reinterpretation of mass-culture theory, *Journal of Popular Culture,* 11(2), 436–52.

Edmondson, A. C., & Harvey, J. (2018). Cross-boundary teaming for innovation: Integrating research on teams and knowledge in organizations. *Human Resource Management Review*, 28(4), 347–360.

Florida, R. (2003). *The rise of the creative class*. New York: Basic.

Frodeman, Robert, Julie Thompson Klein, and Carl Mitcham, eds. (2010), *The Oxford Handbook of Interdisciplinarity*. Oxford: Oxford University Press.

Fuller, Steven (2003) "Interdisciplinarity: The loss of the heroic vision in the marketplace of ideas." October 1, 2003, http://www.academia.edu/1161664/Rethinking_Interdisciplinarity, 1 (accessed on 13/03/2022).

Graff, H.J. (2016), The "Problem" of Interdisciplinarity in Theory, Practice, and History, *Social Science History*, Vol. 40, No. 4, Special Issue Introduction.

Graff, H.J. (2015) *Undisciplining Knowledge: Interdisciplinarity in the Twentieth Century*. Baltimore: Johns Hopkins University Press.

Guildford, J. (1967) *The Nature of Human Intelligence*, New York: McGraw Hill.

Henry J (2001) *Creativity and Perception in Management*, London: Sage.

Huws, U. (2006) 'The spark in the engine: Creative workers in a global economy', *Work Organisation, Labour and Globalisation*, 1(1): 1–12.

Jacobs, Jerry (2013) *In Defense of Disciplines: Interdisciplinarity and Specialization in the Research University*. Chicago: University of Chicago Press.

Jacobs, Jerry A., and Scott Frickel (2009) "Interdisciplinarity: A critical assessment." *Annual Review of Sociology*, 35: 43–65.

Moirano, R., Sánchez, M.A., Štěpánek, L. (2020). *Creative interdisciplinary collaboration: a systematic literature review. Thinking Skills and Creativity, Vol-35.*

Parjanen, S., & Hyypiä, M. (2019). Innotin game supporting collective creativity in innovation activities. *Journal of Business Research*, 96, 26–34.

Rawlinson, J. (1981) *Introduction to Creative Thinking*, London: British Institute of Management Foundation.

Reckwitz, A (2017). *The Invention qf Creativity*, Cambridge, Polity.

Robinson, K. (2001) *Out of our Minds: Learning to be Creative*, Oxford: Capstone.

Timmis, S., & Williams, J. (2017). Playing the interdisciplinary game across education—medical education boundaries: Sites of knowledge, collaborative identities and methodological innovations. *International Journal of Research and Method in Education*, 40(3), 257.

Trow, Martin (1984) "Interdisciplinary studies as a counterculture: Problems of birth, growth and survival." *Issues in Integrative Studies* 3: 1–16.

Index[1]

---

[1] Note: Page numbers followed by 'n' refer to notes.

© The Author(s), under exclusive license to Springer Nature Switzerland AG 2022
P. Powell, B. Shankar Nayak (eds.), *Creative Business Education*,
https://doi.org/10.1007/978-3-031-10928-7

Printed by Printforce, the Netherlands